ECONOMY

MCQs 450

"This booklet contains 450 MCQs with detailed explanation and notes on ECONOMY covering the basic and static concepts, Budget and Economic Survey, and other current updates from various sources.

Specially designed for UPSC Prelims 2025

VIVEK SING

S. CHAND PUBLISHING

S Chand And Company Limited

(ISO 9001 Certified Company)

S Chand And Company Limited

(ISO 9001 Certified Company)

Head Office: D-92, Sector–2, Noida 201301, U.P. (India), Ph. 91-120-4682700

Registered Office: A-27, 2nd Floor, Mohan Co-operative Industrial Estate, New Delhi – 110 044
Phone: 011-49731800

www.schandpublishing.com; e-mail: **info@schandpublishing.com**

Marketing Offices:

Chennai : Ph: 23632120, chennai@schandpublishing.com
Guwahati : Ph: 2738811, 2735640 guwahati@schandpublishing.com
Hyderabad : Ph: 40186018, hyderabad@schandpublishing.com
Jalandhar : Ph: 4645630, jalandhar@schandpublishing.com
Kolkata : Ph: 23357458, 23353914, kolkata@schandpublishing.com
Lucknow : Ph: 4003633, lucknow@schandpublishing.com
Mumbai : Ph: 25000297, mumbai@schandpublishing.com
Patna : Ph: 2260011, patna@schandpublishing.com

First Edition 2025

ISBN: 978-93-6468-767-6 **Product Code:** H1E4547ECON10ENAA25O

PRINTED IN INDIA

By Vikas Publishing House Private Limited, Plot 20/4, Site-IV, Industrial Area Sahibabad, Ghaziabad – 201 010 and Published by S Chand And Company Limited, A-27, 2nd Floor, Mohan Co-operative Industrial Estate, New Delhi – 110 044

CONTENTS

Macro Fundamentals, GDP, Investment, Growth

1. Consider the following statements regarding Gross Domestic Product:

   1. It is the sum total of domestic final consumption and investment expenditure plus net of exports and imports
   2. It is the sum total of final domestic consumption and investment expenditure plus exports
   3. It is the sum total of final consumption and investment expenditure plus net of exports and imports
   4. It is the sum total of final consumption and investment expenditure plus exports

   Select the correct answer using the code given below:
   (a) 1 & 2 only
   (b) 2 & 3 only
   (c) 3 & 4 only
   (d) 1, 2 & 3 only

2. If India is experiencing economic growth, then which of the following statements must hold true:

   1. Real GDP will increase
   2. Nominal GDP will increase
   3. Rate of growth of real GDP will increase
   4. Increase in employment generation

   Select the correct answer using the code given below:
   (a) 1 only
   (b) 1 & 2 only
   (c) 2 & 3 only
   (d) 1 & 4 only

3. If a country is experiencing recession, then which of the following must be true:

   (a) Decrease in real GDP
   (b) Decrease in nominal GDP
   (c) Decrease in rate of growth of GDP
   (d) All of the above

4. The National Income of a country (India) is equal to which of the following:

   (a) Gross National Product (GNP)
   (b) Net National Product at Market Prices
   (c) Net National Product at Factor Cost
   (d) Income going to the household sector

5. Which of the following statements are true regarding Gross National Income:

   1. It is the income earned by a country's Residents
   2. It is the income earned by a country's residents and non-residents both
   3. It is calculated at market price by NSO
   4. It is equal to GDP plus exports minus imports

   Select the correct answer using the code given below:
   (a) 1 & 3 only
   (b) 1 & 4 only
   (c) 2 & 3 only
   (d) 2, 3 & 4 only

6. Consider the following statements:

   1. Product taxes and production taxes both are included as part of GDP calculation
   2. Net Factor Income from Abroad is equivalent to net of exports & imports

   Select the correct answer using the code given below:
   (a) 1 only
   (b) 2 only
   (c) Both 1 & 2
   (d) Neither 1 nor 2

7. Welfare of the people of a country is best represented by which of the following parameter:

(a) Per capita net national income at constant prices
(b) Per capita net national income at current prices
(c) Per capita GDP at constant prices
(d) Per capita GDP at current prices

8. There is a Chinese company doing business in India. The profit made by the company will be part of:

1. India's GDP
2. China's GNP

Select the correct answer using the code given below:
(a) 1 only
(b) 2 only
(c) Both 1 & 2
(d) Neither 1 nor 2

9. Consider the following statements regarding Gross National Income (GNI)/GNP:

1. It includes production taxes
2. It includes transfer payment from rest of the world

Select the correct answer using the code given below:
(a) 1 only
(b) 2 only
(c) Both 1 & 2
(d) Neither 1 nor 2

10. Which of the following constitutes investment in the economy?

1. Production of consumption goods
2. Production of capital goods
3. Production of services
4. Buying and selling of shares

Select the correct answer using the code given below:
(a) 1 & 2 only
(b) 2 only
(c) 2 & 4 only
(d) All of the above

11. Consider the following statements:

1. Imported capital equipment are part of investment in Indian economy
2. Capital goods exported out of India are not part of India's investment

Select the correct answer using the code given below:
(a) 1 only
(b) 2 only
(c) Both 1 & 2
(d) Neither 1 nor 2

12. Which of the following statements could be true for a high savings rate in an economy?

1. Higher investment
2. Higher consumption
3. Higher exports

Select the correct answer using the code given below:
(a) 1 & 2 only
(b) 1 & 3 only
(c) 2 & 3 only
(d) All of the above

13. Which of the following are part of gross fixed capital formation:

1. Machinery and equipment
2. Construction of buildings and other infrastructure
3. Intellectual property rights

Select the correct answer using the code given below:
(a) 1 only
(b) 1 & 3 only
(c) 2 only
(d) All of the above

14. Despite being a high saving economy, capital formation may not result in significant increase in output due to:

(a) weak administrative machinery
(b) illiteracy

(c) high population density
(d) high capital-output ratio

15. Consider the following statements regarding Incremental Capital Output Ratio (ICOR):

1. It shows how efficiently the new capital is being used to produce output
2. It is the extra unit of capital required to produce one additional unit of output
3. It is the extra unit of output produced from one additional unit of capital
4. It is the ratio of change in capital to change in output

Select the correct answer using the code given below:
(a) 1 only
(b) 1 & 2 only
(c) 1, 2 & 4 only
(d) 1, 3 & 4 only

16. Capital formation in a country will lead to which of the following:

1. Increase in ICOR
2. Decrease in ICOR
3. Economic growth

Select the correct answer using the code given below:
(a) 1 & 3 only
(b) 2 & 3 only
(c) 3 only
(d) None of the above

17. Consider the following statements:

1. Capital output ratio depends on governance, quality of labour, technology etc.
2. Economic output increases with decrease in capital output ratio

Select the correct answer using the code given below:
(a) 1 only
(b) 2 only
(c) Both 1 & 2
(d) Neither 1 nor 2

18. For a sustained high growth, which of the following statements will be true:

(a) Raising the investment by keeping the incremental capital output ratio minimum
(b) Raising the investment and incremental capital output ratio both
(c) Increasing capital output ratio and keeping investment at a constant rate
(d) All of the above

19. If the capacity utilization in the economy is decreasing then consider the following statements:

1. Capital to output ratio will decrease
2. Per unit cost of production will increase

Select the correct answer using the code given below:
(a) 1 only
(b) 2 only
(c) Both 1 & 2
(d) Neither 1 nor 2

20. If factories are running at full capacity utilization, then the marginal productivity of capital will be:

(a) Positive
(b) Negative
(c) Zero
(d) One

21. If a country's growth rate is good but there is no corresponding growth in employment, then which of the following could be the reasons:

(a) The growth is coming from better utilization of existing capacity and not because of increase in investment
(b) The growth is coming from increase in investment but not because of better utilization of existing capacity

(c) The growth is coming from both as a result of increase in investment and increase in capacity utilization
(d) None of the above

22. Economic growth in a country will necessarily have to occur if:

(a) There is technological progress in the country
(b) There is population growth in the country
(c) There is capital formation in the country
(d) The country's exports are increasing

23. A country is going through a phase of industrialization. Which of the following statements are correct?

(a) Capital to labour ratio increases
(b) Productivity of labour increases
(c) Total factor productivity increases
(d) All of the above

24. Which of the following statements are correct about CPI rural, CPI urban and CPI combined index?

1. Inflation data is published by NSO
2. The base year is 2011-12
3. It is released for all India and for states and UTs separately on a monthly basis

Select the correct answer using the code given below:
(a) 1 only
(b) 2 only
(c) 2 & 3 only
(d) All of the above

25. Consider the following statements regarding CPI Combined:

1. It captures/reflects the impact of monthly change in prices of various commodities

2. It does not capture/reflect the impact of monthly change in consumption pattern of various commodities

3. It captures/reflects the impact of yearly change in consumption pattern of various commodities

4. It captures the impact of consumption pattern of people through their expenditure on various items

Select the correct answer using the code given below:
(a) 1 only
(b) 1, 2 & 4 only
(c) 2 & 3 only
(d) All of the above

26. Consider the statements regarding the various inflation indices published in the country:

1. Wholesale Price Index (WPI) does not represent the inflation in services
2. Consumer Price Index (CPI) represents the inflation in goods and services
3. CPI and WPI represent the inflation of imported goods also
4. CPI does not represent the inflation in capital and intermediate goods.

Select the correct answer using the code given below:
(a) 1 & 2 only
(b) 1, 2, 3 only
(c) 2, 3 & 4 only
(d) All of the above

27. Wholesale Price Inflation (WPI) index includes price change of which of the following sectors:

1. Agriculture
2. Mining
3. Manufacturing
4. Electricity

Select the correct answer using the code given below:
(a) 2 & 3 only
(b) 3 only
(c) 1, 2 & 3 only
(d) All of the above

28. Central Government employee's salary (dearness allowance) is linked with which CPI inflation index?

(a) CPI – combined
(b) CPI – Industrial Workers
(c) Both (a) & (b)
(d) None of the above

29. Consider the following statements regarding the current "Wholesale Price Index (WPI)" series with base year 2011-12:

1. The weights of the commodities in WPI basket are fixed till the revision/change in base year

2. The weights of the commodities in WPI basket are determined based on domestic production plus net of exports

3. The weights of the commodities in WPI basket are determined based on domestic production plus net of imports

4. "Manufactured Products" have the highest weight in WPI basket

Select the correct answer using the code given below:
(a) 1 only
(b) 1, 2 & 4 only
(c) 1, 3 & 4 only
(d) 3 & 4 only

30. If economic growth in 2022-23 is 8% and nominal growth in GDP over the same period is 12%, then 'GDP Deflator' in this period would be:

(a) 4%
(b) Less than 4%
(c) More than 4%
(d) Can't be calculated

31. Consider the following statement with reference to 'Income Elasticity of Demand':

1. It measures the responsiveness of demand for a particular good to changes in consumer income.
2. Using this concept, it is possible to tell if a particular good represents a necessity or a luxury.

Which of the statements given above is/are correct?
(a) 1 only
(b) 2 only
(c) Both 1 & 2
(d) Neither 1 nor 2

32. Which of the following is a common measure of degree of 'openness of an economy'?

(a) Exports and imports share in world GDP
(b) Balance of Payments as a percentage of GDP
(c) Trade balance as a percentage of GDP
(d) Exports and imports of goods and services as a percentage of GDP

33. The dependence of an economy (X) on another economy (Y) is measured as:

(a) Ratio of imports of X from Y to total imports of X
(b) Ratio of imports of X from Y to GDP of X
(c) Bilateral trade of X with Y to X's total trade
(d) Bilateral trade of X with Y to GDP of X

34. Consider the following statements regarding India:

1. Exports (of goods and services) as a percent of GDP has steadily decreased in the last decade
2. Imports (of goods and services) as a percent of GDP has steadily increased in the last decade

3. Trade as a percent of GDP has steadily decreased in the last decade
4. Services trade balance has consistently been positive in the last 10 years

Select the correct answer using the code given below:
(a) 2 only
(b) 1 & 2 only
(c) 4 only
(d) All of the above

35. Which of the following commodities had the highest share in merchandise exports in 2024-25?

(a) Petroleum products
(b) Gold and other metal jewellery
(c) Marine products
(d) Rice including basmati rice

Money, Banking and Financial Institutions

36. What were the reasons which led to bank nationalization of 1969?

1. Expansion of bank branches was mostly in urban areas
2. Agriculture and small-scale industries were not getting proper access to banking facilities
3. Bank credit was not utilized for financing projects according to Plan priorities
4. Easy and cheap availability of credit to a few industrial houses had encouraged growth of monopolies

Select the correct answer using the code given below:
(a) 1 & 2 only
(b) 1, 2 & 3 only
(c) 2 & 4 only
(d) All of the above

37. Which of the following are part of "Seigniorage"?

1. Interest income on reserves kept with RBI for money creation
2. Interest accruing from bank balances kept with central bank as interest-free balances in order to meet the reserve requirements
3. Inflation tax

Select the correct answer using the code given below:
(a) 1 only
(b) 2 only
(c) 1 & 2 only
(d) All of the above

38. If a country has 'Pegged' (fixed but adjustable) exchange rate, then consider the following statements:

1. Inflation in the country may make its exports less competitive
2. If the country devalues its currency in proportion to the inflation, then its exports may remain competitive

Select the correct answer using the code given below:
(a) 1 only
(b) 2 only
(c) Both 1 & 2
(d) Neither 1 nor 2

39. Which of the following statements are true regarding India's present exchange rate system:

1. RBI regulates the Rupee dollar rate
2. RBI generally intervenes in the forex market indirectly
3. RBI regulates the forex market

Select the correct answer using the code given below:
(a) 1 only
(b) 1 & 2 only
(c) 3 only
(d) 2 & 3 only

40. RBI intervenes in the foreign exchange market to:
   1. To contain the volatility in the rupee
   2. To set a price band for Rupee in terms of Dollar

   Select the correct answer using the code given below:
   (a) 1 only
   (b) 2 only
   (c) Both 1 & 2
   (d) Neither 1 nor 2

41. Consider the following statements regarding purchasing power parity (PPP) exchange rates:

   1. If two countries have same rate of inflation, their PPP exchange rates will remain constant
   2. The prices of goods will be same in both the countries when converted at PPP exchange rate

   Select the correct answer using the code given below:
   (a) 1 only
   (b) 2 only
   (c) Both 1 & 2
   (d) Neither 1 nor 2

42. Which of the following statements are true in case "the currency of two countries are at purchasing power parity":

   (a) PPP exchange rate is equal to Nominal exchange rate
   (b) PPP exchange rate is equal to Real exchange rate
   (c) Nominal exchange rate is equal to Real exchange rate
   (d) PPP, Nominal and Real exchange rates become equal

43. If Mr. X has Rs. 20 crores in India and Mr. Y has $1 crore in US and whatever Mr. X can consume in India with Rs. 20 crores, the same items can be consumed by Mr. Y in $ 1 crore in US.

   If both of them, with their money, met at a place other than India and US then who will be richer?

   (a) Mr. X
   (b) Mr. Y
   (c) Equally rich
   (d) Will depend on Nominal Exchange Rate

44. Increase in India's trade deficit may lead to which of the following:

   (a) Increase in money supply in the economy
   (b) Depreciation of rupee
   (c) Appreciation of rupee
   (d) Increase in GDP

45. Which of the following situation will lead to depreciation of a country's currency:

   (a) Foreign Investment inflow
   (b) Rise in the interest rate
   (c) Increase in exports
   (d) None of the above

46. The export competitiveness of a country with its trading partners can be best measured through which of the following exchange rates:

   (a) Nominal Exchange Rate
   (b) Real Exchange Rate
   (c) Nominal Effective Exchange Rate
   (d) Real Effective Exchange Rate

47. If rupee is appreciating in real terms with respect to US dollars, then:

   (a) India's exports competitiveness will decrease
   (b) India's exports competitive will increase
   (c) India's exports will be more competitive than US
   (d) India's exports will be less competitive than US

48. Consider the following statements:

1. If rupee is depreciating, then it leads to increase in cost of imports in dollars

2. If rupee is depreciating, then it leads to earning more dollars per unit of exports

Select the correct answer using the code given below:

(a) 1 only
(b) 2 only
(c) Both 1 & 2
(d) Neither 1 nor 2

49. Which of the following will be the impact of rupee depreciation?

1. Exports will become more competitive
2. Exporters will fetch more dollars for the same amount of goods exported
3. Demand for domestic goods and services will increase

Select the correct answer using the code given below:

(a) 1 only
(b) 2 only
(c) 1 & 3 only
(d) All of the above

50. Suppose due to higher domestic inflation, rupee started depreciating but RBI used the Forex reserves to prevent the depreciation of Rupee. Then consider the following statements:

1. REER will increase
2. REER will decrease
3. Exports will become more competitive
4. No impact on trade competitiveness

Select the correct answer using the code given below:

(a) 1 only
(b) 4 only
(c) 2 & 3 only
(d) 1 and 3 only

51. Consider the following statements regarding the transactions happening at the international level for trade and financial flows.

1. There is an international authority with the power to force the use of a particular currency
2. There is a basket of currencies which can only be used to settle international transactions
3. Currencies which maintain a stable purchasing power are generally accepted
4. Freely convertible currencies are generally accepted

Select the correct answer using the code given below:

(a) 1 only
(b) 2 & 4 only
(c) 3 & 4 only
(d) 2, 3 & 4 only

52. Consider the following statements regarding 'internationalization of rupee'?

1. It means use of rupee for transactions between non-residents
2. It means use of rupee transactions between residents and non-residents
3. Military capability of a country plays role in internationalization of currency

Select the correct answer using the code given below:

(a) 1 only
(b) 2 only
(c) 1 & 2 only
(d) All of the above

53. Retail investors are allowed to directly access Govt. securities market. Consider the following statements:

1. Retail investors will be allowed in both primary and secondary Govt. securities market

2. Individuals participate in the non-competitive auctioning process of G-Securities in Primary Market
3. It will help in reducing the cost of borrowing for government

Select the correct answer using the code given below:
(a) 1 & 2 only
(b) 3 only
(c) 1 & 3 only
(d) All of the above

54. Consider the following statements regarding government securities market:

1. G-Secs are issued through auctions conducted on E-Kuber which is the core banking solution platform of RBI

2. Negotiated Dealing System-Order Matching is a secondary market for G-Secs

Select the correct answer using the code given below:
(a) 1 only
(b) 2 only
(c) Both 1 & 2
(d) Neither 1 nor 2

55. Consider the following statements regarding "State Development Loans"

1. It can be used under SLR by banks
2. It is a tradable instrument
3. RBI manages the public debt of states

Select the correct answer using the code given below:
(a) 2 only
(b) 1 & 2 only
(c) 1 & 3 only
(d) All of the above

56. Which of the following statements are true regarding "Cash Management Bills"?

1. Issued by Central Government and not by state governments
2. It is used to fund fiscal deficit
3. It can be used for temporary mismatches in the cash flow of the government

Select the correct answer using the code given below:
(a) 1 & 2 only
(b) 2 & 3 only
(c) 3 only
(d) 1 & 3 only

57. Consider the following statements regarding the 'Statutory Liquidity Ratio (SLR)' maintained by Scheduled Commercial Banks:

1. It is maintained as per the RBI Act 1934
2. Can be maintained as cash balance with RBI
3. Cash Management Bills, Treasury Bills, Dated Securities and State Development Loans (SDL), all are considered as SLR securities

Select the correct answer using the code given below:
(a) 1 only
(b) 2 & 3 only
(c) 2 only
(d) 3 only

58. Consider the following statements regarding 'ways and means' advance:

1. It is available for both Central and State governments
2. Government needs to pay interest on ways and means advance
3. It is to meet the temporary mismatches of receipts and payments

Select the correct answer using the code given below:
(a) 1 only
(b) 1 & 3 only
(c) 2 & 3 only
(d) All of the above

59. Consider the following statements regarding 'Ways and Means Advance':

1. It is used to fund government's fiscal deficit
2. It is tradable government security

Select the correct answer using the code given below:
(a) 1 only
(b) 2 only
(c) Both 1 & 2
(d) Neither 1 nor 2

60. Which of the following statements will be true if the inflation in the economy is increasing?

1. Bond price will decrease
2. Bondholders will loose
3. The yield on bonds will increase

Select the correct answer using the code given below:
(a) 1 only
(b) 1, & 2 only
(c) 3 only
(d) All of the above

61. The price of government securities in India is influenced by which of the following?

1. Repo rate
2. US Federal Bank benchmark interest rate
3. Liquidity in the market

Select the correct answer using the code given below:
(a) 1 only
(b) 2 only
(c) 1 & 2 only
(d) All of the above

62. Which one of the following statements correctly describes the meaning of legal tender money?

(a) The money which is tendered in courts of law to defray the fee of legal cases
(b) The money which a creditor is under compulsion to accept in settlement of his claims
(c) The bank money in the form of cheques, drafts, bills of exchange, etc.
(d) The metallic money in circulation in a country

63. Consider the following statements:

1. Currencies and coins are fiat money
2. Currencies do not have intrinsic value, but coins have
3. Currencies and coins are legal tenders
4. Currency notes are guaranteed by Govt. of India

Select the correct answer using the code given below:
(a) 1 only
(b) 1 & 3 only
(c) 3 & 4 only
(d) 1, 3 & 4 only

64. Consider the following statements:

1. All the currency in circulation is the liability of RBI
2. All the currency in circulation is part of money supply
3. Notes and coins are circulated in the economy only through RBI

Select the correct answer using the code given below:
(a) 1 only
(b) 1 & 2 only
(c) 3 only
(d) None of the above

65. Who has the authority to issue currency notes in India?

(a) Central Government
(b) Ministry of Finance
(c) RBI
(d) RBI governor

66. Consider the following statements regarding currency circulation in India:

1. Govt. of India has the sole right to mint coins

2. The coins are issued for circulation only through RBI in terms of the RBI Act 1934
3. Coins can be issued up to the denomination of Rs. 1000 as per the Coinage Act 1906

Select the correct answer using the code given below:
(a) 1 only
(b) 1 & 2 only
(c) 3 only
(d) All of the above

67. If new currency is being issued, then who has the authority to decide its "Denomination":

(a) RBI Governor
(b) RBI Central Board of Directors
(c) Central Government
(d) Monetary Policy Committee

68. Who is the final authority in approving the design, form and material of bank notes:

(a) Governor of RBI
(b) Central Board of RBI
(c) Central Government
(d) Governor of RBI in consultation with Central Government

69. Prime Minister, on 8th of Nov 2016, declared that the existing Rs. 500 and Rs. 1000 notes will not be legal tender. This was done under which of the following Act.

(a) RBI Act 1934
(b) Banking regulation Act 1949
(c) Payment and Settlement Systems Act 2007
(d) Does not require any statutory backing

70. RBI targets the growth of money supply in the economy based on:

1. Expected real GDP growth
2. Normal level of inflation

Select the correct answer using the code given below:
(a) 1 only
(b) 2 only
(c) Both 1 & 2
(d) Neither 1 nor 2

71. Which of the following statements are true regarding RBI?

1. As per the RBI Act 1934, RBI is bound to undertake the receipt and payments and other banking operations of the central government
2. As per the RBI Act 1934, RBI is obliged to act as banker to State governments

Select the correct answer using the code given below:
(a) 1 only
(b) 2 only
(c) Both 1 & 2
(d) Neither 1 nor 2

72. Consider the following statements regarding 'Agency Banks' of RBI:

1. RBI Act 1934 allows RBI to appoint agency banks
2. Scheduled payment banks and small finance banks can act as 'Agency Banks'
3. Only those private banks which are of certain size are allowed to act as 'Agency Banks'

Select the correct answer using the code given below:
(a) 1 only
(b) 1 & 2 only
(c) 1 & 3 only
(d) 2 & 3 only

73. Which of the following functions are part of the Reserve Bank of India (RBI) acting as Banker to Banks?

1. Enabling banks to maintain their accounts with RBI for statutory reserve requirements
2. Enabling settlement of interbank transfer of funds

3. RBI provides short term loans and advances to banks
4. Acting as lender of last resort

Select the correct answer using the code given below:
(a) 1 only
(b) 1 & 2 only
(c) 1, 2 & 3 only
(d) All of the above

74. Consider the following statements regarding RBI acting as 'lender of last resort' for banks:
1. It is done to prevent possible failure of the banks and to protect the interest of the depositors
2. RBI does it only if the troubled financial institution has exhausted all the resources it can obtain from the market and from the RBI's regular liquidity facilities like LAF, MSF
3. To ensure financial stability in the economy

Select the correct answer using the code given below:
(a) 1 only
(b) 1 & 2 only
(c) 1 & 3 only
(d) All of the above

75. Which of the following statements are true regarding lender of last resort?
1. It is provided to banks which have been declared bankrupt
2. RBI provides funds for long period
3. RBI provides fund against collateral and at a penal rate

Select the correct answer using the code given below:
(a) 1 only
(b) 2 & 3 only
(c) 3 only
(d) 1 & 3 only

76. Which of the following functions are part of the RBI acting as Banker to Central Government?
1. RBI maintains the account for the various central government funds like Consolidated Fund of India, Contingency Fund and Public Account of India
2. RBI acts as advisor to the government on monetary and banking related matters
3. RBI provides Ways and Means Advances to the government
4. RBI floats loan and manages them on behalf of the government

Select the correct answer using the code given below:
(a) 1 & 2 only
(b) 2 & 3 only
(c) 1, 2 & 3 only
(d) All of the above

77. Consider the following statements regarding 'Notice Money':
1. It is a money market instrument for overnight lending
2. It is issued by commercial banks and other financial institutions
3. It is generally a secured instrument

Select the correct answer using the code given below:
(a) 1 only
(b) 1 & 2 only
(c) 2 only
(d) 2 & 3 only

78. Consider the following statements regarding "Commercial Papers":
1. It is an unsecured debt instrument
2. It is a short-term money market instrument
3. NBFCs issue commercial papers

Select the correct answer using the code given below:
(a) 1 only
(b) 2 & 3 only
(c) 2 only
(d) All of the above

79. Consider the following statements regarding "Certificate of Deposits":

1. It is not a tradable instrument
2. It is a secured instrument issued by banks
3. It is a money market instrument

Select the correct answer using the code given below:
(a) 1 & 2 only
(b) 2 only
(c) 2 & 3 only
(d) 3 only

80. Which of the following are instrument/s of money market?

1. Cash management bills
2. Treasury bills
3. Certificate of Deposits
4. State Development Loans

Select the correct answer using the code given below:
(a) 1 & 2 only
(b) 2 & 3 only
(c) 1 & 4 only
(d) 1, 2 & 3 only

81. Mergers and Acquisitions of commercial banks may require approval of which of the following agency/ies?

1. Reserve Bank of India (RBI)
2. Competition Commission of India (CCI)

Select the correct answer using the code given below:
(a) 1 only
(b) 2 only
(c) Both 1 & 2
(d) Neither 1 nor 2

82. Consider the following statements regarding the "Financial Services Institutions Bureau (FSIB)" constituted in 2022:

1. It is responsible for appointment of heads in PSBs and Financial Institutions
2. It helps PSBs in developing strategies and capital raising plans
3. It has been constituted under Banking Regulation Act 1949

Select the correct answer using the code given below:
(a) 1 only
(b) 1 & 2 only
(c) 2 & 3 only
(d) All of the above

83. Consider the following statements regarding Financial Services Institutions Bureau (FSIB):

1. It selects the chiefs of LIC, NABARD and public financial institutions
2. The persons selected by the FSIB require approval of Appointments Committee of the Cabinet (ACC)

Select the correct answer using the code given below:
(a) 1 only
(b) 2 only
(c) Both 1 & 2
(d) Neither 1 nor 2

84. Consider the following statements regarding the insurance cover provided to depositors by Deposit Insurance and Credit Guarantee Corporation (DICGC)

1. All commercial banks and urban cooperative banks have to register with DICGC for providing insurance to depositors
2. RBI incurs the insurance premium burden
3. Government incurs the insurance premium burden
4. DICGC provides insurance only in case the bank has gone bankrupt

Select the correct answer using the code given below:
(a) 1 only
(b) 1 & 2 only
(c) 3 only
(d) 1 & 4 only

85. Consider the following statements regarding payment banks:

1. They can open demand and time deposit accounts both
2. They are set up as differentiated banks
3. They may act as Business Correspondents for other banks
4. They will provide payments / remittance services to migrant labour workforce and small businesses

Select the correct answer using the code given below:
(a) 1 & 4 only
(b) 1 & 2 only
(c) 2, 3 & 4 only
(d) All of the above

86. Consider the following statements regarding "India Post Payment Bank":

1. It allows demand and fixed deposit both
2. It allows savings and current account both
3. It is a public sector company

Select the correct answer using the code given below:
(a) 1 only
(b) 1 & 3 only
(c) 2 & 3 only
(d) None of the above

87. What is the purpose of setting up of Small Finance Banks (SFBs) in India?

1. To supply credit to small business units
2. To supply credit to small and marginal farmers
3. To encourage young entrepreneurs to set up business particularly in rural areas.

Select the correct answer using the code given below:
(a) 1 & 2 only
(b) 2 & 3 only
(c) 1 & 3 only
(d) All of the above

88. Consider the following statements regarding Cooperative Banks:

1. All cooperative banks are under dual regulation of RBI and government
2. RBI regulates the cooperative banks under Banking Regulation Act 1949
3. All cooperative banks are supervised by NABARD

Select the correct answer using the code given below:
(a) 1 only
(b) 2 only
(c) 2 & 3 only
(d) 1 & 3 only

89. NABARD provides refinance to which of the following types of financial institutions:

1. Commercial Banks
2. Regional Rural Banks
3. State Cooperative Banks & Land Development Banks
4. Non-Banking Financial Companies

Select the correct answer using the code given below:
(a) 2 only
(b) 2 & 3 only
(c) 1, 2 & 3 only
(d) All of the above

90. Which of the following are the sources of finance for National Bank for Agriculture and Rural Development (NABARD)

1. RBI
2. Borrowing from commercial banks
3. Issuing bonds which are fully serviced by Govt. of India
4. Foreign currency borrowings

Select the correct answer using the code given below:

(a) 1 only
(b) 1 & 3 only
(c) 3 only

(d) All of the above

91. Consider the following statements regarding MUDRA Bank:

1. It provides direct lending to small entrepreneurs
2. MUDRA loans are available to small and marginal farmers
3. MUDRA loan is available for manufacturing, trading and service activities

Select the correct answer using the code given below:
(a) 1 only
(b) 2 & 3 only
(c) 3 only
(d) 1 & 3 only

92. Consider the following statements regarding National Housing Bank (NHB):

1. NHB regulates Housing finance companies
2. NHB is owned by Govt. of India and regulated by RBI
3. NHB provides direct finance for individual housing loans

Select the correct answer using the code given below:
(a) 1 only
(b) 1 & 2 only
(c) 2 only
(d) 1 & 3 only

93. Which of the following statements are true regarding Housing Finance Companies (HFC)?

1. HFCs are under direct regulation of RBI
2. HFCs are a category of Non-Banking Financial Companies (NBFCs)

Select the correct answer using the code given below:
(a) 1 only
(b) 2 only
(c) Both 1 & 2
(d) Neither 1 nor 2

94. Consider the following statements regarding "Peer to Peer Lending Platforms" in India:

1. They are regulated by RBI as Non-Banking Financial Companies
2. They can lend on their own
3. They provide credit guarantee

Select the correct answer using the code given below:
(a) 1 only
(b) 2 only
(c) 1 & 3 only
(d) All of the above

95. NBFCs raise their resources from which of the following:

1. Loans from Banks
2. By issuance of bonds in the financial markets
3. Money market
4. Through External Commercial Borrowing (ECB)

Select the correct answer using the code given below:
(a) 1 only
(b) 1 & 2 only
(c) 1 & 3 only
(d) All of the above

96. Which of the following are risk factors for NBFCs in their lending process?

1. Relying on short term financing to fund long-term investments
2. Asset liability mismatch (ALM)
3. Rollover risk of commercial papers

Select the correct answer using the code given below:
(a) 1 only
(b) 1, 2 only
(c) 2, 3 only
(d) All of the above

97. Consider the following statements regarding 'Digital Banking Units

(DBUs)' launched by the Scheduled Commercial Banks:

1. It is fixed point business unit / hub housing certain minimum digital infrastructure for delivering digital banking products & services
2. It offers banking services in both self-service and assisted mode
3. It provides services without requiring paper

Select the correct answer using the code given below:
(a) 1 only
(b) 2 only
(c) 2 & 3 only
(d) All of the above

98. Consider the following statements regarding "Real Estate Investment Trusts (REITs):

1. They are regulated by respective Real Estate Regulatory Authorities (RERA) of every State
2. It will make real estate sector accessible to small investors

Select the correct answer using the code given below
(a) 1 only
(b) 2 only
(c) Both 1 & 2
(d) Neither 1 nor 2

99. Which of the following statements are true regarding "Angel Investors":

1. Angel investors generally invest their own money
2. They invest in small start-ups and entrepreneurs
3. They provide more favourable terms and conditions as compared to other lenders
4. Angel investment is regulated by SEBI

Select the correct answer using the code given below:
(a) 1 & 2 only
(b) 3 only
(c) 2 & 3 only
(d) All of the above

100. Consider the following statements regarding 'Anchor Investors':

(a) They are high net worth individual investors who invest in startups
(b) They are individual investors investing first time in the stock market
(c) They are institutional investors who invest in startups and unlisted companies
(d) They are institutional investors who are invited to invest just before the initial public offer

101. Consider the following statements regarding 'Alternative Investment Fund' (AIF):

1. Its privately pooled investment vehicle established in India and regulated by SEBI
2. It collects fund from sophisticated investors from India or Foreign
3. Venture capital comes under AIF

Select the correct answer using the code given below:
(a) 1 only
(b) 1 & 2 only
(c) 3 only
(d) All of the above

102. Which of the following statements are true regarding the term "Crowd funding"?

1. It is a method of financing through the internet/social media
2. Small amounts of money are raised from large number of investors
3. It is also referred as marketplace financing

Select the correct answer using the code given below:
(a) 1 & 2 only
(b) 2 & 3 only

(c) 3 only
(d) All of the above

103. Consider the following statements regarding "Exchange Traded Funds (ETF)":

1. ETFs are traded like stocks and can be bought and sold throughout the day
2. ETFs can be used as a vehicle for disinvestment
3. ETFs offers the benefit of diversification of risks

Select the correct answer using the code given below:

(a) 1 only
(b) 1 & 2 only
(c) 2 & 3 only
(d) All of the above

104. Which of the following statements are true regarding 'impact bonds':

1. Subscribed by government
2. Private sector finances the bond issuance
3. Repayment is based on agreed upon outcomes
4. This instrument is used to fund social and development initiatives

Select the correct answer using the code given below:
(a) 1 & 3 only
(b) 2 & 3 only
(c) 2, 3 & 4 only
(d) 1 & 4 only

105. Consider the following statements regarding 'surety bonds':

1. Insurance companies are allowed to issue surety bonds for infrastructure projects
2. It can be used as a substitute for bank guarantee
3. It will reduce indirect cost for contractors

Select the correct answer using the code given below:
(a) 1 & 2 only
(b) 1 & 3 only
(c) 2 & 3 only
(d) All of the above

106. Consider the following statements regarding the 'India International Bullion Exchange (IIBX)':

1. It has been launched in the GIFT City in Gandhinagar
2. It is the first such bullion exchange in the country to trade physical gold.

Select the correct answer using the code given below:
(a) 1 only
(b) 2 only
(c) Both 1 & 2
(d) Neither 1 nor 2

107. Consider the following statements regarding the term of appointment of RBI Governor:

(a) As fixed by the Central Government while appointing, not exceeding five years and eligible for re-appointment
(b) As fixed by the Central Government while appointing, not exceeding three years and eligible for re-appointment
(c) As fixed by the Central Government while appointing, not exceeding five years and not eligible for re-appointment
(d) As fixed by the Central Government while appointing, not exceeding three years and not eligible for re-appointment

108. Consider the following statements:

1. Banks require prior approval of RBI for appointment of directors
2. Management of Public Sector banks is under dual regulation of Central Govt. & RBI

Select the correct answer using the code given below:
(a) 1 only
(b) 2 only
(c) Both 1 & 2
(d) Neither 1 nor 2

109. Consider the following statements:

1. RBI is a wholly owned by Govt. of India
2. RBI's surplus transfer to the central government has steadily decreased in the last 5 years

Select the correct answer using the code given below:
(a) 1 only
(b) 2 only
(c) Both 1 & 2
(d) Neither 1 nor 2

110. Consider the following statements regarding the 'Economic Capital Framework' of RBI:
1. RBI Act 1934 specifies to keep some contingency buffer
2. RBI Act 1934 specifies that the surplus needs to be transferred to Government of India
3. The transfer of surplus to Govt. of India may result in inflation

Select the correct answer using the code given below:
(a) 1 only
(b) 1 & 2 only
(c) 3 only
(d) All of the above

111. Consider the following statements regarding liquidity crisis in the debt markets:

1. It may be caused due to defaults in the debt market
2. It may be caused due to FPIs running out of Indian markets
3. It may result in hardening of interest rates
4. RBI may do OMO to resolve the liquidity crisis

Select the correct answer using the code given below:
(a) 1 & 2 only
(b) 1 & 3 only
(c) 2, 3 & 4 only
(d) All of the above

112. Which of the following could be the after effects of demonetization?

1. RBI's liability would reduce to the extent the old notes does not come to the banking system
2. Transfer of wealth from holders of illicit black money to the public sector
3. Decrease in liquidity

Select the correct answer using the code given below:
(a) 1 & 2 only
(b) 1 & 3 only
(c) 2 & 3 only
(d) All of the above

113. Which of the following is part of Monetary Base of an economy?

1. Currency notes and coins with the public
2. Vault cash of commercial banks
3. Deposits of commercial banks with RBI

Select the correct answer using the code given below:
(a) 1 only
(b) 1 & 2 only
(c) 2 & 3 only
(d) All of the above

114. Reserves of commercial banks includes which of the following:

1. All deposits of Public
2. Government securities held by banks
3. Cash held by banks in their vaults
4. Money deposited with RBI

Select the correct answer using the code given below:
(a) 2 & 3 only
(b) 2, 3 & 4 only
(c) 4 only

(d) All of the above

115. Money can be created in the economy in which of the following ways?

1. Full reserve banking
2. Fractional reserve banking

Select the correct answer using the code given below:
(a) 1 only
(b) 2 only
(c) Both 1 & 2
(d) Neither 1 nor 2

116. Consider the following statements regarding Money Multiplier:

1. It increases with increase in reserve requirements of banks
2. It decreases with increase in reserve requirements of banks
3. It increases with Monetary Base
4. It decreases with Monetary Base

Select the correct answer using the code given below:
(a) 1 only
(b) 2 only
(c) 2 & 3 only
(d) 2 & 4 only

117. Which of the following will increase 'Monetary Base'?

1. Creation of more credit by banks
2. Public withdrawing more cash from the banks

Select the correct answer using the code given below:
(a) 1 only
(b) 2 only
(c) Both 1 & 2
(d) Neither 1 nor 2

118. Money Multiplier depends on which of the following?

1. Currency deposit ratio
2. Reserve deposit ratio

Select the correct answer using the code given below:
(a) 1 only
(b) 2 only
(c) Both 1 & 2
(d) Neither 1 nor 2

119. Consider the following statements regarding 'money supply':

1. It can be increased by increasing the money multiplier
2. It can be increased by increasing the monetary base

Select the correct answer using the code given below:
(a) 1 only
(b) 2 only
(c) Both 1 & 2
(d) Neither 1 nor 2

120. Consider the following statements regarding "Open Market Operations":

1. It changes the monetary base
2. It changes the money supply
3. It changes the money multiplier

Select the correct answer using the code given below:
(a) 1 & 2 only
(b) 2 only
(c) 1 & 3 only
(d) All of the above

121. Which of the following is not part of the money supply in the economy?

1. Money lying with the government
2. Deposits of commercial banks with other commercial banks
3. Money lying with the Central bank
4. Deposits of pubic with commercial banks

Select the correct answer using the code given below:
(a) 1 only
(b) 2 & 4 only
(c) 1 & 2 only
(d) 1, 2 & 3 only

122. Which of the following are part of money supply in the economy?

1. Cash and deposits of public

2. Corporate bonds held by public
3. Government securities held by public
4. Shares held by public

Select the correct answer using the code given below:
(a) 1 only
(b) 1, 2 & 3 only
(c) 2 & 3 only
(d) All of the above

123. Consider the following statements regarding 'Open Market Operations (OMO)':

1. Outright OMOs are directed at influencing enduring liquidity
2. Liquidity Adjustment Facility (LAF) OMO operations target the temporary liquidity in the system

Select the correct answer using the code given below:
(a) 1 only
(b) 2 only
(c) Both 1 & 2
(d) Neither 1 nor 2

124. If RBI is pumping more money in the economy, then which of the following is true?

1. Monetary base is increasing
2. Money supply is increasing
3. Money Multiplier is increasing
4. RBI's balance sheet is increasing

Select the correct answer using the code given below:
(a) 1 only
(b) 1 & 2 only
(c) 2 & 3 only
(d) 1, 2 & 4 only

125. Which of the following actions will lead to immediate increase in money supply in the economy?

1. Individuals purchasing government securities in the primary market
2. Banks purchasing government securities in the primary market
3. Banks purchasing government securities from the public in the secondary market
4. Long Term Repo Operation by RBI to commercial banks

Select the correct answer using the code given below:
(a) 1 only
(b) 1 & 2 only
(c) 3 only
(d) 3 & 4 only

126. Consider the following statements:

1. Open Market Operation is a monetary policy tool
2. Open Market Operations take place in secondary market
3. Sterilization is a monetary policy tool

Select the correct answer using the code given below:
(a) 1 only
(b) 1 & 3 only
(c) 3 only
(d) All of the above

127. Which of the following are part of Liquidity Adjustment Facility (LAF):

1. Marginal Standing Facility
2. Standing Deposit Facility
3. Long term repo operation
4. Overnight repo operation

Select the correct answer using the code given below:
(a) 1 only
(b) 1 & 2 only
(c) 3 & 4 only
(d) All of the above

128. Consider the following statement regarding 'Market Stabilization Bonds' (MSBs):

1. These are Treasury bills and Dated securities
2. RBI is empowered to issue MSBs
3. The interest payment on these bonds is made by government from its budgetary resources

Select the correct answer using the code given below:
(a) 1 only
(b) 2 only
(c) 2 & 3 only
(d) All of the above

129. Consider the following statements regarding Cash Reserve Ratio (CRR):

1. It helps in securing monetary stability and managing liquidity in the economy
2. RBI can change the CRR to any level without any floor or ceiling limit

Select the correct answer using the code given below:
(a) 1 only
(b) 2 only
(c) Both 1 & 2
(d) Neither 1 nor 2

130. Consider the following statements regarding Cash Reserve Ratio (CRR) kept with RBI by commercial banks:

1. It ensures safety to the people's deposits in banks
2. It ensures solvency of banks
3. It increases the cost of funds for the banks
4. Banks earn interest on CRR

Select the correct answer using the code given below:
(a) 1 only
(b) 1 & 2 only
(c) 1, 2 & 3 only
(d) All of the above

131. In the context of Indian economy, which of the following is/are the purpose/purposes of "Statutory Reserve Requirements"?

1. To enable the Central Bank to control the amount of advances the banks can create
2. To make the people's deposits with banks safe and liquid
3. To prevents the commercial banks from making excessive profits
4. To force the banks to have sufficient vault cash to meet their day-to-day requirements

Select the correct answer using the code given below.
(a) 1 only
(b) 1 & 2 only
(c) 2 & 3 only
(d) 1, 2, 3 & 4 only

132. Consider the following statements regarding the 'Monetary Policy Framework' that exists between Govt. of India and Reserve Bank of India:

1. The primary objective of Monetary Policy is price stability
2. There is a flexible target for inflation that RBI needs to achieve
3. Monetary Policy Framework is operated by RBI
4. If RBI fails to achieve the target, it needs to submit report to the Govt. of India stating reasons of failure

Select the correct answer using the code given below:
(a) 1 & 2 only
(b) 3 only
(c) 1, 2 & 4 only
(d) All of the above

133. Consider the following statements regarding the 'Monetary Policy Framework':

1. The operating target is the money market rate
2. RBI tries to keep the operating target around the government securities yield rate

Select the correct answer using the code given below:
(a) 1 only
(b) 2 only
(c) Both 1 & 2
(d) Neither 1 nor 2

134. Which of the following statements are true regarding the Monetary Policy Committee (MPC)?

1. It has the authority to decide repo rate, CRR, SLR
2. Its decision is binding on RBI

Select the correct answer using the code given below:
(a) 1 only
(b) 2 only
(c) Both 1 & 2
(d) Neither 1 nor 2

135. While deciding the repo rate, Monetary Policy Committee may keep in mind the following factors:

1. Inflation
2. Economic Growth
3. Rupee appreciation/depreciation

Select the correct answer using the code given below:
(a) 1 only
(b) 1 and 2 only
(c) All of the above
(d) None of the above

136. Consider the following statements regarding MPC and its members:

1. Three members are appointed by Central Government and three are appointed by Central Board of RBI
2. The three members appointed by the Central Government hold office for a period of four years
3. There should be at least six meetings of the MPC in a year

Select the correct answer using the code given below:
(a) 1 & 2 only
(b) 1 & 3 only
(c) 2 only
(d) 3 only

137. Which of the following statements are true regarding 'Marginal Standing Facility' (MSF)?

1. Scheduled commercial banks borrow additional amount for overnight
2. The banks can dip into their SLR portfolio to borrow from RBI
3. It provides a safety valve against unanticipated liquidity shocks

Select the correct answer using the code given below:
(a) 1 & 2 only
(b) 1 & 3 only
(c) 3 only
(d) All of the above

138. Consider the following instruments:

1. Reverse Repo Rate
2. Marginal Standing Facility
3. Standing Deposit Facility

Which of the following facility/instruments is/are available at RBI's discretion and not banks?

(a) 1 only
(b) 1 and 2 only
(c) 3 only
(d) 2 and 3 only

139. The "Consumer Confidence Survey" in India is conducted by which of the following:

(a) Reserve Bank of India
(b) National Statistical Office (NSO)
(c) Department of Consumer Affairs
(d) Ministry of Labour & Employment

140. Which of the following agencies conducts 'inflation expectation survey' of households in India?

(a) Ministry of Statistics and Programme Implementation
(b) National Statistical Office
(c) Reserve Bank of India
(d) Ministry of Finance

141. Which of the following situations may lead to increase in repo rate by RBI?

1. Inflation in the economy is high

2. Inflation expectation in the economy is high

Select the correct answer using the code given below:
(a) 1 only
(b) 2 only
(c) Both 1 & 2
(d) Neither 1 nor 2

142. If the US Central Bank raises their interest rate, then it may lead to which of the following in the Indian economy:

(a) Rupee depreciation
(b) Rupee appreciation
(c) Investors moving to India
(d) Increase in money supply

143. Which of the following RBI may do to curb the rupee depreciation?

1. Allowing importers to directly buy foreign currency from RBI
2. Increasing the repo rate
3. Selling dollars in foreign exchange market
4. Buying dollars in foreign exchange market

Select the correct answer using the code given below:
(a) 1 & 3 only
(b) 2 & 3 only
(c) 1, 2 & 3 only
(d) 1, 2 & 4 only

144. Consider the following statement regarding the term "Operation Twist":

1. It is a kind of open market operation
2. RBI pumps additional money into the system to increase liquidity
3. It helps in monetary transmission

Select the correct answer using the code given below:

(a) 1 & 2 only
(b) 2 & 3 only
(c) 1 & 3 only
(d) All of the above

145. Which of following statements are true regarding "Long Term Repo Operations"?

1. It comes under liquidity adjustment facility
2. The interest rate should be at or above the repo rate
3. It is long term lending by RBI

Select the correct answer using the code given below:

(a) 1 & 3 only
(b) 2 & 3 only
(c) 2 only
(d) All of the above

146. Which of the following could be the impact of Long-Term Repo Operation (LTRO) conducted by RBI:

1. Increase in money supply
2. Increase in inflation
3. Increase in interest rate
4. Increase in liquidity with banks

Select the correct answer using the code given below:
(a) 1, 2 & 3 only
(b) 1 & 4 only
(c) 1, 2 & 4 only
(d) 2, 3 & 4 only

147. Which of the following could be the reasons for the deficit in banking system liquidity?

1. An uptick in the bank credit
2. Advance tax payments by corporates
3. Incremental deposit growth not keeping pace with credit demand
4. Intervention of the RBI into the forex market to prevent rupee depreciation

Select the correct answer using the code given below:
(a) 2 & 3 only
(b) 3 & 4 only
(c) 1, 2 & 4 only
(d) All of the above

148. Consider the following statements regarding the "Monetary Policy" followed by RBI:

1. It follows flexible inflation target
2. While inflation is in control, RBI can focus on growth
3. Financial Stability is the explicit mandate of monetary policy
4. Achieving monetary policy objective will ensure financial stability

Select the correct answer using the code given below:
(a) 1 only
(b) 1 & 2 only
(c) 2 & 4 only
(d) 2, 3 & 4 only

149. Which of the following monetary policy tools are used at RBI's discretion rather than banks availing the facility as per their own requirement?

1. Open market operation
2. Long Term Repo Operation
3. Overnight fixed rate repo lending
4. Reverse repo auction

Select the correct answer using the code given below:
(a) 1 & 2 only
(b) 2, 3 & 4 only
(c) 1 & 4 only
(d) All of the above

150. Which of the following indicators is/are used to observe the monetary transmission mechanism in the economy?

1. Weighted average lending rate
2. Weighted average domestic term deposit rate
3. 1-year median MCLR
4. MSF rate

Select the correct code:
(a) 1 and 2 only
(b) 1, 2 and 3 only
(c) 3 and 4 only
(d) 4 only

151. Which of the following statements are true regarding the Marginal Cost of Funds based Lending Rate (MCLR):

1. Banks will do lending at or above MCLR
2. MCLR may increase because of increase in CRR/SLR
3. MCLR helps in better transmission of policy rate as compared to base rate

Select the correct answer using the code given below:
(a) 1 & 2 only
(b) 1 & 3 only
(c) 3 only
(d) All of the above

152. Consider the following statements regarding the interest rates linked with an external benchmark rate:

1. External benchmark rate can be repo rate or yield on government securities
2. Once repo rate changes the lending rate of banks will automatically change
3. Banks are mandated by RBI to link the deposit and lending rate with external benchmark rate

Select the correct answer using the code given below:
(a) 1 only
(b) 1 & 2 only
(c) 2 only
(d) 1 & 3 only

153. Consider the following statements regarding the "spread" charged over the external benchmark rate by the banks:

1. The spread will be decided by the banks
2. The spread will change with the change of external benchmark rate
3. The spread may be different for different category of loans

Select the correct answer using the code given below:
(a) 1 & 2 only

(b) 2 & 3 only
(c) 1 & 3 only
(d) All of the above

154. Consider the following statements regarding Non-Banking Finance Companies (NBFCs):

1. RBI mandates NBFCs to link their lending rates with an anchor rate
2. MCLR is an anchor rate which acts as external benchmark rate

Select the correct answer using the code given below:

(a) 1 only
(b) 2 only
(c) Both 1 & 2
(d) Neither 1 nor 2

155. Which of the following could create a hindrance in achieving the objective of inflation targeting by RBI?

1. Government deviating from the fiscal road map
2. Impediments in monetary policy transmission
3. Supply side bottlenecks

Select the correct answer using the code given below:
(a) 1 only
(b) 1 & 2 only
(c) 2 & 3 only
(d) All of the above

156. Which of the following market plays the major role in transmission of monetary policy?

(a) Government Securities market
(b) Money Market
(c) Forex market
(d) Capital Market

157. Consider the following statements regarding real and nominal interest rate:
1. Real Interest Rate must be positive to encourage savings and reduce consumption
2. Nominal interest rate must be positive to attract savings in banks
3. Real interest rate is always positive

Select the correct answer using the code given below:
(a) 1 only
(b) 1 & 2 only
(c) 2 & 3 only
(d) 2 only

158. Which of the following factors may lead to increase in savings in the economy?

1. Positive real interest rate
2. Low inflation rate
3. Rise in per capita income
4. Growth of financial intermediaries

Select the correct answer using the code given below:
(a) 3 only
(b) 3 & 4 only
(c) 2 & 3 only
(d) All of the above

159. The term 'Inflation Premium' refers to:

(a) Higher nominal return that equity investors get due to increase in inflation
(b) It is the risk that investors have to face because of higher inflation
(c) It the higher return that investors demand in exchange for investing in a long-term security because of higher inflation risk
(d) It is the high return that short term bond investors demand due to higher inflation risk

160. Inflation in the economy generally leads to which of the following:

1. Depreciation of currency
2. Appreciation of currency
3. Increase in real interest rate
4. Increase in nominal interest rate

Select the correct answer using the code given below:
(a) 1 & 3 only
(b) 2 & 3 only

(c) 1 & 4 only
(d) 1, 3 & 4 only

161. If an economy is in "Liquidity Trap", then which of the following statements shall be true:

1. The interest rate in the market will be very low/zero
2. People and businesses both will hold on to their cash and don't spend
3. Yield on bonds will be very less
4. Demand Deposits of banks increases

Select the correct answer using the code given below:
(a) 1 only
(b) 2 & 4 only
(c) 1, 2 & 4 only
(d) All of the above

162. Consider the following statements:
1. Inflation benefits creditors
2. Inflation benefits debtors
3. Inflation benefits bondholders
4. Inflation benefits depositors

Select the correct answer using the code given below:
(a) 1 & 3 only
(b) 2 only
(c) 3 only
(d) 1, 3 & 4 only

163. If a country is experiencing inflation, then what will decrease:

(a) Wage level
(b) The output of goods and services
(c) The amount of money needed to purchase a given quantity of goods and services
(d) Purchasing Power

164. Which of the following will be the outcome if an economy is under the inflationary pressure?

1. Domestic currency heads for depreciation
2. Exports become less competitive with imports getting costlier
3. Cost of borrowing decreases

Select the correct answer using the code given below:
(a) 1 only
(b) 1 & 2 only
(c) 2 & 3 only
(d) 1 & 3 only

165. Which of the following may lead to an increase in the overall prices?

1. Increase in effective demand
2. Decrease in the aggregate level of output
3. Increase in aggregate output
4. An increase in overall employment

Select the correct answer using the code given below:
(a) 1 & 4 only
(b) 2 & 4 only
(c) 1, 2 & 4 only
(d) All of the above

166. Which of the following will necessarily lead to inflation?

(a) Increase in aggregate demand
(b) Increase in effective demand
(c) Decrease in aggregate output
(d) Increase in government spending

167. If the supply of money is increased in the economy, then which of the following statements are true:

(a) It may lead to increase in interest rates
(b) It may lead to decrease in interest rates
(c) It will necessarily lead to economic growth
(d) None of the above

168. Which of the following scenarios can support sustainable economic growth?

1. Deflation
2. Low and moderate inflation
3. Galloping inflation

4. Hyperinflation

Select the correct answer using the code given below:
(a) 2 only
(b) 1 & 2 only
(c) 2 & 3 only
(d) All of the above

169. Which of the following are the reasons that make a moderate level of inflation good for the economy?

1. It increases consumption levels
2. It keeps businesses profitable
3. It induces people to save more

Select the correct answer using the code given below:

(a) 2 only
(b) 1 & 2 only
(c) 3 only
(d) All of the above

170. Consider the following statements regarding an economy facing deflation:

1. Companies defer their investments
2. People defer their expenditures
3. Demand decreases
4. Unemployment increases

Select the correct answer using the code given below:
(a) 1 & 2 only
(b) 3 only
(c) 3 & 4 only
(d) All of the above

171. Which of the following factors could potentially contribute to stagflation in the Indian economy:

1. High inflationary pressures due to increased Government spending
2. Expansionary monetary policy
3. Decline in industrial production and sluggish economic growth
4. Decrease in aggregate demand and consumer spending

Select the correct answer using the code given below:

(a) 1 & 2 only
(b) 1, 2 & 3 only
(c) 4 only
(d) All of the above

172. Which of the following are supply side factor/s responsible for inflation?

1. Increase in exports
2. Increase in government expenditure
3. Increase in credit creation

Select the correct answer using the code given below:
(a) 1 only
(b) 2 & 3 only
(c) 1 & 3 only
(d) None of the above

173. Which of the following are causes of demand-pull inflation?

1. Lower interest rate
2. Higher government expenditure
3. Higher cost of inputs

Select the correct answer using the code given below:
(a) 1 & 2 only
(b) 2 only
(c) 3 only
(d) All of the above

174. If the interest rate is decreased in an economy, it will

(a) Decrease the consumption expenditure in the economy
(b) Increase the tax collection of the Government
(c) Increase the investment expenditure in the economy
(d) Increase the total savings in the economy

175. Consider the following statements:
1. High output leads to high unemployment
2. High unemployment leads to high inflation

Select the correct answer using the code given below:

(a) 1 only
(b) 2 only
(c) Both 1 & 2
(d) Neither 1 nor 2

176. Consider the following statements in the context of inflation:

1. An overheating economy is an economy that is expanding at an unsustainable rate
2. Increasing interest rate by RBI is more effective in case of demand pull- inflation rather than in cost push

Select the correct answer using the code given below:
(a) 1 only
(b) 2 only
(c) Both 1 & 2
(d) Neither 1 nor 2

177. The term 'Reflation' of economy is related to which of the following?

1. Fiscal stimulus to expand the output
2. It tries to curb the effects of deflation
3. Monetary stimulus by reducing the interest rate

Select the correct answer using the code given below:
(a) 1 only
(b) 3 only
(c) 1 & 3 only
(d) All of the above

178. Consider the following statements regarding an economy facing disinflation:

1. Companies defer their investments
2. People defer their expenditures
3. Demand decreases
4. Unemployment increases

Select the correct answer using the code given below:
(a) 1 only
(b) 1 & 3 only
(c) None of the above
(d) All of the above

179. Consider the following statements regarding "Sovereign Gold Bonds":

1. These are government securities denominated in grams of gold
2. Issued by RBI on behalf of Govt. of India
3. Investors will receive fixed interest rate
4. If the market price of gold declines, investors will be protected against capital loss

Select the correct answer using the code given below:
(a) 1 & 2 only
(b) 2 & 3 only
(c) 1, 2 & 3 only
(d) All of the above

180. Consider the following statements regarding the recently launched 'Sovereign Green Bonds (SGB)':

1. These bonds will be part of Govt. borrowing and will be debt. on Govt. of India
2. The proceeds will be deployed in public sector projects which help in reducing the carbon intensity of the economy
3. The proceeds of SGB can be used for investment, subsidies, grant-in-aid or tax forgone

Select the correct answer using the code given below:
(a) 1 & 2 only
(b) 2 & 3 only
(c) 1 & 3 only
(d) All of the above

181. The recently constituted Green Finance Working Committee (GFWC) will be chaired by:

(a) Union Finance Minister
(b) RBI Governor
(c) Chief Economic Advisor
(d) None of the above

182. Which of the following will help in reducing the current account deficit?

1. Adopting suitable policies to attract FDI/FPI
2. The foreign currency earnings of India's IT sector
3. Foreign investments in Govt. securities

Select the correct answer using the code given below:
(a) 1 & 2 only
(b) 1 & 3 only
(c) 3 only
(d) 2 & 3 only

183. Integrated Ombudsman Scheme is applicable on:

1. Banks
2. NBFCs
3. Payment System Providers
4. Credit Information Companies (CIC)

Select the correct answer using the code given below:
(a) 1 only
(b) 1 & 2 only
(c) 2 & 3 only
(d) All of the above

184. Consider the following statements regarding the 'Integrated Ombudsman Scheme, 2021':

1. RBI will appoint the Ombudsman for a period not exceeding five years at a time
2. There is a limit to the dispute value that can be brought before the Ombudsman

Select the correct answer using the code given below:
(a) 1 only
(b) 2 only
(c) Both 1 & 2
(d) Neither 1 nor 2

185. Consider the following statements regarding "Kisan Credit Card (KCC)" scheme:

1. It provides short term credit for cultivation of crops as well as long term credit
2. It provides credit for consumption requirements of farmers household
3. Available to owner cultivator, tenant farmers and share croppers

Select the correct answer using the code given below:

(a) 1 only
(b) 1 & 3 only
(c) 2 & 3 only
(d) All of the above

186. Which of the following category of financial institutions are not involved in the implementation of Kisan Credit Cards (KCC)?

(a) Regional Rural Banks (RRBs)
(b) Cooperative Banks
(c) Small Finance Banks
(d) Non-Banking Financial Institutions (NBFCs)

187. Which category of financial institutions have the highest share in agricultural credit:

(a) Commercial Banks (excluding regional rural banks)
(b) Regional Rural banks
(c) Cooperative Banks
(d) Non-Banking Financial Companies

188. Which of the following statements are true regarding the "Prompt Corrective Action (PCA)" framework for banks:

1. It is a supervisory tool of RBI for effective market discipline
2. It applies once financial institutions reach certain threshold level regarding Capital, asset quality and leverage

Select the correct answer using the code given below:
(a) 1 only
(b) 2 only
(c) Both 1 & 2
(d) Neither 1 nor 2

189. Which of the following actions RBI can take once it declares a particular bank under Prompt Corrective Action?

1. Prohibit lending
2. Increase in provisioning
3. Bring in new management or supersede the bank's board
4. Bank merger

Select the correct answer using the code given below:

(a) 1 & 2 only
(b) 2 & 4 only
(c) 3 & 4 only
(d) All of the above

190. Consider the following statements regarding the 'Supervisory Action Framework':

1. It is applicable for Urban-Cooperative banks
2. It can be initiated in case of serious governance issues

Select the correct answer using the code given below:
(a) 1 only
(b) 2 only
(c) Both 1 & 2
(d) Neither 1 nor 2

191. RBI manages its forex reserves as:

1. Deposits with Bank for International Settlement (BIS)
2. Deposits with Foreign Commercial banks
3. Deposits with foreign Central banks

Select the correct answer using the code given below:
(a) 1 only
(b) 2 only
(c) 1 & 3 only
(d) All of the above

192. Which of the following statements is true regarding "Line of Credit":

(a) It is issued by one bank to another
(b) It is issued mainly in case of international transactions
(c) It is a preset amount of money that a bank has agreed to lend
(d) The company will have to pay interest on the amount for which line of credit has been issued

193. Which of the following statements are true regarding "Teaser Loans"?

1. It is a fixed cum floating loan product
2. These are short term loans
3. These loans are banned by RBI

Select the correct answer using the code given below:
(a) 1 only
(b) 1 & 2 only
(c) 3 only
(d) 2 & 3 only

194. The term "provisioning" in the banking sector is related to which of the following:

(a) It is the loss that the bank incurs on sale of bad assets
(b) It is the amount of fund that the bank needs to set aside when the loan turns NPA
(c) It is the minimum amount of funds that the depositors will receive when the bank goes bankrupt
(d) It is the minimum amount which the borrower will have to pay even if the loan turns NPA

195. Consider the following statements regarding 'First Loss Default Guarantee (FLDG)':

1. It has been approved by RBI
2. It's a contractual agreement between banks and Fintechs under which Fintechs give guarantee for loss due to default
3. The loan is shared on the books of banks and Fintechs

Select the correct answer using the code given below:
(a) 1 & 2 only
(b) 2 & 3 only
(c) 3 only
(d) All of the above

196. Consider the following statements:

1. Capital Adequacy Ratio (CAR) is the amount that banks have to maintain in the form of their own funds to offset any loss that banks incur if the accountholders fail to repay dues.
2. CAR is decided by each individual bank.

Which of the statements given above is/are correct?
(a) 1 only
(b) 2 only
(c) Both 1 & 2
(d) Neither 1 nor 2

197. Consider the following statements regarding 'Additional Tier 1 bonds':

1. They are part of capital under Basel III norms
2. They are perpetual in nature and have no maturity period
3. They can be written down in case of bank failure

Select the correct answer using the code given below:
(a) 2 only
(b) 3 only
(c) 1 & 3 only
(d) All of the above

198. Which of the following statements are true regarding the "Liberalized Remittance Scheme" (LRS)?

1. It is applicable for Individuals only and not companies
2. It is applicable for both current and capital account
3. Foreign exchange trading is not permitted in this scheme

Select the correct answer using the code given below:
(a) 1 only
(b) 1 & 3 only
(c) 2 & 3 only
(d) All of the above

199. Which of the following instruments are permitted for receiving 'foreign investment' in an Indian Company?

1. Equity shares
2. Debentures
3. Preference Shares
4. Share Warrants

Select the correct answer using the code given below:
(a) 1 only
(b) 1 & 3 only
(c) 2 & 3 only
(d) All of the above

200. Which of the following can be treated as FDI:
1. Investment in Central and State Govt. securities
2. Foreign Currency Convertible Bonds (FCCB)
3. Global Depository Receipts (GDRs)
4. Financial Lease

Select the correct answer using the code given below:
(a) 1 & 2 only
(b) 2 & 3 only
(c) 2, 3 & 4 only
(d) All of the above

201. Foreign Direct Investment (FDI) in India can happen by which of the following ways:

1. Subsidiary
2. Joint Venture
3. Acquisition of shares

Select the correct answer using the code given below:
(a) 1 & 2 only
(b) 2 & 3 only
(c) 1, 2 & 3 only
(d) 3 only

202. Consider the following statements regarding Foreign Direct Investment (FDI):

1. FDI investment happens mainly through primary market
2. FDI investment is about equity securities
3. FDI investment can happen through convertible debentures

Select the correct answer using the code given below:
(a) 1 only
(b) 1 & 2 only
(c) 1 & 3 only
(d) All of the above

203. Consider the following statements regarding Foreign Portfolio Investors (FPI):

1. FPI is mainly into secondary market
2. FPI investment may happen through primary market
3. They can invest both in debt and equity

Select the correct answer using the code given below:
(a) 1 only
(b) 2 only
(c) 2 & 3 only
(d) All of the above

204. Consider the following statements:

1. Foreign Portfolio investments are more volatile than FDI
2. FDI investors can easily sell their holdings and quit the market
3. Foreign Portfolio investment is sector specific
4. FDI investment in general target the capital market

Select the correct answer using the code given below:
(a) 1 only
(b) 1 & 3 only
(c) 3 & 4 only
(d) 4 only

205. Consider the following statements:

1. A Foreign Portfolio Investor can maximum invest 10 per cent in an Indian Company
2. When Foreign Investment in an Indian company is more than 10 per cent it is treated as FDI

Select the correct answer using the code given below:
(a) 1 only
(b) 2 only
(c) Both 1 & 2
(d) Neither 1 nor 2

206. Consider the following statements regarding Foreign Direct Investment (FDI):

1. FDI is mostly in non-debt instruments
2. If an earlier FDI investment of more than 10% comes below 10% then it will be treated as FPI

Select the correct answer using the code given below:
(a) 1 only
(b) 2 only
(c) Both 1 & 2
(d) Neither 1 nor 2

207. Consider the following statements
1. FDI requires SEBI approval/license
2. FPI requires SEBI approval/license
3. FDI & FPI both require RBI approval/license

Select the correct answer using the code given below:

(a) 1 & 2 only
(b) 2 only
(c) 3 only
(d) All of the above

208. Consider the following statements regarding FDI/FPI:

1. FDI get attracted by higher economic growth
2. FPI get attracted by higher economic growth as well as higher interest rate
3. FPI get attracted by interest rate differential

Select the correct answer using the code given below:
(a) 1 & 3 only
(b) 2 & 3 only
(c) 1 & 2 only
(d) All of the above

209. Which of the following will make Foreign Direct Investment (FDI) inflow attractive in a country:

1. If that country's Real Effective Exchange Rate (REER) depreciates

2. If that country's Nominal Effective Exchange Rate (NEER) depreciates (because of higher inflation)

(a) 1 only
(b) 2 only
(c) Both 1 and 2
(d) FDI inflow becomes attractive in a country if REER or NEER of that country appreciates

210. Consider the following instruments:

1. Overseas Direct Investments
2. Reserve assets
3. India's portfolio investments

Which of the above are part of 'Overseas financial assets of Indian Residents'?

(a) 1 only
(b) 1 and 2 only
(c) 2 and 3 only
(d) All of the above

211. Which of the following statements are true regarding Foreign Portfolio Investors (FPIs):

1. They fund India's Current Account Deficit (CAD)
2. They help in achieving governments disinvestment target
3. They are liable to pay capital gain tax in India

Select the correct answer using the code given below:
(a) 1 only
(b) 2 & 3 only
(c) 3 only
(d) All of the above

212. Foreign Direct Investment in India under "Government Route" is approved by which of the following agency/body:
(a) Department of Economic Affairs
(b) Department for Promotion of Industry and Internal Trade (DPIIT)
(c) Reserve Bank of India (RBI)
(d) Respective administrative Ministry/ Department

213. Which of the following instruments can be considered as part of External Commercial Borrowing (ECB)?

1. Trade credits
2. Preference shares
3. Fully and compulsorily convertible debentures

Select the correct answer using the code given below:
(a) 1 only
(b) 2 and 3 only
(c) 1 and 2 only
(d) All of the above

214. Consider the following statements regarding External Commercial Borrowing (ECB):

1. All ECB requires approval
2. Approval is not required but RBI needs to be informed
3. It requires approval of RBI
4. It requires approval of Department of economic Affairs, Ministry of Finance

Select the correct answer using the code given below:

(a) 1 & 3 only
(b) 1 and 4 only
(c) 2 only
(d) 3 only

215. Consider the following statements:

1. External Commercial Borrowing is a part of 'Foreign Investment' in India
2. Financial Leases are instruments of External Commercial Borrowing
3. Foreign Currency Convertible Bonds (FCCB) can be included in both ECB and 'Foreign Investment'

Select the correct answer using the code given below:
(a) 1 only
(b) 1 & 2 only
(c) 2 & 3 only
(d) All of the above

216. Consider the following statements regarding 'Masala' bonds:

1. Through masala bonds, capital is raised in foreign currency
2. Repayment is made in foreign currency
3. By issuance of masala bonds, the exchange risk is transferred to the investor

Select the correct answer using the code given below:
(a) 1 only
(b) 2 & 3 only
(c) 1 & 3 only
(d) All of the above

217. Which of the following measures will help in preventing rupee depreciation:

1. Easing restriction on ECB
2. Easing restrictions on raising funds through Masala Bonds
3. Restricting imports of non-essential commodities
4. Restricting FPI investments in India

Select the correct answer using the code given below:
(a) 1 & 2 only
(b) 1 & 3 only
(c) 1, 2 & 3 only
(d) 3 & 4 only

218. Consider the following statements regarding "GIFT-SEZ":

1. All transactions are in foreign currency only
2. It is the only place in India designated as 'International Financial Services Centre'
3. It provides financial services to residents and non-residents both

Select the correct answer using the code given below:
(a) 1 only
(b) 2 only
(c) 2 & 3 only
(d) All of the above

219. Consider the following statements regarding "GIFT-SEZ":

1. GIFT-SEZ units are treated as non-resident in India
2. Indian companies can list their shares on international exchanges in GIFT-SEZ
3. Overseas Direct Investment (ODI) rules will be applicable on Indian entities investing in GIFT-SEZ

Select the correct answer using the code given below:
(a) 1 only
(b) 2 only
(c) 2 & 3 only
(d) All of the above

220. Consider the following statements regarding 'Masala Bonds':

1. It may be listed in India
2. It is part of India's external debt
3. Masala bonds help in financing India's current account deficit

Select the correct answer using the code given below:
(a) 1 only
(b) 2 only
(c) 2 & 3 only
(d) All of the above

221. Consider the following statements regarding "strategic disinvestment" of PSUs:

1. Government sells up to 50% or higher percentage of shares to a strategic partner
2. Management control must be transferred to the strategic partner
3. Other PSUs can bid in the strategic disinvestment process

Select the correct answer using the code given below:
(a) 1 only
(b) 2 only
(c) 1 & 2 only
(d) All of the above

222. Which of the following ministries/departments identify PSUs for "Strategic Disinvestment"?

(a) Department of Investment and Public Asset Management (DIPAM)
(b) NITI Aayog
(c) Jointly by DIPAM and NITI Aayog
(d) Inter-Ministerial body called 'Alternative Mechanism'

223. Which of the following are the objectives of the 'Strategic Disinvestment Policy' of Govt. of India announced recently?

1. Financing of social sector and developmental programmes of Govt.
2. Creating new space for private sector
3. Post disinvestment PSUs will be able to create more jobs and contribute to economic growth through private capital and technology

Select the correct answer using the code given below:
(a) 2 only
(b) 3 only
(c) 1 & 2
(d) All of the above

224. Which of the following will be included in the balance of payments of India?
1. It records transactions between the citizens of a country and the rest of the world
2. Factor income of Indian residents from abroad
3. Gift received by a family in India from his NRI son

Select the correct answer using the code given below:
(a) 1 only
(b) 1 & 2 only
(c) 2 & 3 only
(d) All of the above

225. Which of the following constitute Capital Account in BoP?

1. Global Depository Receipts (GDRs)
2. NRI deposits
3. Government securities purchased by foreign Investors
4. Securities purchased by foreign portfolio investors

Select the correct answer using the code given below:
(a) 1 & 2 only
(b) 3 & 4 only
(c) 1, 2 & 4 only
(d) All of the above

226. Consider the following statements regarding 'Global Depository Receipts':

(a) It is a form of equity investment in listed Indian companies
(b) These are investments in banks through debt papers
(c) These are a way for external borrowing by Indian companies
(d) It is a way of borrowing by Govt. of India from external sources

227. Which of the following are parts of capital account transaction?

1. Masala bonds
2. Purchase of capital equipment's from abroad
3. NRI deposits in Indian banks

Select the correct answer using the code given below:
(a) 1 only
(b) 1 & 2 only
(c) 3 only
(d) 1 & 3 only

228. Which of the following statements are parts of 'Transfer Payments' in balance of payment?

1. Gift sent by an NRI to his friend in India
2. Money sent by an Indian employee to his family in India who has gone abroad temporarily

Select the correct answer using the code given below:
(a) 1 only
(b) 2 only
(c) Both 1 & 2
(d) Neither 1 nor 2

229. Arrange the countries in the decreasing order of remittances received (in dollars) last year (2024):

(a) India>China>Mexico>Philippines
(b) China>India>Mexico>Philippines
(c) India>China>Philippines>Mexico
(d) India> Mexico> China>Philippines

230. The Current Account Deficit in Balance of Payment can be financed through:

1. Net capital inflow
2. Foreign exchange reserve transaction

Select the correct answer using the code given below:
(a) 1 only
(b) 2 only
(c) Both 1 & 2
(d) None of the above

231. Consider the following statements regarding currency swap agreement between two countries:

1. The countries can exchange their own currencies or a third currency
2. It is an open-ended credit line from one country to another at a fixed exchange rate

Select the correct answer using the code given below:
(a) 1 only
(b) 2 only
(c) Both 1 & 2
(d) Neither 1 nor 2

232. Consider the following statements regarding Reserve Bank of India (RBI) Act 1934:

1. As per the RBI Act 1934, RBI, in public interest can supersede the management of a non-banking financial company
2. The Central Government can supersede the 'Central Board' of RBI under RBI Act 1934

Select the correct answer using the code given below:
(a) 1 only
(b) 2 only
(c) Both 1 & 2
(d) Neither 1 nor 2

233. Consider the following statements regarding resolution of stressed assets:

1. RBI can issue directions to banking companies for resolution of stressed assets
2. RBI can direct banking companies to move through IBC 2016 for resolution of stressed assets only upon authorization of Govt. of India
3. Lenders require RBI authorization for resolution of stressed assets under IBC Code 2016

Select the correct answer using the code given below:
(a) 1 only
(b) 1 & 2 only
(c) 2 & 3 only
(d) All of the above

234. Which of the following statements are true regarding the Insolvency and Bankruptcy Code 2016?

1. Committee of Creditors consist of only financial creditors
2. Operational creditors do not share the resolution proceeds
3. NCLT will decide the distribution of proceeds between financial and operational creditors

Select the correct answer using the code given below:
(a) 1 only
(b) 1 & 2 only
(c) 2 & 3 only
(d) 3 only

235. Consider the following statements regarding Insolvency and Bankruptcy Code (IBC) 2016:

1. IBC is applicable for Financial Service Providers like NBFCs
2. Central Government has the authority to decide which type of financial service providers will be included for resolution under IBC
3. IBC has not been made applicable for insolvency of banks

Select the correct answer using the code given below:
(a) 1 only
(b) 1 & 2 only
(c) 3 only
(d) All of the above

236. Consider the following statements regarding resolution of Financial Service Providers (FSP) under IBC 2016.

1. Govt. of India in consultation with appropriate regulator will decide which category of FSPs can be taken up for resolution under IBC 2016
2. To initiate resolution of FSPs under IBC 2016, the appropriate regulator should make an application

Select the correct answer using the code given below:
(a) 1 only
(b) 2 only
(c) Both 1 & 2
(d) Neither 1 nor 2

237. Who cannot bid for companies put up for sale under the new Insolvency and Bankruptcy Code (IBC):
1. A wilful defaulter
2. Promoters of the company

Select the correct answer using the code given below
(a) 1 only
(b) 2 only
(c) Both 1 & 2
(d) Neither 1 nor 2

238. Which of the following statements are true regarding the SARFAESI Act 2002?

1. It is applicable to banks and NBFCs both
2. It allows selling of the security in case of secured lending

Select the correct answer using the code given below:
(a) 1 only
(b) 2 only
(c) Both 1 & 2
(d) Neither 1 nor 2

239. Consider the following statements regarding the recently created 'bad bank':

1. It will help in the resolution of bad assets of only public sector banks
2. The bad bank will purchase bad assets from banks in cash
3. Govt. of India is giving guarantee on the securities issued by the bad bank

Select the correct answer using the code given below:
(a) 1 & 3 only
(b) 2 only
(c) 3 only
(d) None of the above

240. Consider the following statements regarding "Pre-Pack" scheme under IBC 2016:

1. It is applicable for defaults by MSMEs of less than Rs. 1 crore
2. The management will remain with the promoters of the distressed firm
3. Only debtors can initiate pre-pack insolvency resolution

Select the correct answer using the code given below:
(a) 1 & 2 only
(b) 1 & 3 only
(c) 2 & 3 only
(d) All of the above

241. "Liquidity Coverage Ratio" is defined as a ratio of:

(a) High quality liquid assets to cash outflow for 30 days period
(b) High quality liquid assets to deposits of the public in the bank
(c) High quality liquid assets to net cash outflow amount over a 30 days period
(d) High quality liquid assets to total lending of banks

242. Consider the following statements regarding crypto currencies in India:

1. They are treated as virtual digital assets rather than a legal currency
2. Income from transfer of these crypto currencies are taxed at rate of 30%
3. Levy of tax on cryptos does not legalise crypto trade

Select the correct answer using the code given below:
(a) 1 only
(b) 1 & 2 only
(c) 2 & 3
(d) All of the above

243. Consider the following statements regarding Central Bank Digital Currency (CBDC) e-Rupee:

1. It will be a fiat currency and legal tender and will not have intrinsic value
2. It will exist only in digital form
3. CBDCs held by people will be reflected as liability on the RBI balance sheet rather than banks
4. It could lead to instantaneous payment without any processing delays

Select the correct answer using the code given below:
(a) 1 & 3 only
(b) 2 & 4 only
(c) 3 & 4 only
(d) All of the above

244. Consider the following statements regarding CBDC (e-Rupee):

1. It is a bearer instrument
2. It would offer features of physical cash like trust, safety and settlement facility
3. RBI Act 1934 has been amended to include e-Rupee as legal tender

Select the correct answer using the code given below:
(a) 1 & 2 only
(b) 2 & 3 only
(c) 1 & 3 only
(d) All of the above

245. A reduction in repo rate by RBI may not be transmitted into lending rate in the economy because of:

1. Banks cost of funds remaining high
2. Government offering higher interest on its own savings schemes
3. Liquidity crunch in the economy

Select the correct answer using the code given below:
(a) 1 & 2 only
(b) 2 & 3 only
(c) 1 & 3 only
(d) All of the above

246. Which of the following statements are true regarding the 'Co-lending' by Banks and NBFCs for lending to priority sector:

1. The banks can claim the total amount of loan given under co-lending as priority sector lending
2. The banks and NBFCs have to keep the same price for their part of the loan
3. In this model banks can leverage their strong presence in local markets while NBFCs will have the cheap availability of funds

Select the correct answer using the code given below:

(a) 1 only
(b) 2 only
(c) None of the above
(d) All of the above

247. Which of the following will deter investments in the economy?

1. High real interest rate
2. High-capacity utilization

Select the correct answer using the code given below:
(a) 1 only
(b) 2 only
(c) Both 1 & 2
(d) Neither 1 nor 2

248. Consider the following statements in a market determined exchange rate system:

1. Imposing tariff may not help in improving trade balance as the exchange rate moves to offset the tariff
2. The exchange rate depends on the demand and supply of the two currencies

Select the correct answer using the code given below:
(a) 1 only
(b) 2 only
(c) Both 1 & 2
(d) Neither 1 nor 2

249. Consider the following statements regarding rupee-dollar rate in foreign exchange market:

1. Inflation in the domestic economy will lead to rupee depreciation
2. Rupee depreciation will lead to inflation in the domestic goods in the economy

Select the correct answer using the code given below:
(a) 1 only
(b) 2 only
(c) Both 1 & 2
(d) Neither 1 nor 2

250. Which of the following activities will increase liquidity in the economy?

1. Advance tax payment
2. Input tax credit on GST
3. Front loading of government expenditure
4. Recapitalization of public sector banks

Select the correct answer using the code given below:
(a) 1 & 3 only
(b) 2, 3 & 4 only
(c) 3 & 4 only
(d) All of the above

251. The problem of international liquidity is related to the non-availability of:

(a) Goods and services
(b) Gold and silver
(c) Dollars and other hard currencies
(d) Exportable surplus

252. Surplus liquidity in the economy may result in which of the following:

1. Reduction in cost of capital
2. Depreciation of currency
3. Softening of bond yield

Select the correct answer using the code given below:
(a) 2 only

(b) 1 & 3 only
(c) 2 & 3 only
(d) All of the above

253. Consider the following statements:

1. If interest rate goes up, bond yield goes up
2. Bond yield can change even if interest rate does not change

Select the correct answer using the code given below:
(a) 1 only
(b) 2 only
(c) Both 1 & 2
(d) Neither 1 nor 2

254. If there is a surge in bond yields in the domestic economy, then:

1. Bondholders will gain
2. It will attract FPI debt investors
3. It will positively impact Government's disinvestment plan

Select the correct answer using the code given below:
(a) 1 only
(b) 2 only
(c) 1 & 2 only
(d) All of the above

255. Consider the following statements regarding bond yield:

1. Generally, the yield curve of bonds is upward sloping
2. Bond yield inversion happens when yield on short duration bonds are higher than long duration bonds
3. Generally, the inversion in bond yield curve indicates a trouble in the economy

Select the correct answer using the code given below:
(a) 1 & 2 only
(b) 3 only
(c) 2 & 3 only
(d) All of the above

256. Consider the following statements regarding microfinance loans:

1. It should be collateral free loan
2. Interest rate is regulated by RBI
3. These are loans availed by households having annual income up to Rs. 3,00,000

Select the correct answer using the code given below:
(a) 1 only
(b) 2 only
(c) 1 & 3 only
(d) All of the above

257. Which of the following type of institutions provide the maximum microfinance credit:

(a) Banks
(b) NBFCs
(c) MFI-NBFCs
(d) Others

258. Consider the following statements:

1. Debt overhang refers to a debt burden so large that an entity cannot take on additional debt to finance future projects.
2. Debt trap is a situation in which it becomes difficult or impossible to repay the debt

Select the correct answer using the code given below:
(a) 1 only
(b) 2 only
(c) Both 1 & 2
(d) Neither 1 nor 2

259. Which of the following can be considered as a case of 'financial repression'?

1. Banks requiring to maintain statutory liquidity ratio
2. Cap on banks interest rates
3. Issuance of non-marketable debt by the government
4. Regulation of cross border capital movement

Select the correct answer using the code given below:
(a) 1 only
(b) 2 & 3 only
(c) 1, 2 & 3 only
(d) All of the above

260. In the recent times, Indian companies have aggressively pursued 'deleveraging', which refers to:

(a) Converting their debt into equity

(b) Reducing the debt by selling assets of the companies

(c) Reducing the promoter's equity in the company

(d) Increasing debt to fund business expansion plans

261. Consider the following statements regarding 'Circuit Breaker':

1. Circuit breaker applies when the stock or indices moves too much in either direction
2. Circuit breakers when triggered may bring about a coordinated trading halt in all the equity markets nationwide

Select the correct answer using the code given below:
(a) 1 only
(b) 2 only
(c) Both 1 & 2
(d) Neither 1 nor 2

262. The term 'Transfer Pricing' was recently in the news, it is related to which of the following?

(a) The price at which one company sells intermediate goods to other companies
(b) The price at which goods are transferred within group companies
(c) The price at which goods are transferred between shell companies
(d) The price at which one company transfers its goods from one state to another state for stocking purpose

263. Consider the following statements regarding 'Advance Pricing Agreement':

1. It is an agreement between a tax authority and a taxpayer
2. It is an agreement between two governments
3. It is an agreement to discover the pricing methodology between related company transactions
4. It helps in making a country an attractive destination for foreign investments

Select the correct answer using the codes given below the lists:
(a) 1 & 3 only
(b) 2 & 3 only
(c) 2 & 4 only
(d) 1, 3 & 4 only

264. Consider the following statements regarding 'Financial Stability Report':

(a) Released annually by Dept. of Economic Affairs
(b) Released biannually by Dept. of Economic Affairs
(c) Released annually by RBI
(d) Released biannually by RBI

265. Consider the following statements regarding 'National Financial Reporting Authority (NFRA)':

1. It has been established under Company's Act 2013
2. It recommends accounting and auditing policies and standards to the Central Government for adoption by companies
3. It has the power to enforce compliance with accounting/auditing standards and undertake investigation of the auditors

Select the correct answer using the code given below:
(a) 1 only
(b) 1 & 2 only
(c) 2 & 3 only
(d) All of the above

266. Consider the following statements regarding the National Bank for Financing Infrastructure Development (NaBFID):

1. It will provide long term non-recourse infrastructure financing
2. It will seek to attract private sector investors and institutional investors in infrastructure projects in India
3. It has been established as a development financial institution by an act of Parliament

Select the correct answer using the code given below:
(a) 1 & 2 only
(b) 2 & 3 only
(c) 3 only
(d) All of the above

Budgeting Process and Tax

267. Which of the following figures are presented as part of the Budget presentation in Parliament?

1. Budgeted receipts and expenses for the next Financial Year (FY)
2. Budgeted receipts and expenses for the current FY
3. Revised receipts and expenses for the current FY
4. Actual receipts and expenses for the last FY

Select the correct answer using the code given below:
(a) 1 only
(b) 1 & 2 only
(c) 1, 2, & 3 only
(d) All of the above

268. Consider the following statements:

1. Supplementary demand is presented before the end of the financial year to which it relates for any additional expenditure
2. Demand for excess grants is presented once the expenditure has been done and the financial year to which it relates has passed

Select the correct answer using the code given below:
(a) 1 only
(b) 2 only
(c) Both 1 & 2
(d) Neither 1 nor 2

269. Consider the following statements regarding presentation of Budget in the Parliament:

1. Finance Bill is introduced on the very first day when the Finance Minister presents Budget in the Parliament
2. Appropriation Bill is introduced after the voting on demand for grants is over

Select the correct answer using the code given below:
(a) 1 only
(b) 2 only
(c) Both 1 & 2
(d) Neither 1 nor 2

270. Consider the following statements:

1. Demand for Grants are not approved in Vote-on-Account
2. Demand for Grants of UTs without assembly are approved as part of Union budget
3. Rajya Sabha does not vote on Demand for Grants but can discuss

Select the correct answer using the code given below:
(a) 1 & 2 only
(b) 2 & 3 only
(c) 1 & 3 only
(d) All of the above

271. Which of the following department prepares outcome budget?

(a) Public finance division under department of expenditure
(b) Budget division under department of Economic affairs
(c) Department of financial services
(d) NITI Aayog

272. Which of the following statement is not true regarding "Outcome Budget":

(a) It is not presented in parliament
(b) It measures development outcomes of govt. programmes
(c) It helps in better service delivery
(d) It reduces unnecessary expenses

273. Surplus reserves of RBI transferred to Government of India (GOI) will come under which of the following?

(a) Market borrowings and other liabilities
(b) Non-tax revenue receipts
(c) Non-debt capital receipts
(d) Debt receipts

274. The Grants-in-aid given by the Central Government to the State Governments and local bodies for creation of capital assets are classified in the Union budget under?

(a) Revenue expenditure
(b) Capital Expenditure
(c) Both Revenue and Capital expenditure
(d) None of the above

275. The term 'Effective Capital Expenditure' is equal to Centre's capital expenditure plus:

(a) Central PSUs Capital Expenditure
(b) Grants given to States for creation of capital assets
(c) Finance Commission transfers to States for creation of capital assets
(d) Loans given to States for creation of capital assets

276. Which of the following are Non-Tax Revenue Receipts of Govt. of India?

1. Spectrum Auction
2. Revenues of IRCTC
3. Examination Fee of Union Public Service Commission

Select the correct answer using the code given below:
(a) 1 only
(b) 1 & 3 only
(c) 3 only
(d) All of the above

277. Which of the following are non-debt capital receipts of Govt. of India?

1. Disinvestment of PSUs
2. Recovery of loans
3. Public Account receipts
4. Cash Management Bills

Select the correct answer using the code given below:
(a) 1 only
(b) 1 & 2 only
(c) 3 & 4 only
(d) 1, 2 & 3 only

278. Which of the following are part of Capital Budget of Govt. of India?

1. Proceeds received in the public account of India
2. PSUs purchasing capital equipment
3. Establishment of “India Post Payment Bank”

Select the correct answer using the code given below:
(a) 1 only
(b) 2 & 3 only
(c) 1 & 3 only
(d) None of the above

279. Which of the following is/are included in the capital budget of the Government of India?

1. Expenditure on acquisition of assets like roads, buildings, machinery, etc.
2. Loans received from foreign governments
3. Loans and advances granted to the States and Union Territories

Select the correct answer using the code given below.

(a) 1 only
(b) 2 & 3 only
(c) 1 & 3 only
(d) All of the above

280. Which of the following are parts of capital budget of Govt. of India?

1. Issuance of Sovereign Gold Bonds
2. Receipt from Gold Monetization
3. Issuance of Sovereign Green Bonds

Select the correct answer using the code given below:

(a) 1 only
(b) 2 only
(c) 1 & 2 only
(d) All of the above

281. Which of the following are revenue receipts of Central Government budget?

1. RBI paying dividend to govt. of India
2. PSUs paying dividend to govt. of India
3. PSUs earnings
4. Proceeds from sale of govt. land

Select the correct answer using the code given below:

(a) 1 only
(b) 1 & 2 only
(c) 1, 2 & 3 only
(d) All of the above

282. Consider the following statements:

1. Central Government revenue (tax + non-tax) receipts/collection is more than all States and UTs combined revenue collection
2. Central Government expenditure is more than all States and UTs combined expenditure

Select the correct answer using the code given below:

(a) 1 only
(b) 2 only
(c) Both 1 & 2
(d) Neither 1 nor 2

283. Govt. of India is financing the 'National Infrastructure Pipeline' through which of the following ways?

1. Establishment of National Bank for Financing Infrastructure and Development (NaBFID)
2. Creation of a 'National Monetization Pipeline' of potential brownfield infrastructure assets which can be monetized
3. Nudging States to spend more on infrastructure

Select the correct answer using the code given below:

(a) 2 only
(b) 2 & 3 only
(c) 1 & 3 only
(d) All of the above

284. "Tax Buoyancy" in the economy is defined as:

1. Ratio of percentage change in tax revenue to percentage change in GDP
2. Ratio of change in tax revenue to change in GDP
3. Percentage increase in tax revenues as measured from previous year
4. Incremental change in tax revenues required to increase the GDP by one percent

Select the correct answer using the code given below:
(a) 1 only
(b) 1 & 2 only
(c) 3 only
(d) 2 & 4 only

285. Which of the following factors may lead to increase in 'Tax Buoyancy'?

1. Increase in GDP
2. Improvement in tax administration
3. Formalization of Economy
4. Bringing agriculture income under tax

Select the correct answer using the code given below:
(a) 1, 2 & 3 only
(b) 3 & 4 only
(c) 2, 3 & 4 only
(d) All of the above

286. Consider the following statements regarding 'Service Charge' levied by hotels and restaurants:
1. It is a kind of indirect tax collected by Government
2. Presently hotels and restaurants have been denied to collect 'service charge'
3. Hotels and restaurants can levy service charge but not on takeaway orders

Select the correct answer using the code given below:
(a) 1 only
(b) 2 only
(c) 3 only
(d) 1 & 2 only

287. Consider the following statements regarding Tax Deducted at Source (TDS) and Tax Collected at Source (TCS):

1. TDS is part of Income tax while TCS is outside the purview of income tax
2. TCS payments cannot be adjusted against TDS

Select the correct answer using the code given below:
(a) 1 only
(b) 2 only
(c) Both 1 & 2
(d) Neither 1 nor 2

288. Which of the following receipts goes to Public Account of India:

1. Dated securities
2. Kisan Vikas Patra
3. Sukanya Samriddhi Account
4. Public Provident Fund

Select the correct answer using the code given below:
(a) 1 & 4 only
(b) 2 & 3 only
(c) 2, 3 & 4 only
(d) All of the above

289. Consider the following statements regarding the various 'Small Savings Schemes' offered by Govt. of India

1. The money collected goes into the National Small Savings Fund (NSSF) under Public Account of India
2. The interest rate on these schemes have been linked with G-securities of similar maturities
3. The NSSF fund is used to lend money to Govt. of India and other Govt. agencies like FCI/NHAI

Select the correct answer using the code given below:
(a) 1 only
(b) 1 & 2 only
(c) 3 only
(d) All of the above

290. Fiscal Deficit is equal to:

1. Total expenditure minus total receipts
2. Total expenditure minus total receipts excluding borrowing
3. Revenue deficit plus capital expenditure minus non debt creating capital receipts

4. Total borrowing

Select the correct answer using the code given below:
(a) 1 & 4 only
(b) 2 & 3 only
(c) 2, 3 & 4 only
(d) All of the above

291. Fiscal Deficit of the Government of India is equal to which of the following:

(a) Debt creating capital receipts
(b) Non-Debt capital receipts
(c) Debt and non-debt capital receipts
(d) Capital receipts less of revenue receipts

292. There has been a persistent deficit budget year after year. Which of the following actions can be taken by the Government to reduce the deficit?

1. Reducing revenue expenditure
2. Introducing new welfare schemes
3. Rationalizing subsidies

Select the correct answer using the code given below.
(a) 1 & 3 only
(b) 2 & 3 only
(c) 1 only
(d) All of the above

293. Consider the following statements regarding the government's fiscal deficit:

1. It may be inflationary
2. It may not be inflationary
3. It raises effective demand

Select the correct answer using the code given below:
(a) 1 only
(b) 2 only
(c) 1 & 2 only
(d) All of the above

294. Fiscal Slippage may result in which of the following:

1. Increase in bond yield
2. decrease in market interest rates
3. Increase in aggregate demand

Select the correct answer using the code given below:
(a) 1 & 2 only
(b) 1 & 3 only
(c) 2 & 3 only
(d) All of the above

295. Which of the following directly finances Govt. of India's fiscal deficit?

1. Foreign Direct Investors
2. Foreign Portfolio Investors
3. NRIs
4. RBI

Select the correct answer using the code given below:
(a) 1 only
(b) 2 only
(c) 2 & 3 only
(d) 2, 3 & 4 only

296. Which of the following statements are true regarding "fiscal stimulus":

1. It is a strategy to boost sluggish economy
2. RBI pumps money into the economy
3. Government reduces subsidies
4. Public spending increases

Select the correct answer using the code given below:
(a) 1 & 2 only
(b) 1, 2, & 4 only
(c) 1, 3 & 4 only
(d) 1 & 4 only

297. Change in the fiscal policy can have impact on which of the following?

(a) Current Account in BoP
(b) Capital Account in BoP
(c) Both (a) & (b)
(d) Neither (a) nor (b)

298. Consider the following statements regarding "counter-cyclical" fiscal policy:

1. Government uses the counter cyclical policy to cool down the economy during boom period
2. In counter cyclical policy, government increases spending and reduces taxes during economic slowdown

Select the correct answer using the code given below:
(a) 1 only
(b) 2 only
(c) Both 1 & 2
(d) Neither 1 nor 2

299. Consider the following statements regarding 'Fiscal Consolidation' policy:

1. It is an effort by the government to bring down fiscal deficit
2. It is an effort to reduce public debt
3. It is an effort to reduce current account deficit
4. It is an effort to raise revenues and bring down wasteful expenses

Select the correct answer using the code given below:
(a) 1, 2 & 3 only
(b) 1, 2 & 4 only
(c) 4 only
(d) All of the above

300. Select the correct statement regarding the term 'Fiscal Dominance':

(a) Greater influence of fiscal policy in handling the economy as compared to monetary policy
(b) Fiscal policy creating obstacles in achieving the monetary objectives
(c) Crowing out of the private sector because of higher government borrowing
(d) Fiscal considerations limiting the scope for an independent monetary policy

301. As per the Fiscal Responsibility and Budget Management (FRBM) Act 2003, which of the following statement is not presented in the budget session of the parliament?

(a) Medium Term Fiscal Policy Statement
(b) Fiscal Policy Strategy Statement
(c) Macro-economic Framework Statement
(d) Medium-term Expenditure Framework Statement

302. Consider the following statements regarding "Monetisation of Deficit":

1. RBI purchases government bonds in the primary market
2. It is allowed as per FRBM Act 2003 but only under exceptional circumstances
3. It may lead to inflation and macroeconomic instability

Select the correct answer using the code given below:
(a) 1 & 2 only
(b) 2 & 3 only
(c) 1 & 3 only
(d) All of the above

303. Which of the following may lead to rupee depreciation?

1. Expansionary fiscal policy
2. Expansionary monetary policy
3. Monetisation of Deficit
4. Debasement of currency

Select the correct answer using the code given below:

(a) 1 & 2 only
(b) 1, 2 & 3 only
(c) 3 & 4 only
(d) All of the above

304. Which of the following policies help to raise interest rate unambiguously and thereby lead to appreciation of currency?

(a) Expansionary fiscal and monetary policy
(b) Contractionary fiscal and monetary policy

(c) Contractionary fiscal policy and expansionary monetary policy
(d) Contractionary monetary policy and expansionary fiscal policy

305. Consider the following statements:

1. Before 1997, central government used to directly monetise its deficit from RBI
2. The primary objective of OMO is to support government borrowing by purchase of govt bonds in the open market

Select the correct answer using the code given below:
(a) 1 only
(b) 2 only
(c) Both 1 & 2
(d) Neither 1 nor 2

306. Which of the following statement is true regarding "Tax Base"?

(a) It is the number of taxpayers
(b) It is the number of people and business units under tax net
(c) It is the income of people which can be taxed by the government
(d) It is the aggregate value of financial streams on which tax can be imposed by the government

307. Which of the following taxes are regressive in nature?
1. Income Tax
2. Sales Tax
3. Goods & Services Tax (GST)
4. Value Added Tax (VAT)

Select the correct answer using the code given below:
(a) 1 only
(b) 2 only
(c) 1 & 2 only
(d) 2, 3 & 4 only

308. Consider the following with respect to regressive taxation:

1. It's the taxation system where the tax% is less for the rich and more for the poor
2. Inflation Tax is not regressive, rather a proportional tax in nature

Select the correct answer using the code given below:
(a) 1 only
(b) 2 only
(c) Both 1 & 2
(d) Neither 1 nor 2

309. Consider the following statements regarding Goods and Services Tax (GST):
1. Taxes need to be paid at each point in the value chain
2. It will have input tax credit mechanism
3. The total taxes will be passed on to the consumers
4. It is a value added tax

Select the correct answer using the code given below:
(a) 1 & 2 only
(b) 1 & 3 only
(c) 2 & 3 only
(d) All of the above

310. Consider the following statements regarding IGST:

1. It is levied by the Centre on inter-state supply of goods
2. The IGST rate is equal to CGST plus the SGST/UTGST rate
3. The tax revenue is shared equally among the Centre and the consuming State/UT

Select the correct answer using the code given below:
(a) 1 only
(b) 2 only
(c) 1 & 3 only
(d) All of the above

311. Consider the following statements regarding the GST Compensation Cess:

1. It is levied and collected by the Centre
2. GST compensation fund has been established in Consolidated Fund of India
3. GST Compensation Cess has been extended till March 2026 to compensate States for any shortfall in tax revenue growth below 14%

Select the correct answer using the code given below:
(a) 1 only
(b) 2 only
(c) 1 & 3 only
(d) All of the above

312. Consider the following statements regarding Goods and Services Tax?
1. It has led to harmonization of taxes
2. There is no GST levied in the entire supply chain in case of exports

Select the correct answer using the code given below:
(a) 1 only
(b) 2 only
(c) Both 1 & 2
(d) Neither 1 nor 2

313. Consider the following statements:

1. Central Government levies National Calamity Contingent Duty to finance National Disaster Response Fund (NDRF)
2. NDRF has been established under Public Account of India

Select the correct answer using the code given below:
(a) 1 only
(b) 2 only
(c) Both 1 & 2
(d) Neither 1 nor 2

314. Consider the following statements regarding import of goods in India:

1. They are treated as inter-state supplies for GST
2. Customs duty and IGST both are applicable
3. Imports are zero-rated

Select the correct answer using the code given below:
(a) 1 & 2 only
(b) 1 & 3 only
(c) 3 only
(d) All of the above

315. Which of the following statements are true regarding the "Electronic - Way Bill"?

1. It is mandatory as per the GST law
2. It is required for goods transported worth more than Rs. 50,000/-
3. It will check tax evasion

Select the correct answer using the code given below:
(a) 1 only
(b) 1 & 4 only
(c) 1 & 3 only
(d) All of the above

316. Consider the following statements regarding "Composition Scheme" in GST:

1. It exempts small taxpayers from payment of GST
2. It allows small businesses to pay tax at a fix percent of their turnover
3. It reduces the compliance cost for small businesses

Select the correct answer using the code given below:
(a) 1 only
(b) 1 & 3 only
(c) 2 only
(d) 2 & 3 only

317. Which agency deals with the complaints related to GST profiteering?
(a) National Anti-Profiteering Authority
(b) GST Council

(c) Central Board of Indirect Taxes and Customs
(d) Competition Commission of India

318. Consider the following statements regarding the recommendations of the GST Council:

1. It will be binding on Centre and State for tax rate changes or framing of rules under CGST/SGST
2. It will not be binding on primary legislation like amendments in CGST/SGST

Select the correct answer using the code given below:
(a) 1 only
(b) 2 only
(c) Both 1 & 2
(d) Neither 1 nor 2

319. The term 'Crowd-out' in economy is related to which of the following:

1. Increased public sector spending replaces private sector spending
2. Governments deficit spending through borrowed money leads to hardening of interest rates
3. Government spending uses up financial resources that would otherwise be used by private firms
4. Government providing a service or good that would otherwise be a business opportunity for private industry

Select the correct answer using the code given below:
(a) 1 only
(b) 1 & 2 only
(c) 2 & 3 only
(d) All of the above

320. The term 'Crowd-in' in the economy is related to which of the following?

1. Targeted government spending acts as an engine of growth in the short run
2. Government spending complements the private investment
3. Government spending substitutes the private investment
4. Government spending boosts demand for goods which in turn increases private demand

Select the correct answer using the code given below:
(a) 1 & 2 only
(b) 1 & 3 only
(c) 1, 2 & 4 only
(d) 1, 3 & 4 only

321. Consider the following statements

1. Higher growth rate relative to interest rate makes the debt sustainable
2. Long maturity profile of debt reduces the rollover risk

Select the correct answer using the code given below:
(a) 1 only
(b) 2 only
(c) Both 1 & 2
(d) Neither 1 nor 2

322. Consider the following statements regarding inverted duty structure in GST:

1. It is the result of several tax slabs in our GST structure
2. It results in loss of revenue for the government

Select the correct answer using the code given below:
(a) 1 only
(b) 2 only
(c) Both 1 & 2
(d) Neither 1 nor 2

323. Consider the following statements regarding use of Aadhar for benefit transfer:

1. The money can be drawn only by Central Govt. from the Consolidated Fund of India

2. The States can also use Aadhar to transfer benefit from Consolidated Fund of States
3. Central government can make Aadhar mandatory for authentication to provide any subsidy
4. It can be used for transfer of benefit to individuals who are residing in India for more than 182 days

Select the correct answer using the code given below:
(a) 1 only
(b) 2 & 4 only
(c) 1, 3 & 4 only
(d) 2, 3 & 4 only

324. When a portion of public debt falls due, refinancing of public debt is done by:

(a) Selling new bonds and using proceeds to pay off holders of maturity bonds
(b) Extending maturity of debt by raising the interest payable on rate maturing debt
(c) Raising taxes to provide funds to repay the maturing bonds
(d) Print additional paper currency to meet maturing obligations

325. Which of the following statements are true regarding "Deficit Financing"?

1. It raises aggregate demand in the economy
2. It may result in inflation in the economy
3. It is used as a developmental tool by developing countries
4. It is done by issuing government bonds

Select the correct answer using the code given below:
(a) 1 & 2 only
(b) 1, 2 & 3 only
(c) 3 & 4 only
(d) All of the above

326. Inflation acts as a tax in the economy. This tax is:

(a) Progressive
(b) Proportional
(c) Regressive
(d) None of the above

327. Consider the following statements regarding the Corporate Income Tax which the government reduced effectively to 25.17%:

1. It is applicable for domestic companies
2. It is applicable only if the companies are not availing various tax exemptions
3. The above rate is including Cess and Surcharge

Select the correct answer using the code given below:
(a) 1 only
(b) 1 & 2 only
(c) 2 & 3 only
(d) All of the above

328. Consider the following statements regarding 'Equalisation Levy':

1. It is a direct tax
2. It is imposed as a percentage of profit
3. It is applicable on Non-resident entities

Select the correct answer using the code given below:
(a) 3 only
(b) 1 & 3 only
(c) 1 & 2 only
(d) 2 & 3 only

329. Once the Global Minimum Corporate Tax becomes effective (let the rate be "GMT") then:

(a) The countries will not be allowed to keep the tax rate below GMT

(b) A country can keep the tax rate below GMT but the foreign firms operating in that country will have to pay tax to the level of GMT

(c) A country can keep the tax rate below GMT but the foreign firms operating in that country will have to pay tax to the level of tax rate prevalent in their home country

(d) A country can keep the tax rate below GMT but the foreign firms operating in that country can be asked to pay the difference of GMT and the country's tax rate to their home country

330. Which department decides the outlay for Centrally Sponsored Scheme (CSS)

(a) NITI Aayog
(b) Public Finance Division under department of Expenditure
(c) Economic Division under department of Economic Affairs
(d) None of the above

331. The pool of tax resources of the Union Government which is shared with the States (Vertical Devolution as per FC) is called 'Divisible Pool'. Which of the following are not part of the Divisible Pool?

1. Cess and Surcharge
2. Cost of collection of taxes
3. Tax Revenue of the Union Territories
4. National Calamity Contingency Duty

Select the correct answer using the code given below:

(a) 1 & 4 only
(b) 3 & 4 only
(c) 1, 2 & 3 only
(d) All of the above

332. Consider the following statements regarding the Fifteenth Finance Commission (FFC) recommendations for 2021 to 2026:

1. It has recommended a devolution of 41% of the divisible pool from Central taxes to States
2. It has recommended 'State specific grants, based on their special needs
3. It has recommended 'sector specific grants' which are mostly performance-based incentives

Select the correct answer using the code given below:
(a) 1 only
(b) 2 & 3 only
(c) 1 & 3 only
(d) All of the above

333. Which UT/State's per capita SGDP has been taken as the reference by the Fifteenth Finance Commission for calculating the 'income distance' for horizontal distribution?

(a) Goa
(b) Haryana
(c) Delhi
(d) Maharashtra

334. "Central Government Debt" includes which of the following?

1. Outstanding liabilities on the security of the Consolidated Fund of India
2. Outstanding liabilities in the Public Account of India
3. Off-budget liabilities

Select the correct answer using the code given below:
(a) 1 only
(b) 1 & 2 only
(c) 2 & 3 only
(d) All of the above

335. The Public Debt of Government of India includes which of the following:
1. Treasury Bills & Dated securities
2. External Commercial Borrowing (ECB)
3. NRI deposits
4. Foreign Direct Investment in India (FDI)

Select the correct answer using the code given below:
(a) 1 only

(b) 1 & 3 only
(c) 1, 2 & 3 only
(d) 2 & 4 only

336. Which of the following is the largest holder of Public Debt?

(a) Commercial banks
(b) Provident Funds
(c) Reserve Bank of India
(d) Insurance companies

337. Which of the following is part of India's External Debt?

1. External Commercial Borrowing (ECB)
2. NRI Deposits
3. Investments made by Portfolio Investors in debt securities
4. Portfolio Investors purchasing government securities

Select the correct answer using the code given below:

(a) 1 only
(b) 4 only
(c) 1, 3 & 4 only
(d) All of the above

338. Consider the following regarding India's external debt:

1. It is around 20% of GDP
2. Sovereign Debt is less than 5% of GDP
3. Commercial Borrowings has the highest share in India's external debt

Select the correct answer using the code given below:
(a) 1 & 2 only
(b) 3 only
(c) 1 & 3 only
(d) All of the above

339. Which of the following is rupee denominated India's external debt?

1. FPIs purchasing corporate and Govt. bonds
2. Masala bonds
3. Non-Resident External (NRE) deposits in Indian banks

Select the correct answer using the code given below:
(a) 1 only
(b) 2 & 3 only
(c) 1 & 3 only
(d) All of the above

340. Consider the following statements regarding currency composition of India's external debt:

1. More than 50% debt is denominated in US dollars
2. Less than 10% debt is denominated in Indian Rupee

Select the correct answer using the code given below:
(a) 1 only
(b) 2 only
(c) Both 1 & 2
(d) Neither 1 nor 2

341. Consider the following statements:

1. Centre's accumulated debt is consistently higher than all State's combined debt in the last decade
2. Out of the total debt of Central Govt., public debt is around 90%
3. Public debt is primarily contracted at fixed interest rate

Select the correct answer using the code given below:
(a) 1 only
(b) 1 & 2 only
(c) 2 & 3 only
(d) All of the above

342. Which of the following statements are true regarding FRBM Act 2003?

1. RBI generally subscribes to the primary issues of Central government securities
2. RBI finances Central government fiscal deficit
3. Central government can take advance from RBI in case there is

a mismatch in cash disbursements and cash receipts

Select the correct answer using the code given below:
(a) 1 only
(b) 1 & 3 only
(c) 2 & 3 only
(d) 3 only

343. States need to take prior approval from the Centre for their borrowing:

1. If they have taken debt from Centre and there are pending dues
2. If there is any outstanding loan on State Govt. with respect to which Central Govt. has given guarantee
3. If States are breaching their FRBM targets (every state has enacted their own fiscal responsibility and budget management act)

Select the correct answer using the code given below:
(a) 1 & 2 only
(b) 1 & 3 only
(c) 3 only
(d) All of the above

344. The General Govt. Debt (Centre and States combined) as on 31st March 2023 is:
(a) More than the GDP
(b) Equal to GDP
(c) Less than 90% of the GDP
(d) Half of the GDP

345. Consider the following statements regarding Forex Reserves of India:

(a) If the foreign currencies other than dollars in our forex reserve appreciates then forex reserve will increase
(b) If the foreign currencies other than dollars in our forex reserve appreciates then forex reserve will decrease
(c) Appreciation/depreciation of Foreign currencies other than dollars (in our forex reserve) do not have any impact on our forex reserves
(d) Our forex reserves do not include foreign currencies other than dollars

346. Consider the following statements regarding 'Net International Investment Position (NIIP)':

1. It measures the difference between a nation's stock of foreign assets and foreigner's stock of that nation's assets at a specific point of time
2. The FDI inflow in a country will worsen the NIIP position of that country
3. It represents the debt and equity service burden
4. Increase in our forex reserves will improve NIIP position

Select the correct answer using the code given below:
(a) 1 & 4 only
(b) 2 & 3 only
(c) 1, 3 & 4 only
(d) All of the above

347. India's external liabilities include which of the following?

1. FDI investment in India
2. FPI's debt and equity investments in India

Select the correct answer using the code given below:
(a) 1 only
(b) 2 only
(c) Both 1 & 2
(d) Neither 1 nor 2

348. Which of the following statement is true regarding the 'Scheme for Financial Assistance to States for Capital Investment':

(a) These are interest free loans to States
(b) These are grants to States
(c) These are within the borrowing limits allowed/ fixed for States
(d) None of the above

349. Consider the following statements regarding the "e-assessment scheme":

1. It allows faceless assessment of taxpayers
2. It is for direct taxpayers
3. The national e-assessment centre is based in Mumbai

Select the correct answer using the code given below:
(a) 1 only
(b) 2 only
(c) 1 & 2 only
(d) All of the above

Agriculture, Subsidy and Food Processing

350. Consider the following statements:

1. Agriculture GVA at constant prices has steadily increased in the last 5 years
2. Horticulture production has surpassed food grain production consistently in the last ten years

Select the correct answer using the code given below:
(a) 1 only
(b) 2 only
(c) Both 1 & 2
(d) Neither 1 nor 2

351. Select the correct code arranging the production of foodgrains in descending order:
(a) Rice> Wheat> Coarse grain> Pulses
(b) Rice >Wheat > Pulses > Coarse grain
(c) Wheat> Rice> Coarse grain> Pulses
(d) Wheat> Rice> Pulses> Coarse Grains

352. Consider the following statements regarding agriculture trade:

1. India's agriculture trade has consistently been in surplus in the last 5 years
2. Agriculture exports in value terms has steadily increased in the last 5 years

Select the correct answer using the code given below:
(a) 1 only
(b) 2 only
(c) Both 1 & 2
(d) Neither 1 nor 2

353. Consider the following statements regarding agriculture trade:

1. USA is our top exporter
2. China is our top importer
3. India's highest import commodity is vegetable oil in terms of value

Select the correct answer using the code given below:
(a) 1 only
(b) 1 & 2 only
(c) 2 & 3 only
(d) 1 & 3 only

354. Consider the following statements regarding millets:

1. India is the largest producer of millets in the world
2. Among states, Rajasthan is the largest producer of millets

Select the correct answer using the code given below:

(a) 1 only
(b) 2 only
(c) Both 1 & 2
(d) Neither 1 nor 2

355. Consider the following statements regarding Jute:

1. National Jute Board has been constituted under an act of parliament to promote jute production and its products

2. Govt. mandates packaging of commodities in jute packaging materials through 'Jute Packaging Materials Act 1987'

Select the correct answer using the code given below:
(a) 1 only
(b) 2 only
(c) Both 1 & 2
(d) Neither 1 nor 2

356. Which of the following factors are taken into account by CACP for recommending MSP of agriculture crops?

1. Demand and supply
2. Price trends in domestic and international markets
3. Terms of trade between agriculture and non-agriculture sector
4. Inter-crop price parity
5. Cost of production
6. Likely implications of MSP on the consumers of that product

Select the correct answer using the code given below:

(a) 5 only
(b) 1, 2 and 5 only
(c) 2, 3 & 6
(d) All of the above

357. Government declares MSP which is at least 50% over cost of production. This cost includes:

1. Actual paid out cost on rentals
2. Rentals forgone on owned land
3. Depreciation on agricultural implements
4. Actual storage cost post-harvest

Select the correct answer using the code given below:
(a) 1 only
(b) 1 & 4 only
(c) 2 & 3 only
(d) 1 & 3 only

358. Consider the following statements regarding electronic National Agriculture Market (e-NAM)

1. It will ensure one nation one price of agri commodities for the consumers
2. Farmers can sell their agri-produce through e-NAM sitting at their homes without bringing it in the physical APMC mandis

Select the correct answer using the code given below:
(a) 1 only
(b) 2 only
(c) Both 1 & 2
(d) Neither 1 nor 2

359. Consider the following statements regarding organic foods in India:

1. FSSAI regulates organic foods in India
2. Any food to be sold as 'organic' in India must be certified through National Program for Organic Production (NPOP)
3. 'Jaivik Bharat' is a logo developed by FSSAI for organic products in India

Select the correct answer using the code given below:
(a) 1 only
(b) 3 only
(c) 1 & 3 only
(d) All of the above

360. Which of the following statements are true regarding "Farmer Producer Organization" (FPO):

1. It can be a company, a cooperative society or any other legal entity
2. It should provide sharing of benefits/profit to the farmers
3. Ownership control is always with the farmers
4. NABARD is providing support for promotion of FPOs

Select the correct answer using the code given below:
(a) 1 only
(b) 2 & 4 only
(c) 1, 2 & 4
(d) All of the above

361. FCI stores the food grains procured for the central pool in the following:

1. FCI's own godowns
2. Central Warehousing Corporation's godowns
3. State Warehousing Corporation's godowns
4. Godowns hired from private sector

Select the correct answer using the code given below:
(a) 1 only
(b) 1, 2 & 3 only
(c) 2 & 4
(d) All of the above

362. "Economic Threshold Limit" is related to which of the following?

(a) Potential GDP growth
(b) Capacity utilization of the economy
(c) Pest management for crops
(d) Underground water level

363. The term 'under-recovery' seen in the news, is related to which of the following?

(a) Government spending more on the subsidies than the budgeted amount
(b) Loss of Oil Marketing Companies (OMCs) in providing fuel at cheaper rate to the public
(c) Government giving exemptions on certain types of taxes
(d) Central government getting less repayment on loans given to States

364. Consider the following statements regarding Urea subsidy:

1. The subsidy amount is transferred directly into farmer's account
2. The per kg subsidy amount is fixed and does not change with market fluctuation
3. Price of Urea is regulated by the government

Select the correct answer using the code given below:
(a) 1 & 2 only
(b) 2 & 3 only
(c) 3 only
(d) All of the above

365. Consider the following statements regarding the 'Nutrient Based Subsidy' (NBS) Scheme.

1. It is given for phosphatic, potassic and complex fertilizers
2. It is given for urea
3. The prices of fertilizers under nutrient based scheme are regulated by the government
4. Subsidy is based on per kg of nutrients present in the fertilizer

Select the correct answer using the code given below:
(a) 1 & 3 only
(b) 2 & 3 only
(c) 1 & 4 only
(d) 3 & 4 only

366. Consider the following statements regarding 'Liquid Nano Urea':

1. Liquid Nano Urea has been developed and Patented by Indian Farmers Fertilizer Cooperative (IFFCO)
2. Govt. provides subsidy on liquid nano urea
3. Liquid Nano Urea contains 4% nitrogen by volume and needs to be sprayed on leaves of the crops

Select the correct answer using the code given below:
(a) 1 & 2 only
(b) 2 only
(c) 2 & 3 only
(d) 1 & 3 only

367. Consider the following statements regarding 'One Nation One Fertilizer Scheme':

1. Fertilizers will be sold under the single brand name 'BHARAT'
2. Companies will not be allowed to put their own name on fertilizer bags
3. The BHARAT logo has a tractor and drone in its image

Select the correct answer using the code given below:
(a) 1 & 2 only
(b) 2 only
(c) 2 & 3 only
(d) 1 & 3 only

368. Consider the following statements regarding 'Kerosene'.

1. Central Govt. allocates States kerosene for PDS
2. Central Govt. does not provide any subsidy on kerosene
3. Some states have been declared as Kerosene free states

Select the correct answer using the code given below:
(a) 2 only
(b) 2 & 3 only
(c) 1 & 3
(d) All of the above

369. Consider the following statements:

1. Minimum Export Price (MEP)/Minimum Import Price (MIP) restrictions are imposed under "The Foreign Trade (Dev. & Reg.) Act 1992"
2. "The Foreign Trade (Dev. & Reg.) Act 1992" can be used to put quantitative restrictions on export/import

Select the correct answer using the code given below:
(a) 1 only
(b) 2 only
(c) Both 1 & 2
(d) Neither 1 nor 2

370. Which of the following statements are true regarding Central Government's procurement policy of wheat and rice?

1. It is an open-ended procurement policy
2. Under the centralized procurement policy, all the wheat and rice is procured by FCI
3. Under decentralized procurement policy, States procure wheat and rice and distribute under NFSA

Select the correct answer using the code given below:
(a) 1 only
(b) 2 & 3 only
(c) 1 & 3 only
(d) All of the above

371. Consider the following statements regarding "Warehouse Receipts":

1. They are issued as per the Warehousing (Development & Regulation) Act 2007
2. Warehousing Development & Regulatory Authority (WDRA) is under ministry of Commerce and Industry
3. Warehouse receipts are negotiable
4. These receipts are govt. recognized and can be used for taking loan

Select the correct answer using the code given below:
(a) 1 only
(b) 3 & 4 only
(c) 1, 3 & 4 only
(d) All of the above

372. Consider the following statements regarding "Agricultural and Processed Food Products Export Development Authority (APEDA)":

1. It is not a statutory body as it was created through a Govt. resolution
2. Established in early 1990s
3. APEDA is implementing the National Program for Organic Production (NPOP)

Select the correct answer using the code given below:

(a) 1 only
(b) 1 and 2 only
(c) 3 only
(d) 2 and 3 only

373. Consider the following statements regarding 'Ethanol Blended Petrol' Programme:

1. Govt. notifies differential price of ethanol based on different feedstock
2. Ethanol price for blending is approved by Cabinet Committee on Economic Affairs
3. Govt. has set the target of 20% ethanol blending in petrol by 2025-26

Select the correct answer using the code given below:
(a) 1 & 2 only
(b) 2 & 3 only
(c) 3 only
(d) All of the above

374. Under the National Food Security Act 2013, the expenditure towards intra state transportation and handling charges for movement from FCI depots to Fair Price Shops is borne by:

(a) Central Government
(b) State Government
(c) Shared between Central and State Government
(d) Is passed on to the beneficiaries

375. Consider the following Statements regarding under National Food Security Act 2013:

1. Within a state, transportation and distribution cost is incurred by State Govt.
2. The Food subsidy burden is shared equally between Centre and States
3. The Central Issue Price (CIP) at which foodgrains are issued to states are decided by FCI
4. Presently central govt. is transferring the food to states at zero prices

Select the correct answer using the code given below:
(a) 1 & 2 only
(b) 2, 3 & 4 only
(c) 3 & 4 only
(d) 4 only

376. Consider the following statements regarding Price Stabilization Fund (PSF)

1. Govt. provides budgetary support for working capital as well as long term loan
2. The scheme targets intervention in the retail market
3. Sale of 'Bharat Atta' is being done under the PSF scheme

Select the correct answer using the code given below:
(a) 1 only
(b) 1 & 2 only
(c) 2 & 3 only
(d) All of the above

377. Consider the following statements regarding 'Custom Hiring Centre' (CHC)?

1. Government is establishing CHC under National Mission on Agricultural Extension & Technology
2. Government is providing subsidy on purchase of equipment by CHCs
3. CHC provides costly equipment to small farmers on rental basis

Select the correct answer using the code given below:
(a) 2 only
(b) 2 & 3 only
(c) 1 & 3 only
(d) All of the above

Inclusive Growth and Employment

378. Consider the following statements regarding National Sample Survey (NSS):

1. It is conducted by National Statistical Office (NSO)
2. It is a socioeconomic survey conducted annually
3. It is conducted on rotating topics

Select the correct answer using the code given below:
(a) 1 only
(b) 1 & 3 only
(c) 3 only
(d) All of the above

379. Match the following regarding how frequently they are conducted:

(i) Periodic Labour Force Survey
(ii) Economic Census
(iii) Consumer Expenditure Survey
(iv) Census

1. Decadal
2. Quinquennial
3. Annual
4. No fixed periodicity

Select the correct answer using the code given below:
(a) (i) – 4, (ii) – 2, (iii) – 4, (iv) – 1
(b) (i) – 3, (ii) – 4, (iii) – 2, (iv) – 1
(c) (i) – 4, (ii) – 2, (iii) – 3, (iv) – 1
(d) (i) – 3, (ii) – 1, (iii) – 4, (iv) – 2

380. Consider the following statements regarding the "Periodic Labour Force Survey":

1. It is conducted quinquennially
2. It is conducted for both rural and urban labour force
3. It collects data for urban labour on a quarterly basis

Select the correct answer using the code given below:
(a) 1 only
(b) 1 & 2 only
(c) 2 only
(d) 2 & 3 only

381. Consider the following statements regarding 'Quarterly Employment Survey':

1. It is conducted by labour bureau
2. It provides employment scenario from the supply side
3. It provides employment updates in both organized and unorganized segments

Select the correct answer using the code given below:
(a) 1 & 2 only
(b) 1 & 3 only
(c) 2 & 3 only
(d) All of the above

382. The unemployment caused due to the workers living far from the regions and are unable to move to the locations where jobs are available is an example of:
(a) Cyclical
(b) Frictional
(c) Structural
(d) Disguised

383. The unemployment caused due to the workers lacking the requisite job skills is an example of:

(a) Cyclical
(b) Structural
(c) Frictional
(d) Disguised

384. In a country, jobs are available but still people are unemployed as there is a serious mismatch between what companies need and what workers can offer. This kind of unemployment is referred as:

(a) Cyclical
(b) Structural

(c) Seasonal
(d) Frictional

385. A person has left his current job and is looking for another job. He/ she is facing which type of unemployment:

(a) Structural
(b) Cyclical
(c) Frictional
(d) He/ she will not be considered as unemployed

386. An auto worker in Gurgaon lost his job because the company relocated the plant to another country represents an example of:
(a) Frictional
(b) Structural
(c) Cyclical
(d) Seasonal

387. In case of disguised unemployment, which of the following will hold true:

1. Marginal productivity of capital will be zero
2. Productivity of labour will be less

Select the correct answer using the code given below:
(a) 1 only
(b) 2 only
(c) Both 1 & 2
(d) Neither 1 nor 2

388. Consider the following statements regarding an economy facing cyclical unemployment:

1. It may lead to inflation in the economy
2. It may lead to deflation in the economy
3. It can be tackled through expansionary monetary policy
4. It can be tackled through expansionary fiscal policy

Select the correct answer using the code given below:
(a) 1 only
(b) 2 only
(c) 1, 3 & 4 only
(d) 2, 3 & 4 only

389. Which of the following are true for underemployment?

1. Workers in job that are not able to utilize their skills
2. Workers in low paying jobs as relative to their skills
3. Part time workers preferring full time jobs
4. Productivity of labour is low

Select the correct answer using the code given below:
(a) 1 & 2 only
(b) 1, 2 & 3 only
(c) 2, 3 & 4 only
(d) All of the above

390. Consider the following statements:
1. 'Jobless growth' implies labour is becoming more productive
2. If 'employment elasticity' is decreasing that implies labour productivity is increasing

Select the correct answer using the code given below:
(a) 1 only
(b) 2 only
(c) Both 1 & 2
(d) Neither 1 nor 2

391. 'Demographic Dividend' is estimated/calculated in terms of which of the following:

(a) Population
(b) Total Fertility Rate (TFR)
(c) Working Age to Non-Working Age population ratio
(d) Additional per capita income growth

392. Consider the following statements:

1. Human capital considers education and health as a means to increase labour productivity

2. Under human development, human beings are end in themselves

Select the correct answer using the code given below:
(a) 1 only
(b) 2 only
(c) Both 1 & 2
(d) Neither 1 nor 2

393. The term 'ASEEM' is related to which of the following?

(a) Online delivery of government services
(b) An online portal for procurement of goods by MSMEs
(c) Online platform for procurement of defence items
(d) A digital portal to map skills of workers with jobs

394. Consider the following statements regarding the 'e-SHRAM' portal:

1. It is under Ministry of Labour and Employment
2. It is for organized as well as unorganized workers
3. Insurance cover is also being provided to workers registered on this portal

Select the correct answer using the code given below:
(a) 1 only
(b) 1 & 2 only
(c) 2 & 3 only
(d) 1 & 3 only

395. Which organization publishes the 'Gender Gap Index'?

(a) World Economic Forum
(b) World Health Organization
(c) United Nations Development Programme
(d) International Labour Organization

396. Consider the following statements:

1. Insurance penetration is measured as the percentage of insurance premium to GDP
2. Insurance density is measured as the ratio of premium (in US dollar) to total population

Select the correct answer using the code given below:
(a) 1 only
(b) 2 only
(c) 1 & 2 both
(d) Neither 1 nor 2

397. Consider the following statements:

1. Life insurance business wàs nationalized in mid 1950s
2. Life Insurance Corporation (LIC) was established in the early 1960s

Select the correct answer using the code given below:
(a) 1 only
(b) 2 only
(c) Both 1 & 2
(d) Neither 1 nor 2

398. Consider the statements regarding general insurance sector in India:

1. The sector was nationalized in 1970's
2. It was liberalized in early 1990's
3. Insurance Regulatory and Development Authority (IRDA) was established as a statutory body in 2000

Select the correct answer using the code given below:
(a) 1 only
(b) 2 & 3 only
(c) 1 & 3 only
(d) 2 only

399. Which of the following statements are true regarding 'replacement level fertility'?

(a) It is the level of fertility at which population remains constant

(b) It is the level of fertility at which population growth remains constant
(c) It is the level of fertility at which a population exactly replaces itself from one generation to another
(d) None of the above

400. Which of the following statements are true regarding India's Total Fertility Rate (TFR)?
1. It has declined below the 'replacement level of fertility'
2. Since it has gone below the replacement level fertility, the population will stop increasing

Select the correct answer using the code given below:
(a) 1 only
(b) 2 only
(c) Both 1 & 2
(d) Neither 1 nor 2

401. Consider the following statements regarding poverty:

1. Incidence of poverty is defined as the percentage of population which is poor and is also called headcount ratio

2. Intensity of poverty is defined as the average share of deprivations across various indicators which the people experience simultaneously

Select the correct answer using the code given below:
(a) 1 only
(b) 2 only
(c) Both 1 & 2
(d) Neither 1 nor 2

402. Global Multidimensional Poverty Index (MPI) has been developed by:

(a) Oxford Poverty and Human Development Initiative (OPHI)
(b) United Nations Development Program (UNDP)
(c) OPHI in collaboration with UNDP
(d) None of the above

403. Consider the following statements regarding MGNREGA wages:

1. It is decided by respective state governments
2. It is revised annually linked with CPI-Rural labourers

Select the correct answer using the code given below:

(a) 1 only
(b) 2 only
(c) Both 1 & 2
(d) Neither 1 nor 2

404. Consider the following statements regarding the newly enacted 'The Code on Wages 2019':

1. There will be a statutory minimum/floor wage which will be applicable for both organized and unorganized sector labours
2. This code will not be applicable to MGNREGA wages

Select the correct answer using the code given below:
(a) 1 only
(b) 2 only
(c) Both 1 & 2
(d) Neither 1 nor 2

405. Consider the following statements regarding the newly enacted 'The Industrial Relations Code 2020':

1. Permission will not be required from the government to close a factory if the number of workers are less than 300
2. Fixed term employment has been made applicable for all industries

Select the correct answer using the code given below:
(a) 1 only
(b) 2 only
(c) Both 1 & 2
(d) Neither 1 nor 2

406. Consider the following statements regarding the newly enacted 'The Code on Social Security 2020':

1. A social security fund is proposed to be established for workers of unorganized sector
2. Aggregators will have to contribute a small portion of their turnover which will be used to pay gig and platform workers

Select the correct answer using the code given below:
(e) 1 only
(f) 2 only
(g) Both 1 & 2
(h) Neither 1 nor 2

407. Consider the following statements regarding the newly enacted 'The Occupational Safety, Health and Working Conditions Code 2020':

1. An inter-state migrant worker is one whose wages does not exceed Rs. 18,000 per month
2. Employment of women has been allowed in all establishments for all types of works and in the night shift also

Select the correct answer using the code given below:
(a) 1 only
(b) 2 only
(c) Both 1 & 2
(d) Neither 1 nor 2

408. The National Census is conducted by which offices/ agencies:

(a) National Statistical Office (NSO)
(b) Labour Bureau
(c) Registrar General and Census Commissioner, Ministry of Home Affairs
(d) Census Bureau of India

409. Which of the following agency conducts 'Time Use Survey' in India?

(a) National Statistical Office
(b) Reserve Bank of India
(c) Ministry of Labour and Employment
(d) None of the above

International Organizations

410. World Bank has introduced the concept of 'Learning Poverty' which is defined as:
(a) Percentage of youth aged 18 and above who cannot read and write a simple text
(b) Percentage of the children aged 8 and above who are not enrolled in any kind of school education
(c) Percentage of 10-year-old children who cannot read and understand a simple text
(d) Percentage of 12-year-old children who cannot read and write a simple text

411. The 'Logistics Performance Index' is released by which agency?

(a) World Bank
(b) UNCTAD
(c) WTO
(d) OECD

412. Consider the following statements regarding the 'Compulsory Licenses' under the Indian Patent Act 1970:

1. It is given for generic versions of drugs
2. It is given during the protection period of the patent
3. Manufacturers producing drugs under compulsory license need not pay royalty to the patent owner

Select the correct answer using the code given below:
(a) 1 only
(b) 1 & 2 only
(c) 3 only
(d) 2 & 3 only

413. Consider the following statements regarding the "Remission of Duties or Taxes on Export Products (RoDTEP)" scheme:
   1. The scheme will reimburse the levies which are currently out of GST regime
   2. The scheme is for reimbursing the CGST and SGST paid on various products in case of exports
   3. The scheme will make exports zero-rated

   Select the correct answer using the code given below:
   (a) 1 & 2 only
   (b) 2 & 3 only
   (c) 1 & 3 only
   (d) All of the above

414. The term "Certificates of Origin" is related to which of the following?
   (a) It is used in granting of visas to individuals
   (b) It is used in protection of intellectual property rights across the country
   (c) It is used in international trade
   (d) None of the above

415. 'International Debt Statistics' report is released by which of the following institutions?
   (a) World Bank
   (b) IMF
   (c) World Economic Forum
   (d) United Nations Conference on Trade and Development (UNCTAD)

416. "Human Capital Index" is published annually by which of the following agency?
   (a) World Bank
   (b) IMF
   (c) UNDP
   (d) WHO

417. 'World Migration Report' is released by which of the following institution?
   (a) World bank
   (b) IMF
   (c) World Economic Forum
   (d) United Nations

418. "Which countries are eligible to become member of BRICS Bank?"
   (a) Any Country
   (b) Members of United Nations
   (c) Members of World Bank or IMF
   (d) Any 'developing' country

419. Which of the following is dependent on "QUOTA" assigned by IMF to its member countries?
   1. Financial resources that the member country is obliged to provide IMF
   2. Voting Rights
   3. SDR allocation to member countries
   4. Borrowing capacity of a member country

   Select the correct answer using the code given below:
   (a) 2 only
   (b) 2 & 3 only
   (c) 1 & 4 only
   (d) All of the above

420. Consider the following statements regarding Special Drawing Rights (SDR) of IMF:
   1. It is allocated to the member countries based on their economic size
   2. SDR allocation acts as external debt for the respective country's Govt.
   3. SDRs can be held only by Government entities
   4. It forms part of Capital Account under Balance of Payment

   Select the correct answer using the code given below:
   (a) 1, 2 & 3 only
   (b) 1 & 3 only
   (c) 2 & 3 only
   (d) All of the above

421. Consider the following statements regarding the "Most Favoured Nation (MFN)" principle of WTO trade:
   1. A member country can grant more favours to the other member country
   2. MFN is basically a principle of non-discriminatory trade

3. Free Trade Agreements have been exempted from the MFN principle

Select the correct answer using the code given below:
(a) 1 only
(b) 1 & 3 only
(c) 2 only
(d) 2 & 3 only

422. Which of the following measures are considered as prohibitive under the Agreement on 'Trade Related Investment Measures (TRIMS)' under WTO?
1. Local content requirement
2. Export obligation
3. Technology transfer requirement
4. Domestic employment

Select the correct answer using the code given below:
(a) 1 only
(b) 1 & 3 only
(c) 2 & 3 only
(d) All of the above

423. Which of the following statements is true regarding the issue of imposing customs duty on electronic transmission under the ongoing 'Doha Development Agenda'?
(a) Member countries have agreed not to impose customs duty on electronic transmission
(b) Most of the developing countries are demanding a permanent moratorium on imposing customs duty on electronic transmission
(c) India is in support of permanent moratorium on imposing customs duty on electronic transmission
(d) There is a moratorium on imposing customs duty on electronic transmission, but it is temporary in nature

424. Consider the following statements regarding 'Tariff rate quota' (TRQ) system:
(a) It allows a pre-determined quantity of a product to be imported at lower import duty rates than the duty rate normally applicable to that product
(b) It allows a pre-determined quantity of a product to be imported at normal import duty and then the duty increases
(c) It allows only a pre-determined quantity of a particular product to be imported at a particular tariff
(d) None of the above

425. Which of the following are imposed in case a country's government is subsidizing its exporters?
(a) Anti-Dumping Duty
(b) Counter-vailing Duty
(c) Safeguard Duty
(d) Customs Duty

426. Which of the following statements are true regarding 'Safeguard Duty':
1. It is a WTO compliant measure
2. It is imposed when there is an increased import of particular product
3. It is imposed as an additional import duty

Select the correct answer using the code given below:
(a) 1 only
(b) 2 only
(c) 2 & 3 only
(d) All of the above

427. Consider the following statements regarding 'Trademarks':
1. Trademarks can last for indefinite time period
2. Trademarks are assignable
3. Protected through 'Trade Marks Act 1999'

Select the correct answer using the code given below:
(a) 1 only
(b) 1 & 3 only
(c) 3 only
(d) All of the above

428. Consider the following statements regarding 'Trade secrets':

3. Protected through 'Trade Marks Act 1999'

Select the correct answer using the code given below:
(a) 1 only
(b) 1 & 3 only
(c) 3 only
(d) All of the above

428. Consider the following statements regarding 'Trade secrets':

1. No registration is required to protect trade secrets
2. It can be protected for unlimited time period
3. To qualify as a trade secret, the information should have commercial value

Select the correct answer using the code given below:
(a) 1 only
(b) 1 & 3 only
(c) 3 only
(d) All of the above

429. "Annual Observance Report" is published by which institution/agency?

(a) IMF
(b) World Bank
(c) RBI
(d) OECD

430. Which agency/institution releases the "Social Mobility Index"?

(a) World Economic Forum
(b) World Bank
(c) OECD
(d) None of the above

Infrastructure & Industries

431. Consider the following statements regarding 'Startups':

1. An entity is considered startup up to a period of 10 years from the date of its incorporation
2. Turnover of the entity should not be more than 10 crores in any year since incorporation
3. They are included in priority sector lending

Select the correct answer using the code given below:
(a) 1 only
(b) 1 & 3 only
(c) 2 & 3 only
(d) All of the above

432. Parliament passed "Factoring Regulation (Amendment) Bill, 2021". Which of the following statements are true regarding 'factoring'?

(a) It is an unsecured lending facility by banks to generally MSMEs
(b) Banks provide lending facility where receivables act as collateral
(c) It is a way to get immediate liquidity by selling receivables
(d) It is a short-term lending facility by NBFCs to MSMEs

433. Consider the following statements regarding 'Merchanting Trade':

(a) There is no physical delivery of goods
(b) Goods bought and sold does not enter into the merchant territory
(c) It involves trade in services only
(d) Trade does not involve a merchant

434. Which of the following statements are true regarding 'National Monetization Pipeline'?

1. Plans for monetization of core assets of central government and central PSUs

435. Consider the following statements:
1. Private Label products are sold under the name of specific retailers
2. White Label products are sold by multiple sellers under their brand

Select the correct answer using the code given below:
(a) 1 only
(b) 2 only
(c) Both 1 & 2
(d) Neither 1 nor 2

436. Which of the following statements are true regarding 'Production Linked Incentive Scheme'?
(a) Govt. is giving incentive as interest subvention for domestic manufacturing units
(b) Govt is providing guarantee on loan for domestic manufacturing units
(c) Govt. is giving incentive on additional sales from domestic manufacturing
(d) None of the above

437. Which of the following are part of the 'Index of Industrial Production (IIP)'?
1. Mining and quarrying
2. Electricity generation
3. Construction
4. Forestry

Select the correct answer using the code given below:
(a) 1 & 2 only
(b) 2 & 3 only
(c) 1, 2 & 3 only
(d) All of the above

438. 'Industrial Outlook Survey' is conducted by:
(a) Ministry of Commerce and Industry
(b) RBI
(c) National Statistical Office
(d) Dept. of Economic Affairs

439. The term "Graded Surveillance Measure" is related to which of the following:
(a) Security of Indian coastal areas
(b) Companies listed on stock exchanges
(c) ISRO's satellite programme
(d) IMF monitoring various economies

440. Consider the following statements regarding 'Core Industries':
1. It comprises of around 40% of the weight of items included in Index of Industrial production (IIP)
2. Fertilizers have the lowest weight in Core Industries index

Select the correct answer using the code given below:
(a) 1 only
(b) 2 only
(c) Both 1 & 2
(d) Neither 1 nor 2

441. In which of the following sectors FDI is prohibited?
1. Lottery
2. Gambling and betting including casinos
3. Atomic Energy
4. Railway operations

Select the correct answer using the code given below:
(a) 1 & 2 only
(b) 3 only
(c) 3 & 4 only
(d) All of the above

442. The term "Open access" in electricity means which of the following:
(a) Consumers have access to the transmission and distribution network to obtain electricity from the suppliers of their choice
(b) Consumers can choose the distribution company of their choice
(c) Any consumer of electricity can also generate electricity from their own resource and can feed on to the distribution network.
(d) Distribution companies can choose from which of the power producers they want to purchase power without government interference

443. Consider the following statements:
1. Under the Old Pension Scheme (OPS), the monthly pension is exempt from tax
2. Under the New Pension Scheme (NPS), the lump sum amount that someone gets at maturity (60 years) is taxable
3. Under the Unified Pension Scheme (UPS), employees do not need to contribute and there is an assured pension

Select the correct answer using the code given below:
(a) 1 only
(b) 2 only
(c) 3 only
(d) None of the above

444. Arrange the following in the correct the correct chronological order i.e., the one which was established as a statutory body first should come first in the order.
1. Pension Fund Regulatory Development Authority (PFRDA)
2. Insurance Regulatory and Development Authority of India (IRDAI)
3. Securities and Exchange Board of India (SEBI)

Select the correct answer using the code given below:
(a) 2 – 1 - 3
(b) 3 – 2 – 1
(c) 1 – 2 – 3
(d) 2 – 3 – 1

445. As per SEBI, minimum 'Public Shareholding' (the shares which are traded on the stock exchange) for listed companies is:
(a) 5%
(b) 10%
(c) 25%
(d) 35%

446. Which stock exchange has got the approval by SEBI to set up a Social Stock Exchange?

(a) National Stock Exchange
(b) Bombay Stock Exchange
(c) Delhi Stock Exchange
(d) Multi Commodity Exchange of India

447. Arrange the States in decreasing order of merchandise exports (by value):
(a) Maharashtra > Gujarat > Karnataka > Tamil Nadu
(b) Maharashtra > Gujarat > Tamil Nadu > Karnataka
(c) Gujarat > Maharashtra > Karnataka > Tamil Nadu
(d) Gujarat > Maharashtra > Tamil Nadu > Karnataka

448. Consider the following statements:
1. Renewable Energy Certificates (REC) are traded on Indian Energy Exchange and Power Exchange of India
2. Ministry of Power in consultation with ministry of New and Renewable Energy sets target every year for Renewable Purchase Obligation (RPO) for all States/UTs

Select the correct answer using the code given below:
(a) 1 only
(b) 2 only
(c) Both 1 & 2
(d) Neither 1 nor 2

449. 'Project Nexus' is related to which of the following?
(a) Defence
(b) Cross border Payment
(c) Indian Space Research Organization
(d) Artificial intelligence

450. Consider the following statements regarding 'Dabba Trading':
1. Trading of securities outside the purview of stock exchange
2. It is illegal
3. Trading is done in blocks of securities

Select the correct answer using the code given below:
(a) 1 only
(b) 2 only
(c) 1 & 2 only
(d) All of the above

ANSWER SHEET

Q.No.	ANS	Q.No.	ANS	Q.No.	ANS	Q.No.	ANS	Q.No.	ANS
1	B	51	C	101	D	151	D	201	C
2	A	52	D	102	D	152	B	202	D
3	A	53	D	103	D	153	C	203	D
4	B	54	C	104	C	154	D	204	A
5	A	55	D	105	D	155	D	205	C
6	A	56	D	106	C	156	B	206	A
7	A	57	B	107	A	157	B	207	B
8	C	58	D	108	C	158	D	208	D
9	A	59	D	109	A	159	C	209	A
10	B	60	D	110	D	160	C	210	D
11	C	61	D	111	D	161	D	211	D
12	B	62	B	112	D	162	B	212	D
13	D	63	D	113	D	163	D	213	C
14	D	64	C	114	B	164	B	214	D
15	C	65	C	115	B	165	C	215	C
16	C	66	D	116	B	166	B	216	D
17	C	67	C	117	D	167	B	217	C
18	A	68	C	118	C	168	A	218	D
19	B	69	A	119	C	169	D	219	D
20	A	70	C	120	A	170	D	220	D
21	A	71	C	121	D	171	B	221	C
22	C	72	B	122	A	172	D	222	C
23	D	73	D	123	C	173	A	223	D
24	D	74	D	124	D	174	C	224	C
25	B	75	C	125	C	175	D	225	D
26	D	76	C	126	D	176	C	226	A
27	D	77	C	127	D	177	D	227	D
28	B	78	D	128	D	178	C	228	A
29	C	79	D	129	C	179	C	229	D
30	B	80	D	130	C	180	D	230	C
31	C	81	C	131	A	181	C	231	C
32	D	82	B	132	D	182	A	232	C
33	C	83	C	133	A	183	D	233	B
34	C	84	A	134	B	184	D	234	A
35	A	85	C	135	B	185	D	235	D
36	D	86	C	136	C	186	D	236	C
37	D	87	A	137	D	187	A	237	A
38	C	88	B	138	A	188	C	238	C
39	D	89	D	139	A	189	D	239	C
40	A	90	D	140	C	190	C	240	D
41	C	91	C	141	C	191	D	241	C
42	A	92	C	142	A	192	C	242	D
43	D	93	C	143	C	193	A	243	D
44	B	94	A	144	C	194	B	244	D
45	D	95	D	145	D	195	A	245	D
46	D	96	D	146	C	196	A	246	C
47	A	97	D	147	D	197	D	247	A
48	D	98	B	148	B	198	D	248	C
49	C	99	D	149	D	199	D	249	A
50	A	100	D	150	B	200	B	250	B

ANSWER SHEET

Q.No.	ANS	Q.No.	ANS	Q.No.	ANS	Q.No.	ANS	
251	C	301	D	351	A	401	C	
252	D	302	D	352	A	402	C	
253	C	303	D	353	D	403	D	
254	B	304	D	354	C	404	C	
255	D	305	A	355	C	405	C	
256	C	306	D	356	D	406	C	
257	A	307	D	357	D	407	C	
258	C	308	A	358	D	408	C	
259	D	309	D	359	C	409	A	
260	B	310	D	360	D	410	C	
261	C	311	A	361	D	411	A	
262	B	312	C	362	C	412	B	
263	D	313	C	363	B	413	C	
264	D	314	A	364	C	414	C	
265	D	315	D	365	C	415	A	
266	D	316	D	366	D	416	A	
267	D	317	D	367	D	417	D	
268	C	318	C	368	D	418	B	
269	C	319	D	369	C	419	D	
270	D	320	C	370	C	420	D	
271	A	321	C	371	C	421	D	
272	A	322	C	372	C	422	D	
273	B	323	D	373	D	423	D	
274	A	324	A	374	C	424	A	
275	B	325	D	375	D	425	B	
276	B	326	C	376	C	426	D	
277	B	327	D	377	D	427	D	
278	C	328	B	378	D	428	D	
279	D	329	D	379	B	429	A	
280	D	330	B	380	D	430	A	
281	B	331	D	381	B	431	B	
282	A	332	D	382	C	432	C	
283	D	333	B	383	B	433	B	
284	A	334	D	384	B	434	A	
285	D	335	A	385	C	435	C	
286	C	336	A	386	B	436	C	
287	D	337	D	387	B	437	A	
288	C	338	D	388	D	438	B	
289	D	339	D	389	D	439	B	
290	C	340	A	390	C	440	C	
291	A	341	D	391	D	441	D	
292	A	342	D	392	C	442	A	
293	C	343	A	393	D	443	D	
294	B	344	C	394	D	444	B	
295	C	345	A	395	A	445	C	
296	D	346	D	396	C	446	A	
297	C	347	C	397	A	447	D	
298	C	348	A	398	C	448	C	
299	B	349	C	399	C	449	B	
300	D	350	C	400	A	450	C	

1. (b)

GDP is the sum of the final value of all goods and services (consumption and capital) produced in the economy. And this final output is purchased by the household sector, Private sector, government sector and outsiders/foreigners (also called exports) which is written as:

GDP = c + i + g + X

Where **c** is the expenditure by household sector on **domestically** produced consumption goods, **i** is the expenditure by private sector on **domestically** produced investment/capital goods and **g** is the expenditure by government sector on **domestically** produced investment goods and X is the expenditure by outsiders (which is also defined as exports).

[So, first statement will be false and second will be true]

Now the above formula can also be written as:

GDP = [C – Cm] + [I – Im] + [G - Gm] + X

Where C is the expenditure by household sector on domestic and imported both goods and Cm is the expenditure by household sector on imported goods.

So, C – Cm = c

In similar way I – Im = i

And G – Gm = g

So, GDP = C + I + G + X – [Cm + Im + Gm]

GDP = C + I + G + X – M

Where M is the total imports = Cm + Im + Gm

[So, third statement will be true and fourth will be false]

2. (a)

Real GDP growth measures growth in quantity and nominal GDP measures growth in value (which includes quantity as well as price).

Now, suppose an economy produces wheat and rice. The quantities produced and the market price is given in the following table.

	2011-12	2012-13	2013-14	2014-15
Wheat	10kg X Rs. 10/kg	11kg X Rs. 10.5/kg	12kg X Rs. 11/kg	12.5kg X Rs. 12/kg
Rice	8kg X Rs. 12/kg	9kg X Rs. 12.5/kg	10kg X Rs. 13/kg	10.5kg X Rs. 13.5/kg
Nominal GDP	10X10 + 8X12 = Rs. 196	11X10.5 + 9X12.5 = Rs. 228	12X11 + 10X13 = Rs. 262	12.5X12+ 10.5X13.5 = Rs. 291.75
To calculate Real GDP, we take the price of any year as constant and declare it as a base year. So, suppose we declare 2011-12 as base year then we will take price of wheat as Rs. 10/kg and price of rice as Rs. 12/kg as constant in all the subsequent years to calculate the real GDP.				
Real GDP	10X**10** + 8X**12** = Rs. 196	11X**10** + 9X**12** = Rs. 218	12X**10** + 10X**12** = Rs. 240	12.5X**10** + 10.5X**12** = Rs. 251

The base year for calculation of GDP is 2011-12. So, if we want to calculate India's Real GDP for 2014-15 then we will have to take the quantities produced in 2014-15 and the prices of 2011-12 (base year). And if we want to calculate the Nominal GDP of 2014-15 then we will have to take the quantities produced in 2014-15 and the market prices of the same year i.e., 2014-15.

In India, **economic growth is measured by change in real GDP** i.e., GDP at **constant** Market Prices as per the global best practices.

Consider the above table once again.

	2011-12		2012-13		2013-14		2014-15
Nominal GDP	Rs.196		Rs.228		Rs.262		Rs.291.75
Change in Nominal GDP		16.3%		14.9%		11.4%	
Real GDP	Rs.196		Rs.218		Rs.240		Rs.251
Change in Real GDP		11.2%		10.1%		4.6%	

So, Real GDP is steadily/consistently increasing from 2011-12 to 2014-15 but "change in real GDP" is decreasing from 11.2% to 4.6% and change in nominal GDP is also decreasing from 2011-12 to 2014-15.

The above is a case of economic growth as real GDP is increasing. But since the rate of change of real GDP is decreasing (but not negative), we say that economic **growth** is **slowing down. When the "real GDP" decreases or "change in real GDP" is negative then it is a case of recession.**

And if the prices are decreasing more but the production quantity is increasing then the nominal GDP may decrease but Real GDP may increase. So, in case of economic growth, nominal GDP may decrease.

So, only **1st** statement is the required criteria. Because even if **3rd** statement is not true (as in the above example), a country may experience economic growth.

Economic growth can happen even without generation of employment, so it is not a required criterion.

3. (a)
When the "real GDP" decreases or "change in real GDP" is negative then it is a case of recession.
If the nominal GDP decreases because of decrease in prices, real GDP may increase.
If the growth rate is decreasing, GDP may increase.

4. (b)
National Income (NI) and Net National Income (NNI) are same terms and used interchangeably.

National Income = Net National Income (NNI) = Net National Product (NNP)
NNP = GNP - Depreciation

Earlier (before January 2015) NSO was using factor cost to calculate NNP but now it uses Market Prices to calculate NNP.

5. (a)
Gross National Income (GNI) is the income earned by Indian residents only whether in India or abroad. GNI does not include the income earned by Non-Resident Indians (NRIs). And it is equal to GDP plus net factor income from abroad (NFIA).

GNI = GNP = GDP + NFIA

6. (a)
GDP calculation methodology changed slightly in 2015. The new way of GDP calculation is:

$GVA_{\text{basic prices}}$ = $GVA_{\text{factor cost}}$ + *Production Taxes - Production subsidies*

GDP_{MP} = $GVA_{\text{basic prices}}$ + *product taxes - Product subsidies*

Land revenue is a kind of production tax and railway subsidies are a kind of production subsidies. Production taxes and production subsidies are independent of the volume of actual production.

So, both production and product taxes are included in GDP_{MP}.

Goods and services produced in India and sold outside the country i.e., to the foreigners is referred as exports. But the Net Factor Income from Abroad (NFIA) is the income earned by the four factors of production from abroad. In case of NFIA the production happens in abroad but in case of exports the production happens in the domestic country. So NFIA is different from exports and hence statement **2nd** is false

7. (a)
The question talks about "people of a country" which is basically residents of the country and the income coming to residents is represented by National Income rather than GDP.

As the question talks about welfare, so it should be better calculated as '**per capita**' National Income rather than just National Income. Because if GNP/GDP increased but population increased more than GNP/GDP, then people standard of living (welfare) will not improve.

Since increase in price can increase the National Income at market price without increasing the welfare of the people. So, welfare can best be represented by per capita National Income at **constant** market prices rather than current market prices.

8. (c)
If the Chinese company in India produces a BURGER and sells it and earns REVENUE of Rs. 100 then it means the value of production in India is Rs. 100. Then out of this Rs. 100, company pays for the costs and keeps some profit. So, profit is just a part of the value of production and hence it will be part of India's GDP. But this profit belongs to the person in China (whether he takes it away or not does not matter) who owns the company in India and hence the profit will be part of China's GNP also.

9. (a)
GVA basic price = GVA factor cost + (Production taxes – production subsidies)
GDP = GVA basic price + (Product taxes – product subsides)

GNP = GDP + NFIA

So, GNP includes production taxes. These are taxes which does not depend on production.

NFIA is net factor income from abroad and does not include free transfer. Factor income means income received in return of something and not free transfer/payment.

But of course, the free money that we get from abroad increases our disposable income, so for that we have another term called 'Gross National Disposable Income (GNDI)' which includes free transfer from abroad as well.

So, GNDI = GNI + net transfer from abroad

10. (b)
The value of capital goods produced is defined as investment.
Hence, production of consumption goods and services are not investment.
Buying and selling of shares from one person to another person is also not investment for the economy as only the ownership changes and nothing happens on ground.
So, only **2nd** statement is true.

11. (c)
GDP is the goods and services produced within the domestic territory of the country, so imported items are not part of GDP.

Investment in Indian economy means the value of capital goods that are going to **remain** in Indian economy whether it was domestically produced or not does not matter. This is because, whatever capital equipment's are going to remain in the economy will help in increasing domestic production in future. So, investment in India is equal to capital goods produced in India plus imported capital goods minus exported capital goods.

For detailed understanding, you can refer the book on Indian Economy by Vivek Singh.

12. (b)
If an economy's savings (in percentage terms) are high then its consumption (in percentage) will be less and this saving could be turned into investment.

Now, if an economy's savings are high and investments are also high then it will lead to economic growth i.e., increase in production of output. And since output is increasing and savings are high and consumption are low (in percentage terms), so the output must be exported.

For detailed understanding, you can refer the book on Indian Economy by Vivek Singh.

13. (d)
Gross Capital Formation = Gross Fixed Capital Formation *(machinery + equipment + building + cultivated biological resources + intellectual property)* + Valuable Metals + Change in stock/inventory

Cultivated biological resources is defined as animal resources yielding repeat products and tree, crop and plant resources yielding repeat products whose natural growth and regeneration are under the direct control, responsibility and management of institutional units.

The term 'Gross fixed capital formation' is interchangeably used as "gross investment" as valuable metals and change in stock/inventory is less than 1%.

14. (d)

First let us develop the general concept of (average) productivity and marginal productivity.

1 Acre Land
5 Labourers
2 Tonne production

If one acre of land produces 2 Tonnes of food grains, then;

$$\text{Productivity of Land} = \frac{\text{Output}}{\text{Input (land)}} \quad \frac{2 \text{ Tonne}}{1 \text{ acre}} = 2 \text{ Tonne/acre}$$

$$\text{Productivity of Labour} = \frac{\text{Output}}{\text{Input (labour)}} = \frac{2 \text{ Tonne}}{5 \text{ labourer}} = 0.4 \text{ Tonne/labour}$$

The above two are basically **average** productivity.

If by adding one extra labour, production increases by 0.2 tonne (assumption), then

Marginal productivity of labour $= \frac{\text{change in output}}{\text{Change in labour}} = \frac{0.2 \text{ tonne}}{1 \text{ labour}} = 0.2 \text{ tonne/labour}$

In the same way, productivity of capital $= \frac{\text{Output}}{\text{Capital}}$

Higher is the productivity of capital, it is good for the economy.

The inverse of "productivity of capital" is Capital/Output ratio.

Higher the capital/output ratio, it is bad for economy. If Capital/Output ratio is 3/1, that means Rs. 1 unit of output is produced from Rs. 3 units of capital. And if Capital/Output ratio is 4/1, that means to produce Rs. 1 unit of output, Rs. 4 units of capital is required. So, 3/1 is better than 4/1 for the economy.

Generally, if an economy has higher savings, higher capital formation happens. But if Capital/Output ratio in the economy is high, then that means the productivity of the capital is low, so output production may not increase much even if capital formation is high.

'Weak administrative machinery' could also be one of the answers but this parameter is already getting included in 'high capital-output ratio'. Basically, if administrative machinery is weak that will automatically lead to high capital-output ratio.

So, the best possible answer is high capital-output ratio.

15. (c)

Incremental Capital Output Ratio (ICOR) is defined as:-

$$\text{ICOR} = \frac{\text{change in capital}}{\text{change in output}} = \frac{\text{(change in capital/output)}}{\text{(change in output/output)}} = \frac{\text{investment \% in GDP}}{\text{\% change in GDP}}$$

ICOR represents how much **extra** unit of capital is required to produce one **additional** unit of output. It basically represents the (inverse of) efficiency of the **new** capital.

16. (c)
Capital formation means production of capital goods.
Production of capital goods leads to increase in future production of goods and services and hence economic growth. So, statement (iii) is true

Production of capital goods increases the capital stock in the economy but does not tell anything about the productivity/efficiency of the capital whether it will increase or decrease. Efficiency is measured as how much output is produced from how much of inputs. So, we can't say that ICOR (which is a measure of efficiency) will increase or decrease with capital formation.

If you were studying 80 pages in 8 hours, so your productivity was 10 pages per hour. Now if you will study one more hour, then you may study few more pages but whether your marginal productivity will be 10 pages per hour or more or less, that you can't say.

17. (c)
Capital/Output ratio represents (inverse of) productivity of capital. If capital/output ratio is decreasing, that means capital is becoming more productive. And if capital is becoming more productive, then economic output will increase.

Capital/output ratio represents (inverse) productivity of capital. But productivity of capital depends upon multiple factors such as governance, quality of labour which again depends on education and skill development levels and technology etc.

For example, if labour is not well trained and he is not operating the machines properly, then output may be less and we will say that capital/output ratio is high i.e., productivity of capital is low, but there may not be any problem with the capital. So, even if the problem is with the labour who is operating the capital, then also the capital output ratio may be high and productivity of labour will be low.

18. (a)

$$\% \text{ change in GDP} = \frac{\text{Investment } \%}{\text{Incremental Capital Output Ratio (ICOR)}}$$

So, for higher growth rate, we require more investment and less ICOR

19. (b)
If the capacity utilization is decreasing that means the entire capacity of the factory is not being utilized to produce goods and services. And this may be because of less demand.

This means that output decreased even if the same amount of capital was there in the economy. This resulted in decrease in productivity of capital. Because now the same capital is producing less output as some capital was idle. So, this will result in an increase in capital-output ratio.

And since the full capacity was not utilized, the per unit cost of production increased. When the full capacity is utilized, the cost of capital and other fixed costs gets distributed over more goods but if it is not being utilized fully then it gets distributed over less goods produced. This increases the per unit cost of production.

20. (a)

$$\text{Marginal productivity of capital} = \frac{\text{Change in output}}{\text{Change in capital}}$$

When the factories are running at full capacity utilization and we add some extra capital (extra machines) then that will produce some additional output/goods in the economy (assuming there is some additional demand in the economy).

So, marginal productivity of capital will be some positive number.

When the factories are running at less than full capacity and then we add extra capital then that extra capital may not produce additional output because even the earlier capacity is not utilized fully (assuming the demand is less because even the earlier capacity is not utilized).

And if factories are running at full utilization, then the marginal productivity of labour may be zero. Because if you will add extra labour then the output will not increase as the factory is already running at full capacity.

21. (a)
Higher economic growth comes from

- additional investment, or
- increase in capacity utilization of the capital stock (factory)

When economic growth comes from new investment then generally more jobs are created but when economic growth comes from better utilization of the existing capacity (which was earlier not utilized properly) then jobs may not get created in the economy.

22. (c)
Investment in the economy means production of capital goods.
When the economy produces all consumption goods and no capital goods (investment) then its GDP shall remain constant i.e., it will not grow. But till the time there is net production of capital goods i.e., investment in the economy, the production of goods and services (GDP) will keep on increasing.

Capital formation means production of capital goods. So, if there is capital formation, it will necessarily lead to increase in GDP i.e., economic growth (assuming increase in demand).

23. (d)
When a country goes through industrialization, it uses more capital and less labour comparatively or we can say labours are replaced by capital (machinery). That means ratio of capital to labour increases sharply. So, statement **(a)** is true.

Industrialization also leads to increase in production of goods and services (with the same amount of labour or may be less labour). So, production per labour also increases which means increase in labour productivity. So, statement **(b)** is also true.

Total factor productivity means productivity of all factors of production i.e., labour, capital, land etc. During industrialization, since overall production increases, so production per unit of inputs i.e., labour, capital, land etc also increases.
So, statement **(c)** is also true.

$$\text{Productivity of labour} = \frac{\text{Output}}{\text{Labour}}$$

$$\text{Productivity of land} = \frac{\text{Output}}{\text{Land}}$$

We all know that because of industrialization output increased. Now if output increased (with the same land and labour), then as per the above formula, productivity of land and productivity of labour, both will increase. So, in case of industrialization, productivity of all the factors of production increases.

24. (d)

25. (b)
The weights of various items in CPI basket are assigned as per the expenditure by the consumers on different items. Once we started CPI Combined in 2011-12, then we assigned the weights as per the expenditure done by consumers on various items. Inflation (CPI Combined) depends on price and weights of various items in the CPI basket. We measure the price of various items every month but weights are not measured every month (it remains fixed). Weights are changed in 5/6 years and not annually. But this time we have not been able to change weights since 2011-12 due to demonetization, GST, Covid.

So, when CPI combined is being published then it is capturing the price data of various items monthly but weights are old only which were fixed in 2011-12. We are planning to revise the weights. Let us say we revise the weights in 2024-25, then again weights will remain fixed for the next 5/6 years because it is difficult/cumbersome to measure the weights monthly, and weights don't change much so we ignore the change in weights and try to publish the inflation data timely.

26. (d)
Services are not traded/transacted in the wholesale markets. So, WPI data does not include the inflation due to services but CPI includes services and goods both.
So, **1st** statement is true
When goods are imported in India, first they move to the wholesale mandis and then they come in the retail markets. So, wholesale prices and retail prices both get impacted because of the imported goods.
So, **3rd** statement is true.

The goods purchased by consumers in the retail market do not represent all the goods produced in the country (like inputs, intermediates and capital goods are purchased by the companies), so CPI does not include these items but WPI takes into account of all such goods.
So, **4th** statement is true.

27. (d)
WPI is released by Office of Economic Advisor, Department for Promotion of Industry and Internal Trade (DPIIT), Ministry of Commerce and Industry. The Base year has been revised to 2011-12 and includes 697 items. WPI inflation measures the average change in prices of commodities for bulk sale at the level of early stage of transactions pertaining to agriculture, mining, manufacturing and electricity. WPI does not cover services. WPI covers commodities falling under three Major Groups namely:

- "Primary Articles" (weight 22.62%) like agricultural commodities and minerals
- "Fuel and Power" (weight 13.15%) like coal and electricity and
- "Manufactured Products" (weight 64.23%) like textiles, leather, machine tools

The prices tracked are agri-market (mandi) prices for agricultural commodities, ex-factory prices for manufactured products and ex-mines prices for minerals. The prices used for compilation do not include indirect taxes in order to remove the impact of fiscal policy. This is in consonance with best international practices and makes the new WPI conceptually closer to "Produce Price Index" used internationally.

28. (b)

29. (c)
When DPIIT started the new series of WPI with base year 2011-12, then it measured/calculated the "Net traded value" of the 697 different items.

Net traded value = Domestic production plus imports minus exports
= Domestic production plus Net imports

So, the weights of the 697 different items in the WPI basket is based on "Domestic production of that item plus Net imports" which is also called "Net traded value". And this weight is kept constant till the revision of base year. And every month only the price change of 697 different items will be measured in the wholesale mandis/markets and the Index will be calculated. Because, it is very cumbersome process to measure the 'Net traded Value' every month/year and revise the weights. And anyways the 'Net traded Value' does not change much in proportion every month/year.

Now let us say base year is changed to 2021-22, then again, the "Net traded Value" will be measured in 2021-22 and new weights will be assigned.

All the 697 items are divided into three groups
Primary Articles = overall weight 22.62%
Fuel and Power = overall weight 13.15%
Manufactured Products = overall weight 64.23%

30. (b)
Real GDP Growth (2022-23) = 8%
Nominal GDP Growth (2022-23) = 12%

Take 2021-22 as the base year (price constant) and assume that Real GDP and Nominal GDP in 2021-22 is Rs. X (as we have taken 2021-22 as price constant, so real GDP and nominal GDP of 2021-22 will be same and let us assume it to be Rs. X).

	2021-22	2022-23
Nominal GDP	X	X * 1.12
Real GDP	X	X * 1.08

$$\text{GDP Deflator} = \frac{\text{Nominal GDP}}{\text{Real GDP}} = \frac{X * 1.12}{X * 1.08} = \frac{1.037}{1}$$

In percentage terms, the above number (1.037/1) represents an increase of 3.7%

31. (c)
Income elasticity of demand is calculated as the ratio of the percentage change in quantity demanded to the percentage change in income. It measures the responsiveness of the quantity demanded for a good or service to a change in income.

If income elasticity of demand of a commodity is less than 1 that means that with change in income, demand is not changing much, that means, it is a necessity good. If the elasticity of demand is greater than 1, it is a luxury good or a superior good.

32. (d)
Openness is measured as, Exports + Imports of goods and services of a country as a percentage of its GDP.
So, **(d)** is correct
Trade balance means Exports – Imports.
So, statement **(c)** is incorrect.

33. (c)
So, if we have to calculate dependence of Indian economy on Chinese economy then we need to calculate India-China bilateral trade i.e. exports and imports from China divided by total trade of India i.e. equal to India's total exports and imports.

34. (c)
India's services export has consistently been higher than import of services in the last ten years. Hence services trade balance has been consistently positive.

For rest of the options, refer the Trends

35. (a)
Maximum export is 'petroleum products' and maximum import is 'Crude Petroleum'

36. (d)
All were the reasons leading to bank nationalization. And the objectives of bank nationalization were:

- Channelizing bank capital into rural and semi urban areas
- Checking misuse of banking capital for financing speculative activities
- To shift from class banking to mass banking
- Make banks an integral part of socio-economic development

37. (d)
Seigniorage refers to the income from money creation. It is a way for governments to generate revenue without levying conventional taxes. Seigniorage is the profit that accrues to the central banks (which then may be transferred to the central government) in the following ways:

- While issuing currency, the reserves/backup that the RBI keeps with itself, these reserves give RBI interest Income on the total amount of currency in circulation (minus cost of printing currency)
- Interest accruing from bank balances with central banks arises from funds banks have to hold with the central banks to meet their reserve requirements, either as interest-free balances (CRR) or at below market interest rates.
- the inflation tax concept which is measured as the product of the inflation rate and the monetary base. (Because of inflation, the currency note that the public is holding losses value which reduces the liability of RBI)

38. (c)
Pegged exchange rate means a country fixes its exchange rate with another country currency or a basket of currencies and when required changes it accordingly.

Suppose Nominal Exchange Rate is $1 = Rs.60 (Nominal exchange rate means how many Rs. can be purchased in $1)

For example, suppose

	India	US
Burger Price	Rs. 30	$1

In this case US will import the burgers from India as in $1 they will get Rs. 60 and in Rs. 60 they will get 2 burgers from India. So, India will export burgers to US.

But if due to inflation the burger price in India becomes Rs. 60 then exports from India will stop. So, inflation in the country may make its exports less competitive.
Hence, **1st** statement is true.

But when price of burger in India reaches to Rs. 60 and RBI devalues the exchange rate to $1 = Rs. 120 then again exports from India will start. Because now foreigners will get Rs. 120 in $1 and in Rs. 120 they will again get 2 burgers from India.
So, **2nd** statement is also true.

39. (d)
The rate of rupee-dollar is determined in the forex market based on market forces of demand and supply. When rupee becomes highly volatile, then RBI **intervenes** in the forex market, to contain the volatility. But RBI does not regulate or fix the rupee dollar rate. This is called 'Managed Float' or 'Dirt Float'.

RBI intervenes in the forex market indirectly through select public sector banks. These banks, in turn, buy or sell on behalf of RBI in the market. Indirect interventions became the primary mode of intervening in the forex market by RBI since 1997-98.

RBI regulates the Forex Market, Money Market and Govt. securities Market.

40. (a)
RBI intervenes in the forex market to contain volatility in exchange rate of Rupee with respect to dollar/foreign currency. There is no targeted band in which RBI tries to keep the Rupee Dollar exchange rate.

For example, if Rupee starts **depreciating slowly over a period of time** and it moves to $1 = Rs 85, then RBI may not intervene in the forex market. But if it happens in a day or two then RBI may intervene.

41. (c)
Suppose Nominal Exchange Rate is $1 = Rs.60 and India and US produces just burgers.

	India	US
Burger Price	Rs. 30	$1

To calculate PPP exchange rate, we need to compare the prices of a basket of goods in India with US.

In the above case by comparing the prices of burger in India and US, we will get $1 = Rs. 30

So, $1 = Rs. 30 is the PPP exchange rate. It implies that, whatever Rs. 30 can purchase in India, the same item can be purchased in $1 in US i.e., purchasing power of Rs. 30 in India is equal to purchasing power of $1 in US.

So, if inflation rate is different in India and US, then PPP exchange rate will change. But if the inflation percent remains same, then PPP exchange rates will remain same i.e., constant.
So, **1st** statement is true.

When we use PPP exchange ($1 = Rs. 30) rate to convert the price of burger in US in Indian currency then it is Rs. 30 in US which is the same as in India also.
So, **2nd** statement is also true.

42. (a)
When nominal exchange rate becomes equal to PPP exchange rate, then we say that the "currencies of two countries are at purchasing power parity".

43. (d)
From the above question we can derive that PPP exchange rate is: $1 = Rs. 20

Now if NER is: $1 = Rs. 15, then Mr. X will be richer than Mr. Y outside India and US

And if NER is $1 = Rs. 25, then Mr. Y will be richer than Mr. X outside India and US

So, who will be richer at a place outside India and US will depend on Nominal Exchange Rate (NER).

44. (b)
When trade deficit increases that means imports are increasing in the country as compared to exports. Increase in imports causes an increase in demand for dollars which results in decline in value of Indian currency.

Increase in trade deficit results in money going out of the Indian economy.

45. (d)
When foreign investors come to India, they bring dollars and this dollar they sell in forex market and demand rupees which results in increase in demand of rupee and rupee appreciates.

When exports increase, we earn more dollars from the foreign market and this dollar we sell in the forex market to purchase rupees which results in increase in demand of rupees and rupee appreciates.

When the interest rate in India increases, more foreign investors come to India to invest in debt, which results in rupee appreciation.

So, none of the statements are true.

46. (d)
Trade competitiveness between two countries is dependent on the movement of domestic price, abroad price and nominal exchange rate. And real exchange rate includes all these three parameters.

For example, if our currency depreciates in nominal terms then our exports become more competitive but it assumes other parameters to be constant.

For example, if with currency depreciation, the price of our product increases much more then our exports may not be competitive.

But the Real Exchange Rate includes the net effect of all the three parameters and hence it's a better measure.

But real exchange rate is between two countries. If we want to measure export competitiveness with respect to a group of countries (trading partners) then we need to calculate real **effective** exchange rate.

Please refer the Indian Economy book for better understanding.

47. (a)
When a currency appreciates either in nominal or real terms then export competitiveness decreases.

If rupee is appreciating that means India's export competitiveness is decreasing but you cannot say India's exports is less competitive.

Please refer the Indian Economy book for better understanding.

48. (d)
Explanation of **1st** statement:
Suppose $1 was equal to Rs 70. And the price of OIL in the international market was $1 per litre. Now, if I have to import one litre OIL then first, I will purchase $1 from the market by paying Rs.70 and then in $1 I will purchase one litre OIL. BUT if rupee depreciates to $1 = Rs. 80, then I will have to purchase the same $1 by paying Rs. 80 and then from $1 I will purchase one litre OIL. So, rupee depreciation did not increase my cost in dollar terms, because I can still import one litre OIL in one dollar as the price of one litre OIL has not changed and only RUPEE has depreciated. So, my cost in Rupees will increase, but the cost of import of one litre OIL still remains same in terms of dollars and that is $1.

Explanation of **2nd** statement:
Suppose the price of wheat in international market is, 1kg wheat = $1 and suppose rupee dollar rate is $1=Rs.70. Now when I will export wheat then first, I will get $1 and this $1 I will sell in market, and I get Rs. 70. Now if rupee depreciated to $1 = Rs. 80 , then still I can/will sell 1 kg wheat in $1 and then while converting 1$ in rupees I will get Rs. 80. So, when rupee has depreciated, I (can) still earn the same dollars (one dollar) per kg of wheat export, but when I convert in rupees then I get more rupees (Rs. 80).

49. (c)
Suppose (Nominal) exchange rate is $1 = Rs. 60
Now if an Indian exporter exported a particular commodity (1 unit) in the international market whose price is $8, then he will get $8 and after conversion in India he will get ultimately Rs. 480.

But if the rupee depreciated i.e., $1 = Rs. 64 then he can sell his product in the international market at a lesser price of $7.5 and can earn the same Rs. 480 after conversion. *(When a country devalues its currency, then exporters are able to sell their product in the international market at a lesser price **without compromising** their earnings.)* So, we also say that exporters become more competitive and demand for domestic goods and services increases as the price gets reduced.

So, exporter will not earn more dollars when rupee depreciates. He will still get the same dollars (or if he reduces the price, then he will get less dollars) per unit of goods sold.
So, **2nd** statement is false.

50. (a)

When rupee appreciates (either in nominal or real terms) that means it is becoming more valuable then its competitiveness decreases. For example, when potato price is increasing from Rs. 10/kg to Rs. 15/kg that means value of potato is increasing/appreciating and potato is becoming less competitive. When something becomes costlier/appreciates then it becomes less competitive.

Second thing is, when rupee appreciates in nominal terms or real terms then our NER/NEER or RER/REER increases. For example, if "$1 = Rs. 70" then it can be written as $.014/Rs. (abroad w.r.t. domestic is the standard) and if this number .014 is increasing that means we are getting more dollars per rupees and rupee is appreciating.

So, when NEER and REER increases then rupee appreciates in nominal and real terms and rupee becomes less competitive.

Explanation:

Real exchange rate (RER) = (NER* Domestic price)/Abroad Price.

If domestic price (i.e. inflation) is increasing then NER will depreciate (decrease in this formula), so the increase and decrease in the numerator will cancel out and there may not be any impact on trade competitiveness. BUT if there is domestic price increase (inflation) but RBI does not allow NER to depreciating (by selling dollars in Forex) then RER (or REER) will increase.... i.e. Rupee will appreciate and our trade competitiveness will decrease. Hence, only 1st Statement is true.

51. (c)

There is no international authority which directs that trade between two countries should happen only with some specific currencies. Any two countries are free to transact with any currency if they are willing.

Generally, any country will accept that currency for its trade (exports), if that currency is not losing value (less inflation) and it is stable and it is freely convertible in other currencies.

52. (d)

- An international currency is one that is freely available to non-residents, essentially to settle cross-border transactions. It is a process that involves increasing use of the local (rupee) currency in cross border transactions i.e., international markets.
- In this process first current account transactions are allowed and then capital account transactions between resident Indians and non-Resident Indians. The last step is use of rupee for transactions between non-residents.
- Internationalization of a currency is an expression of external credibility in the currency as well as in the economy.
- All truly international currencies belong to large, advanced economies. And their use for international transactions confers substantial economic privileges to the host countries. The privileges/advantages include:
    - Immunity from BoP crises as the country can pay for its external deficits with its own currency
    - The dominance of its financial institutions, markets and policies in the global economy
    - Increased bargaining power of domestic business adding weight to the economy and enhancing the country's global stature and respect

- ➢ Protection for its businesses from currency risk
- ➢ Seigniorage that accrues to it
- ➢ Reduces the need for holding foreign exchange reserves
- ➢ Reducing dependence on foreign currency which makes the country less vulnerable to external shocks

- All of the above privileges flow from its status as the preeminent reserve currency.
- Clearly, very few countries can enjoy such privileges at any given point of time in history. And the preconditions - size of the economy and a dominant share of global GDP, globally dominant businesses, extraordinary military capabilities etc. limit the prospects of owning an international currency to any but the largest few economies.
- The preconditions for owning an international currency are - size of the economy and a dominant share of global GDP, globally dominant businesses, extraordinary military capabilities etc. And these preconditions limit the prospects of owning an international currency to only few largest economies.
- Hence internationalization of rupee cannot just be achieved by financial regulation alone.

53. (d)

Earlier Individuals/Retail Investors were not allowed to purchase G-Secs in the Primary Market although in secondary market they were allowed.

Then after some time Individuals/Retail Investors were allowed to purchase G-Secs in Primary Market but not directly but through Banks/NBFCs.

In 2021, Individuals/Retail Investors have been allowed to purchase G-Secs in Primary Market directly by opening a Gilt Account with RBI under 'Retail Direct Scheme'.

When Govt. wants money it issues G-Secs in Primary Market and Banks/NBFCs (called Primary Dealers) participate in bidding/auctioning process and through this auctioning 'Interest Rate' gets discovered on G-Secs. If there are less Banks/NBFCs interested in purchasing G-Secs then interest rate will move up and it will be costlier for Govt. to borrow.

Now, Individuals/Retail Investors participate in the bidding/auctioning process of G-Secs in Primary Market but are only passive participant (called non-competitive bidding). Banks/NBFCs participate in the bidding/auctioning process (competitive bidding) and interest rate gets discovered and the Individuals/Retail Investors are allotted G-Secs at the discovered interest rate, if they have applied to purchase G-Secs in Primary Market.

Allowing of retail investors will broaden the base of investors who want to invest in Govt. securities. And more the number of people/investors willing to purchase Govt. bonds will result in interest rates coming down on Govt. borrowings.

RBI manages the issuance of Govt. securities through "e-Kuber" platform. Earlier retail investors (like we people) were not allowed to purchase the govt securities (bonds/ debt paper) directly at the time of issuance. But now retail investors can directly purchase the Govt. securities at the time of issuance (in the primary market) and also in the secondary market.

54. (c)

G-Secs are issued through auctions conducted by RBI. Auctions are conducted on the electronic platform called the E-Kuber, the Core Banking Solution (CBS) platform of RBI. So, basically e-Kuber is a platform where primary market transaction happens.

Commercial banks, scheduled UCBs, Primary Dealers insurance companies and provident funds, who maintain funds account (current account) and securities accounts with RBI, are members of this electronic platform. All members of E-Kuber can place their bids in the auction through this electronic platform.

There is an active secondary market in G-Secs and Negotiated Dealing System-Order Matching is such a market/platform. Stock exchanges are also a secondary market for government securities.

55. (d)
A Government Security (G-Sec) is a tradable instrument issued by the Central Government or the State Governments. There are four kinds of government securities.

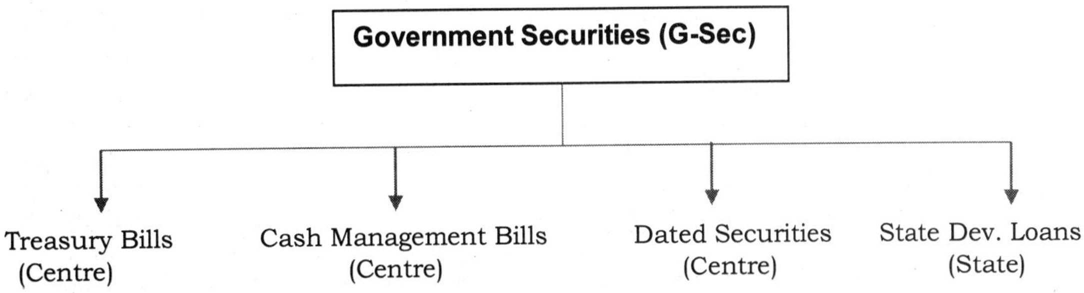

SDLs are allowed to be kept under SLR by banks. SDLs have maturity of more than one year. As per RBI Act 1934, RBI manages the Public Debt of States.

56. (d)
In 2010, Government of India, in consultation with RBI introduced a new short-term instrument, known as Cash Management Bills (CMBs). **It is not used to fund the Fiscal deficit** but is used to meet the temporary mismatches in the cash flow of the **Government of India**. The CMBs have the generic character of T-bills but are issued for maturities less than 91 days. *(Traded in money market also)*

Treasury bills or T-bills: These are short term debt instruments issued by the Government of India for a maturity of less than one year. Treasury bills are zero coupon securities and pay no interest. Instead, they are issued at a discount and redeemed at the face value at maturity. For example, a 91-day Treasury bill of ₹100/- (face value) may be issued at say ₹ 98.20, that is, at a discount of say, ₹1.80 and would be redeemed at the face value of ₹100/-. *(Treasury bills are traded in money market also).*

Dated Securities: Dated central government securities have a tenor of more than one year up to 50 years.

57. (b)
SLR is maintained as per Banking Regulation Act 1949 while CRR is maintained as per RBI Act 1934.

Banks maintain SLR with themselves in the form of Cash, Gold and Govt. securities. But if they want, they can also keep the cash with RBI. In another way, we can say that whatever cash the banks have with RBI in excess of CRR can be treated as SLR.

All the four Govt. securities are eligible under SLR.

58. (d)
The Reserve Bank of India gives temporary loan facilities to the centre and state governments as a banker to government. This temporary loan facility is called Ways and Means Advances (WMA).

The WMA scheme was designed to meet temporary mismatches in the receipts and payments of the government. This facility can be availed by the government if it needs immediate cash from the RBI. The WMA is a loan facility from the RBI for 90 days which implies that the government has to vacate the facility after 90 days. Interest rate for WMA is currently charged at the repo rate. The limits for WMA are mutually decided by the RBI and the Government of India.

59. (d)
Let us understand it with example:
Suppose next year (2023-24), central govt deficit is going to be Rs. 10 lakh crores, then it can plan for issuing bonds worth Rs. 10 lakh crores, which can be Treasury bills or Dated securities. But, suppose on 15th May 2022, govt had some cash requirement (even after this Rs. 10 lakh crore borrowing has been arranged) for 21 days, then Central Govt. can take loan (called ways and means advance) from RBI or it can issue a bond (called cash management bills) of maturity period 21 days. But after 21 days, govt will have to repay this. So, basically, 'ways and means advance' and 'cash management bills' are not issued for the govt's **planned** borrowing requirement (called fiscal deficit), but are used for temporary mismatch in cash receipt and cash payment (disbursement).

The difference between 'Ways and Means Advance' (WMA) and 'Cash Management Bills' (CMB) is WMA is a kind of **loan** facility (which is not tradable) **from RBI** and CMB are bonds of GoI issued **into the market** which are **tradable**. CMB is only for Central Govt. and WMA is for Centre and State both. Govt. pays interest on WMA at repo rate or may be more than that.

60. (d)
A bond (debt paper) holder is expected to get a fix interest regularly and principal at maturity. But if the inflation in the economy starts increasing then interest rate also increases and the (market) price of the bond decreases and bondholders lose. When the price of the bond decreases in the market, the person who will purchase the bond will have to pay less price and hence he will get more return/yield. *(The interest rate on the bond remains fixed but its price fluctuates in the market and hence the return also fluctuates. If the market price of the bond is low, then the return/yield on the bond will be high. This is because the person who will purchase the bond will have to pay less price to get the same bond).*

*For detailed understanding, you can refer the book on **Indian Economy by Vivek Singh**.*

61. (d)
Repo rate acts as benchmark interest rate in the economy and when it moves up/down then the market interest rate also moves up/down impacting G-Sec prices.

When US Federal Bank increases their interest rate then a lot of FPI debt investors in India sell their investments and return to US in search of better return and this leads to decline in G-Sec (bond) prices in India.

If the liquidity in the economy is surplus, the interest rate comes down in the economy resulting in higher bond prices. And if there is liquidity crunch then it moves the interest rate up resulting in decline in bond prices or G-sec prices.

62. (b)
As per the RBI Act 1934, Section 26, rupee notes (and coins) are legal tenders. It means that notes and coins cannot be refused by any person of the country for payment/discharge of debt. Now, Central Bank Digital Currency has also been declared legal tender by amending the RBI Act 1934.

(For example: Is an autowallah obliged to accept your currency note for a ride? Not necessarily! If you are yet to get into the auto, the autowallah can turn you down despite it being a legal tender. But once you make the trip, and you have incurred a debt, then he cannot refuse to take your currency note.)

63. (d)
Currencies and coins are fiat money because they derive their value from government "fiat"/ order and not because of its intrinsic material.

If the coin is melted then it will not fetch the same value in the market and the paper of which the currency note is made of does not have any value in the market. Hence, Currency notes and coins are called fiat money and they do not have intrinsic value.

Currencies and coins are 'Legal tender' which means it is recognized by the law of the land, as valid for payment of debt. It must be accepted for discharge of debt. RBI Act 1934, Section 26 states that "*Every central bank **note** shall be legal tender at any place in India in payment or on account for the amount expressed therein*".
As per the RBI Act 1934, all currency notes are guaranteed by the Central Government

64. (c)
Currency in circulation consists of Notes and Coins. All the currency notes (except one rupee note) are liability of RBI. But one-rupee notes and coins are printed/minted by Govt. of India and hence are liability of Govt. of India.

All the currency in circulation is not part of money supply. Only that currency in circulation which is with the PUBLIC is part of money supply. The currency with bank is not part of money supply.

Currency in circulation = Currency with public + currency with bank

Even if one-rupee notes and coins are minted/printed by Govt. of India, all the currency notes and coins are circulated in the economy by RBI (as per RBI Act 1934).

65. (c)
The RBI Act of 1934, Section 22 gives the central bank the sole right to issue currency notes.

66. (d)
[The Government of India has the sole right to mint coins. The responsibility for coinage vests with the Government of India in terms of the Coinage Act, 1906. The designing and minting of coins in various denominations is also the responsibility of the Government of India. Coins are minted at the India Government Mints at Mumbai, Alipore(Kolkata), Saifabad (Hyderabad), Cherlapally (Hyderabad) and NOIDA (UP).

The coins are issued for circulation only through the Reserve Bank in terms of the RBI Act. Coins can be issued up to the denomination of Rs.1000 as per the Coinage Act, 1906.

The RBI shall ***issue*** *rupee coins on demand and the Govt. of India shall supply/mint such coins to the RBI on demand.*

Ref: https://www.rbi.org.in/scripts/ic_coins.aspx
And RBI Act 1934, section 39

67. (c)

As per section 24 of RBI Act 1934, *"Central Government, on the recommendation of Central Board of Directors of RBI, has the authority to specify the denomination of the new currency note to be issued in the country."*

68. (c)

As per the RBI Act 1934, Section 25, *"the design, form and material of bank notes shall be such as may be approved by the Central Government after consideration of the recommendations made by the Central Board of RBI."*

69. (a)

As per the RBI Act 1934, Section 26, *"on recommendation of the Central Board, the Central Government may, by notification in the Gazette of India, declare that, with effect from such date, any series of bank notes of any denomination shall cease to be legal tender".*

70. (c)

In any particular year, suppose there is some level of output/GDP and some level of money supply in the economy. Now, next year, RBI tries to increase the money supply in the economy based on what will be the real growth in GDP next year and what level of inflation RBI wants to maintain/target (4% +/- 2%) in the economy.

71. (c)

In terms of Section 20 of the RBI Act 1934, RBI has the obligation to undertake the receipts and payments of the Central Government and to carry out the exchange, remittance and other banking operations, including the management of the public debt of the Central Govt. Further, as per Section 21 of the said Act, RBI has the right to transact Government business of the Union in India.

State Government transactions are carried out by RBI in terms of the agreement entered into with the State Governments in terms of section 21 A of the RBI Act. As of now, such agreements exist between RBI and all the State Governments except Government of Sikkim.
Thus, the legal provisions vest RBI with both the right and the obligation to function as banker to the government.

72. (b)

RBI carries out the general banking business of the governments through its own offices and commercial banks, both public and private, appointed as its agents (called Agency Banks). Section 45 of the Reserve Bank of India Act, 1934, provides for appointment of scheduled commercial banks as agents at all places or at any place in India.

A network comprising the Government Banking Division of RBI and branches of agency banks appointed under Section 45 of the RBI Act carry out the government transactions. Only designated branches of agency banks can conduct government banking business.

Recent changes:

- Now any scheduled commercial private bank can act as agency banks without any limit on size (earlier only big private banks were allowed).

- Now RBI has allowed all scheduled Payment Banks and Small Finance Banks also to act as 'Agency Banks'.

73. (d)
As a banker to bank, RBI performs the following functions:

- RBI enables banks to open their (current) accounts with RBI for maintenance of statutory reserve requirements (CRR and may be SLR)
- RBI acts as a common banker for different banks to enable settlement of interbank transfer of funds
- RBI provides short term loans and advances to banks for specific purposes
- RBI acts as lender of last resort for example in case of a bank run situation. *(**Bank Run** is a situation that occurs when everybody wants to take money out of one's bank account before the bank runs out of reserves.)*

74. (d)
RBI comes to the rescue of a bank that is solvent (which has not gone bankrupt) but faces temporary liquidity (funds) problems by supplying it with much needed liquidity when no one else is willing to extend credit to that bank. RBI extends this facility to protect the interest of the depositors of the bank and to prevent possible failure of a bank, which in turn may also affect other banks and institutions and can have an adverse impact on financial stability and thus on the economy.

RBI provides this emergency liquidity assistance only if the troubled financial institution has exhausted all the resources it can obtain from the market and from the RBI's regular liquidity facilities like LAF, MSF etc.

75. (c)
Lender of Last Resort (LOLR): RBI provides emergency liquidity assistance to stressed banks that is solvent but faces temporary liquidity problems by supplying it with much needed liquidity when no one else is willing to extend credit to that bank. The troubled bank is expected to first exhaust all the resources it can obtain from the market and from the Reserve Bank's regular liquidity facilities (like LAF and MSF), before requesting for the Lender of Last Resort (LOLR) support. It typically does so against specified collaterals, preferably the central or state governments' securities. The LOLR support is typically provided for short periods of up to 90 days at a penalty rate above the repo rate. The LOLR facility is provided to a solvent but illiquid bank which is facing temporary liquidity problem.

Bankrupt means who has been adjudged bankrupt by a bankruptcy order/judgement. Once a bank is declared bankrupt then RBI may not come for its protection under lender of last resort.

76. (c)
When RBI floats/raises loans on behalf of government then it is acting as a "Debt Manager" of government and not as a Banker to government. So (iv) statement is not true.

77. (c)
The call/notice money market forms an important segment of the Indian money market. Under call money market, funds are transacted on overnight basis and under notice money market, funds are transacted for the period between 2 days and 14 days. These are unsecured instruments.

Participants in call/notice money market currently include Commercial and Cooperative Banks, Primary Dealers (PDs), development finance institutions, insurance companies and select mutual funds.

78. (d)
Commercial Paper (CP) is an unsecured money market instrument issued in the form of a promissory note (promise to pay in future). The original tenor (time period) of a CP shall be between seven days to one year.

NBFCs, All India Financial Institutions (like NABARD, SIDBI etc.), cooperative societies, Govt. entities (PSUs) and other companies can issue CP to raise money in the money market.

79. (d)
Certificate of Deposits are negotiable/tradable, unsecured money market instruments issued by Scheduled Commercial Banks (and some All-India Financial Institutions like NHB, SIDBI etc. but mostly by banks) for a maturity period up to one year against funds deposited at the bank.

For example, if a bank is issuing a Rs. 100 CD paper to raise money from the money market then it will have to keep some percent (of Rs. 100) as reserves. These Certificate of Deposits are different from the 'deposit certificate' that we individuals get while doing Fixed Deposit in the bank. Our 'deposit certificates' are not tradable.

80. (d)
The money market is a market for short-term (maturity less than one year) financial assets (debt papers) that are close substitutes of money. The most important feature of a money market instrument is that it is liquid and can be turned over (bought/sold) quickly at low cost and provides an avenue for equilibrating the short-term surplus funds of lenders and the requirements of borrowers.

Cash management bills, Treasury bills and Certificate of deposits have less than one-year maturity and are traded in money market.

State Development Loans (SDL) have maturity more than a year and are not traded in money market.

81. (c)
Mergers and Acquisitions of commercial banks require the approval of Competition Commission of India (CCI) and Reserve Bank of India (RBI) both.

CCI is the "Fair Trade Regulator".

CCI looks into the competition part of such deal and RBI looks into the prudential aspects. The RBI is the sector regulator, so the health of banks is its concern. The CCI's concern is their behaviour in the market and the consumers in the market,"

If any merger/amalgamation/acquisition is happening and after the merger/amalgamation/acquisition the combined asset value is more than Rs. 1000 crore or Turnover (sales in a year) is more than Rs 3000 crore then they are required to take approval of Competition Commission of India (CCI) under the Competition Commission of India Act 2002.

But as per section 54 of the CCI Act, Central government may exempt from the application of CCI Act, any class of enterprises, if such exemption is necessary in the interest of security of the State or public interest. So, when SBI and its associates got merged, then Central government had waived of the approval of CCI. When SBI was acquiring 49% stake in Yes Bank then also central government waived off the CCI approval.

82. (b)
In line with the recommendations of the P J Nayak committee and with a view to improve the Governance of Public Sector Banks (PSBs), the GoI appointed an autonomous **Banks Board Bureau (BBB)** but it was later on replaced by Financial Services Institutions Bureau (FSIB) through a Govt. resolution from 1st July 2022. **The following are the functions of the FSIB:**

- To recommend persons for appointment as whole-time directors (WTDs) and non-executive chairpersons (NECs) on the Boards of Directors in Public Sector Banks, financial institutions and Public Sector Insurers (hereinafter referred to as "PSBs", "FIs" and "PSIs" respectively.
- To advise the Government on matters relating to appointments, transfer or extension of term of office and termination of services of the said directors.
- To advise the Government on the desired management structure at the Board level for PSBs, FIs and PSIs
- To advise the Government on a suitable performance appraisal system for WTDs and NECs in PSBs, FIs and PSIs
- To build a databank containing data related to the performance of PSBs, FIs and PSIs
- To advise the Government on formulation and enforcement of a code of conduct and ethics for whole-time directors in PSBs, FIs and PSIs
- To advise the Government on evolving suitable training and development programmes for management personnel in PSBs, FIs and PSIs
- To help PSBs, FIs and PSIs in terms of developing business strategies and capital raising plan etc.
- To carry out such process and draw up a panel for consideration of competent authority for any other bank, financial institution or insurer for which the Government makes a reference

(FIs are basically public sector financial institutions like NABARD, NHB, SIDBI, EXIM, MUDRA etc.)

83. (c)
FSIB is responsible for appointment as whole-time directors (WTDs) and non-executive chairpersons (NECs) on the Boards of Directors in Public Sector Banks, financial institutions and Public Sector Insurers

Once FSIB selects the Directors/Chairman then it is sent for approval by the Appointments Committee of the Cabinet (ACC).

84. (a)
RBI has set up (100% subsidiary) Deposit Insurance and Credit Guarantee Corporation (DICGC) to protect the interest of small depositors in case of bank **failures/bankruptcy**. The DICGC provides insurance cover to all eligible bank depositors up to Rs. 5 lakhs (principal and interest combined) per depositor per bank.

As per "The Deposit Insurance and Credit Guarantee Corporation (DICGC) Act 1961", DICGC must register all commercial banks (scheduled and non-scheduled both) and Urban Cooperative banks (UCB) and State and District Central Cooperative Banks (StCB/DCCB) as an insured bank.

And every insured bank is liable to pay premium to DICGC as may be notified by DICGC after the approval of RBI. As per the rules, premium cost is required to be borne by the bank themselves and cannot be passed on to depositors.

Deposits of foreign governments, deposits of central and state governments, and inter-bank deposits are not covered/insured.

Even if a bank has not gone bankrupt but is **not doing well and** RBI has imposed moratorium/restrictions on withdrawal of deposits to improve the condition of the bank, then in that case also DICGC will have to pay to depositors Rs. 5 lakhs (maximum, depending on what is in your account) within 90 days. This was a major issue for depositors as in the last few years several banks had cases related to fraud and were not doing well and RBI imposed moratorium/restrictions on public deposit withdrawal. *(It was done by amending the DICGC Act in 2021).*

85. (c)
The objectives of setting up of payments banks is to promote financial inclusion by providing small savings accounts and payments/remittance services to migrant labour workforce, low-income households, small businesses, other unorganized sector entities and other users.

The following will be the scope of activities for payment banks:

- Acceptance of demand deposits (savings or current) up to Rs. 2 lakhs only but no time deposits
- **No lending activity**
- Issuance of ATM/debit cards but not credit cards
- Payments and remittance services through various channels
- Acting as Banking Correspondent (BC) of another bank
- Distribution of simple financial products like mutual funds/insurance products, etc.

Payment banks will be required to maintain Cash Reserve Ratio (CRR) and Statutory Liquidity Ratio (SLR). The total deposits of the public must be invested in government securities and/ or deposited in other commercial banks (i.e., no lending is allowed). This makes the public deposit in payment banks safe. Payment banks have been set up as differentiated banks for serving niche interests. *(Differentiated banks have restrictions either in geography or in operation or both. Opposite of differentiated banks are universal banks).*

86. (c)
India Post Payment Bank is a public sector enterprise and comes under the Department of Posts, Ministry of Communications. It is a payment bank and accepts only demand deposits (current and savings account).

'Department of Post' is a department of Govt. of India to provide mail and various services. Now, Govt. of India (through Department of Post, Ministry of Communication) created a wholly owned PSU, 'India Post Payment Bank', to provide banking facilities.

87. (a)
The objectives of setting up of small finance banks are to promote financial inclusion by providing provision of savings vehicles and supply of credit to small business units; small and marginal farmers; micro and small industries; and other unorganized sector entities, through high technology - low-cost operations. They are required to extend 75% of their loans to priority sectors and 50% of their loan portfolio shall constitute loans of up to 25 lacs.

The scope of activities for small finance banks will be basic banking activities of acceptance of deposits and lending to unserved and underserved sections including small business units, small and marginal farmers, micro and small industries and unorganized sector entities and there will not be any restriction in the area of operations. They will be required to maintain CRR and SLR. They will be set up as differentiated banks for serving niche interests

Small Finance Banks are not particularly for rural areas.

RBI released guidelines for 'on-tap' licensing of Small Finance Banks. Urban Cooperative Banks and Payment Banks can apply for conversion into SFB. 'On-tap' means any time they can apply for conversion into SFB and they don't need to wait for a time window when RBI will grant licenses.

88. (b)
Urban cooperative banks (UCB) (also called Primary cooperative banks), State Cooperative Banks (StCB) and District Central Cooperative Banks (DCCB) are under dual regulation of Central/State governments and the RBI.

StCB and DCCB are rural cooperative banks.

Though the Banking Regulation Act came in to force in 1949, the banking laws were made applicable to cooperative societies only in 1966 through an amendment to the Banking Regulation Act, 1949. Since then, there is '**duality of control**' over cooperative banks (UCB, StCB and DCCB) between the State Registrar of Cooperative Societies/Central Registrar of Cooperative Societies and the Reserve Bank of India. The Reserve Bank **regulates and supervises** the banking functions and amalgamation and liquidation of UCBs/StCB/DCCB under the provisions of Section 22 and 23 of Banking regulation Act, 1949 and the non-banking aspects like registration, management, administration and recruitment are regulated by the State/ Central Governments.

PACS and long-term credit co-operatives like SCARDB and PCARDB, which are basically rural cooperative banks, are outside the purview of the Banking Regulation Act, 1949 and are hence not regulated by the Reserve Bank.

Urban Cooperative Banks are under the supervision of RBI but supervision of all rural cooperative banks including StCB/DCCB have been delegated to NABARD by RBI.

For detailed understanding, you can refer the book on ***Indian Economy by Vivek Singh.***

89. (d)
NABARD does not give direct loan to individuals but it gives loan to Commercial Banks, Regional Rural Banks (RRBs), State Cooperative Banks & Land Development Banks **and** Non-Banking Financial Companies (NBFCs) for further lending (refinance) to the agriculture and rural sectors.
[Ref: https://www.nabard.org/english/Longterm.aspx]

90. (d)
NABARD is 100% owned by Govt. of India. Govt. of India keeps on contributing share capital to NABARD time to time.

NABARD raises money by borrowing from RBI (Actually RBI gave Rs. 25,000 crore of special refinance facility at repo rate under Aatma Nirbhar Bharat). This facility is not always available to NABARD and is on discretion of RBI.
NABARD also borrows from commercial banks and it also raises money by issuing bonds and debentures in the financial markets. NABARD also borrows from abroad in foreign currency.

NABARD also borrows money by issuing bonds which are fully serviced (interest and principal are paid) by govt. of India. The purpose of these bonds is to meet expenditure towards Govt. of India schemes by raising 'Extra-budgetary Resources' in the name of NABARD. And hence it is not counted in fiscal deficit of Govt. of India

91. (c)
MUDRA is responsible for **refinancing** all Last Mile Financiers such as Non-Banking Finance Companies, Societies, Trusts, Companies, Co-operative Societies, Small Banks, Scheduled Commercial Banks and Regional Rural Banks which are in the business of lending to micro/small business entities engaged in **manufacturing, trading and services activities but not agriculture.** Refinancing means MUDRA loans will be available through Banks/NBFCs/MFIs and not directly from MUDRA Bank.

MUDRA loans have been designed to cater to customers operating at the lower end of the enterprise spectrum i.e., informal/unorganized sector.

92. (c)
National Housing Bank (NHB) was set up in 1988 under the National Housing Bank Act, 1987. It operates as a principal agency to promote Housing Finance Companies (HFC) both at local and regional levels and to provide financial and other support to such institutions.

National Housing Bank was a wholly owned (100%) subsidiary of RBI. But in 2019, Govt. of India took over the entire stake of NHB from RBI.

NHB is regulated by RBI. Earlier, NHB regulated the activities of HFCs based on regulatory and supervisory authority derived under the NHB Act 1987, but now RBI does it. It does not extend direct credit at individual level but extends indirect financial assistance by way of refinance *(i.e., NHB finances those institutions which provide finance to individual borrowers, builders etc.)*

93. (c)
Housing finance companies (HFCs) are a category of NBFCs and till recently, HFCs were regulated by National Housing Bank (NHB). But this changed in 2019 and now HFCs have come under the direct regulation of RBI. This may have been done because of the bankruptcy issues going on in various housing finance companies like DHFL.

94. (a)
P2P intermediaries are a class of NBFCs and are regulated by RBI that provides the platform which pairs borrowers and individual lenders. With P2P lending, borrowers take loans from individual investors who are willing to lend their own money for an agreed interest rate. The repayments are also made through the NBFC-P2P which processes and forwards the payments to the lenders who invested in the loan. P2P lending is also called social lending or crowd lending.

- NBFC - P2P shall:
  - not raise deposits
  - not lend on its own
  - not provide any credit guarantee
  - not facilitate or permit any secured lending linked to its platform
  - shall not provide any assurance for the recovery of loans.
  - undertake due diligence on the participants;
  - undertake credit assessment and risk profiling of the borrowers and disclose the same to their prospective lenders;
  - provide assistance in disbursement and repayments of loan amount;
  - render services for recovery of loans originated on the platform.
  - all fund transfers shall be through and from bank accounts and cash transaction is strictly prohibited.

95. (d)
NBFCs borrow from banks and then lend. They also issue bonds in financial markets to raise money and then this money they lend at a higher interest rate. NBFCs also borrow from abroad through debt financing (called ECB). NBFCs also issue Commercial Papers (CP) in the money market to raise short term money.

Mutual funds also invest in NBFCs which means, NBFCs issue debt papers to mutual funds and then this money they lend.

But, the main wholesale funding sources of the NBFCs comprise mainly of:
- Banks (primarily via term loans and rest through non-convertible debentures and commercial paper); and
- debt mutual funds (via non-convertible debentures and commercial paper)

Debentures are long-term unsecured debt financial instruments (they are similar to bonds in functioning). Some debentures have a feature of convertibility into shares after a certain point of time. The debentures which can't be converted into shares or equities are called non-convertible debentures (or NCDs) and earn a higher interest rate.

96. (d)
NBFCs rely on short-term financing like commercial papers to fund long-term investments (long term loans to businesses). So, the tenure of liability (the commercial papers issued by NBFCs) is short and the tenure of asset (loans given by NBFCs) is long. This is called Asset Liability Mismatch (ALM). So, NBFCs are required to refinance these commercial papers at short frequencies of a few months. The frequent re-pricing of loans/advances (as they need to be raised again and again and interest rate keeps on changing in the market) exposes NBFCs to the risk of facing higher financing costs, and in the worst case, credit rationing. Such refinancing risks are referred as rollover risks.

Credit rationing is the limiting by lenders of the supply of additional credit to borrowers who demand funds, even if the latter are willing to pay higher interest rates.

97. (d)
In October 2022, 24 Scheduled Commercial Banks launched 75 Digital Banking Units (DBUs) in 75 districts. DBUs would promote financial inclusion and digital literacy, which will boost the formalization of the economy. DBUs are physical banking units that will provide services without requiring paper.

The products and services in these DBUs will be provided in two modes, namely, self-service and assisted modes, with self-service mode being available on 24*7*365 basis. The banks are also free to engage the services of digital business facilitators and business correspondents to expand the footprint of the DBUs.

A **Neo-bank** is a digital bank that does not have any branches. Instead of having a physical presence at a set location, neo banking is entirely online. A broad collection of financial service providers, who primarily target tech-savvy customers, comes under the umbrella of neo banking. Some of the neo banks offering services in India are Jupiter, Fi Money, Niyo, Razorpay X etc.

98. (b)
A "Real estate investment trust" is a trust registered under the Indian Trusts Act, 1882 which manages a fund/ corpus where the funds are invested in real estate property. REITS are mutual fund like institutions that enable investment into the real estate sector by pooling small sums of money from multitude of individual investors. REITS are regulated by Securities and Exchange Board of India (SEBI).

Most middle-class investors presently do not invest in commercial real estate because of the big size of investment. This entry barrier will be removed through REITs as it will make the expensive real estate sector accessible to the middle-class investor. REITS will also help the real estate industry which is currently plagued with problems such as weak demand, cash constraints, stuck projects etc. Now, the developers will be able to sell their property to REITs and move on to execution of new projects.

SEBI has also approved **Infrastructure Investment Trusts (InvITs)** along with REITs which are very similar to REITs but are for infrastructure sector.

99. (d)
- An **angel investor** is a person who invests in highly risky companies, typically before those companies have any revenue or profits. They are often among an entrepreneur's family and friends and invest in small start-ups and entrepreneurs.
- Angel investors provide more favourable terms compared to other lenders, since they usually invest in the entrepreneur starting the business rather than the viability of the business.
- Angel investors are focused on helping start-ups take their first steps, rather than the possible profit they may get from the business.
- Fund-raising with angel investors is typically done more casually, using networking and crowd funding platforms.
- Essentially, angel investors are the opposite of venture capitalists. Angel investors typically use their own money, unlike venture capitalists who take care of pooled money from many other investors and place them in a strategically managed fund.
- Angel Investment in India is regulated by Securities and Exchange Board of India (SEBI) under Category I of Alternative Investment Funds (AIF).

100. (d)
Anchor investor is a concept launched by SEBI in 2009. Anchor investors are institutional investors (not individual) who are invited to subscribe/purchase the shares

before the Initial Public Offer (IPO) opens so that it popularizes the issue and increases the confidence of the other investors and improves the demand of the share. Each anchor investor needs to invest a minimum sum in the issue. The anchor investors are allotted share one day before the IPO opens and there is some lock in period before which they cannot exit their investment.

101. (d)
Alternative Investment Fund (AIF) means any fund established or incorporated in India which is a **privately pooled investment vehicle which collects funds from sophisticated investors**, whether Indian or foreign, for investing it in accordance with a defined investment policy for the benefit of its investors. AIFs are registered with and regulated by SEBI. Angel Investor Funds and Venture Capital Funds come under AIF.

102. (d)
Crowd funding or marketplace financing refers to a method of funding a project or new venture through small amounts of money raised from a large number of people, typically through a portal (internet/social media) acting as an intermediary. Crowd funding makes use of the easy accessibility of vast networks of people through social media and crowd funding websites to bring investors and entrepreneurs together. Crowd funding has the potential to increase entrepreneurship by expanding the pool of investors from whom funds can be raised beyond the traditional circle of owners.

103. (d)
The concept of a mutual fund is that various investors/individuals put their money in a fund and this fund is used to purchase shares or bonds of various companies thus diversifying the risk of the investors. The fund is managed by experts and individuals/investors don't trade the share/bonds directly. The fund managers decide in which companies to invest and from which companies to exit. If the share price or bond price of the companies increase then the value of the fund also increases and investors gain. If some individual wants to put money into the mutual fund, then it can be done only once after the market has closed for that given day.

Exchange Traded Funds (ETFs) are almost similar to that of mutual funds but they differ in the sense that ETFs are traded on the stock exchange throughout the day. So, if any investor wants to purchase an ETF, they can always purchase it from the stock exchange/market throughout the day, just like the shares of any company. [So, basically you can purchase the shares of ETF from the stock exchange and ETF's assets are not physical buildings/machinery rather they have purchased shares/bonds of other companies which are assets for ETF]

The Central government announced in the budget 2018-19 that they will be creating an ETF of various central public sector companies so that to attract investors to purchase ETFs, and through which the disinvestment can be done. So, when an investor is purchasing the shares of the ETF, he is indirectly purchasing the shares of various companies/PSUs which the government is disinvesting.

104. (c)
Impact bonds are innovative financing instruments that leverage private sector capital and expertise, with a focus on achieving results. It shifts the focus from inputs to performance and results. Rather than a government or a donor financing a project upfront, private investors (risk investors) initially finance the initiative and are repaid by 'outcome funders', only if agreed-upon outcomes are achieved.

In an impact bond, a form of results-based financing, an investor provides upfront capital for social services programs, and this investment is repaid—often with interest—based on the program's achievement of predetermined outcomes. In a social impact bond, the repayment is made by government, while in a development impact bond, the repayment is made by a third party, usually a donor organization or a foundation.

National Skill Development Corporation (NSDC), in Oct. 2021, in collaboration with global partners launched first of its kind 'Impact Bonds' involving $14.4 million fund for skilling in India which will benefit 50,000 youth in four years by making them employment ready.

The target group includes 60 per cent women and girls and the objective is to equip them with skills and vocational training and provide access to wage-employment in Covid-19 recovery sectors including retail, apparel, healthcare and logistics. The stakeholders will work towards promoting effective interventions, supporting research and enhancing the impact of the skill development programme. The training will be imparted through NSDC's affiliated training partners.

105. (d)
When a contractor gets a project then he needs to provide a guarantee that he will complete the project as per the stipulated timelines and guidelines. This guarantee is provided in the form of bank guarantee but contractors incur cost in providing guarantee from banks. So, Surety bonds will act as a substitute for bank guarantees and it will reduce the indirect cost for suppliers and work contractors.

Recently, IRDAI allowed issuance of Surety (insurance) bonds which can be offered to infrastructure projects of government and private both.

106. (c)
India is a globally significant market for gold business, but does not produce enough gold that can meet huge domestic demands. India stands at the second position in terms of gold import globally, after China. The country imports gold in the form of gold bars, which is governed by the RBI. According to the RBI circular, only the entities notified by the Directorate General of Foreign Trade (DGFT) are permitted to import gold to India after the issue of license by DGFT.

Gold is tightly regulated in India and currently only nominated banks and agencies approved by RBI can import gold and sell to dealers and jewellers across the country.

The Multi Commodity Exchange (MCX) and National Commodity and Derivatives Exchange (NCDEX) offer gold futures contracts in India, but there wasn't any physical exchange to buy gold.

The launch of the India International Bullion Exchange (IIBX) in GIFT City will bring in the following changes:

- IIBX with its technology-driven solutions, will facilitate transition of Indian bullion market towards a more organised structure by granting qualified jewellers and bullion dealers a direct access to import gold directly through the exchange mechanism.
- Standardization of Gold pricing in India
- It will make India a global price-setter for bullion
- IIBX is India's first International Bullion Exchange set up at International Financial Services Center (IFSC) at GIFT City

107. (a)
The term of appointment can be 5 years, but generally the practise has been to appoint for 3 years and then extend.

108. (c)
RBI issues various guidelines for directors of banks and also has powers to appoint additional directors on the board of a banking company. Banks need prior approval of RBI for appointment/termination of Chairman, Directors and CEO. RBI in consultation with Central Govt., can supersede the Board of Directors of Banks.
Public Sector Banks (PSBs) are under dual regulation of Central Govt. and RBI. RBI's powers are curtailed regarding PSBs, where RBI cannot remove directors and management, cannot supersede banks board and does not have the power to force a merger or trigger liquidation.

109. (a)
RBI is 100% owned by govt. of India but its surplus transfer to Govt. has fluctuated in the previous years.
Refer the Trends

110. (d)
As per RBI Act 1934, Section 47, there are two clear objectives for the Economic Capital Framework (ECF).

- First, the RBI as a macroeconomic institution has the responsibility to fight any crisis in the financial system and to handle such a crisis, the RBI should have adequate funds attached under the capital reserve.
- And, second is transferring the remaining part of the net income to the government.

Till the time, reserves are with RBI, it is not part of money supply. But if RBI gives its surplus reserves to government which will ultimately spend this amount will result in this extra money reaching to public resulting in higher inflation.

Bimal Jalan Committee has recommended that RBI should maintain 5.5% to 6.5% of the balance sheet (value of the assets/liabilities) as Contingency Risk Buffer. The committee also recommended that "there always needs to be harmony in the objectives of the Government and the RBI".

111. (d)
When there is a default in the debt market, everyone wants to sell the debt paper and hold cash which results in shortage of liquidity and increase/hardening of interest rates.
Liquidity crisis may also be caused if foreign portfolio investors are running out and selling their bond holdings in the Indian bond markets.
To resolve the liquidity crisis, RBI may buy government bonds i.e., open market operations and pump liquidity in the economy.

112. (d)
The currency held by public is the liability of RBI as whenever somebody comes with the currency note to the RBI, it needs to return a sum equivalent to the value of currency. So, if some old notes do not come to the banking system, then it will become invalid, and RBI will never have to return equivalent value of those currency notes.

If the black money does not come back to the banking system after demonetization, then RBI's liability would reduce by that amount and its net Assets (net worth) will increase. This ultimately means that the private money has been transferred to the RBI. Hence it is a kind of transfer of illicit black money to the public sector.

Demonetization reduces the legal tender (currency notes) circulating in the economy which basically reduces the liquidity.

"Black economy is the market-based production of goods and services – legal or illegal – that escapes capture in the official GDP statistics. And the tax that the government forfeits on this activity circulates as black money."

113. (d)
Currency = Notes + Coins
Monetary base = Currency held by public + Currency held by bank + deposits of banks with RBI.

114. (b)
When people deposit money in banks (public deposits), then banks keep only a certain portion with them and the rest they lend. Whatever banks keep with themselves is considered as reserves of banks.

The portion that they keep as reserves can be in the form of cash or gold or they can purchase government securities (bonds) or they can also deposit with RBI.
So only **2nd**, **3rd** & **4th** statements are true.

115. (b)
Banks are mandated to keep only a fraction of the deposits as reserves, rest they can lend and this lending creates money in the system.

For example, If I had Rs. 100 cash with me which I deposited in a bank, and let us say the bank kept Rs. 20 in reserves and rest i.e., Rs. 80 it lent to someone else. Now, money with me is still Rs. 100 (in deposit form) and money with the other person is Rs. 80.

So, now total money in the system is Rs. 180, while earlier it was only Rs. 100. And this became possible just because I deposited the money in the bank and the bank kept only a fraction in the reserve and the rest it lent to someone else.
This is called fractional reserve banking.

In the above case monetary base is Rs. 100 (hard cash printed by RBI) and money supply is Rs. 180

Money multiplier = Money Supply/ Monetary Base
=180/100 = 1.8

If banks are mandated to keep all the deposited money i.e., Rs. 100 as reserves (full reserve banking) then banks would not have lent and no new money would have been created in the system. And then;
Money multiplier would have been = 100/100 = 1

For detailed understanding, you can refer the book on Indian Economy by Vivek Singh.

116. (b)
From the above example, money multiplier decreases when banks are required to keep more reserves.

Money supply = (Money Multiplier) X (Monetary Base)

When we increase monetary base then money supply increases by the same proportion and money multiplier remains constant.
Money multiplier depends on reserves (CRR/SLR) and currency deposit ratio.
For better conceptual clarity, you can refer the book on Indian Economy by Vivek Singh.

117. (d)
Creation of more credit leads to increase in money supply but not monetary base.

Monetary base includes 'cash with public' + 'cash with banks' + 'deposits/reserves of banks kept with RBI'

Whether people are holding cash or depositing money in banks, it does not alter monetary base........ it just transfers the cash from public to banks and since both are part of monetary base, it will not change.

In the same way, when public withdraws cash from bank, cash is just transferred from banks to public.

118. (c)
The value of the money multiplier depends on two variables: the currency-deposit ratio and the reserves-deposit ratio.

While currency deposit ratio depends on the behaviour of the public, the reserve deposit ratio depends on RBI regulations on CRR and SLR. Both CRR and SLR are treated as bank reserves.

Currency deposit ratio (c) = currency held by public/deposit of public in banks
Reserve deposit ratio (r) = reserves of banks/deposit of public in banks

Then Money multiplier = (1+c)/(c+r)

119. (c)
Money supply = (Money Multiplier) X (Monetary Base)

From the above formula, money supply can be increased by increasing the money multiplier or monetary base or both.
120. (a)
Money supply = (Money multiplier) X (Monetary base)

When RBI does open market operations, then monetary base changes (RBI buys/sells govt. securities in lieu of cash), due to which money supply also changes. But it does not change money multiplier, which depends on following:

- People's tendency of depositing money in banks (currency deposit ratio)
- Statutory reserve requirement of the banks (reserve deposit ratio)

121. (d)
Money supply is defined as the stock of money in circulation among the **public**.
So, money lying with government, RBI and interbank deposits are not considered as money supply.

122. (a)
Money supply is money with the **public** either in cash form or in deposit form (demand and time both) with the bank (and Post offices). Securities like bonds, G-Secs and shares are tradable instruments and their prices fluctuate and are not part of money supply.

123. (c)
There are two types of Open Market Operations (OMOs). Outright and repo

1) Outright OMOs are permanent in nature: when the central bank buys these securities (thus injecting money into the system), it is without any promise to sell them later. Similarly, when the central bank sells these securities (thus withdrawing money from the system), it is without any promise to buy them in future.

2) Repo and Reverse Repo LAF:

   This is a type of operation in which when the central bank buys the security, the agreement of purchase also has specification about date and price of resale of this security. This type of agreement is called a repurchase agreement or repo.

   Similarly, instead of outright sale of securities RBI may sell the securities through an agreement which has a specification about the date and price at which it will be repurchased by RBI in future. This type of agreement is called a reverse repurchase agreement or reverse repo.

   RBI conducts repo and reverse repo operations at various maturities: overnight, 7-day, 14- day etc.

Whether outright OMOs or LAF, it happens at RBI's discretion i.e., when RBI feels then it will do these operations. And auction happens which decides the price.

124. (d)
If RBI is pumping more money/cash into the economy that means this money is going both to banks and public. This can happen in several ways:

1. RBI purchase physical gold from the market and print extra cash and pay for it. RBI's assets (physical gold) will increase and Liabilities (cash/currency) will also increase that means "monetary base" also increases.

2. RBI purchases "govt bonds" from the market and prints extra cash to pay for the bonds. RBI's assets (govt bonds) will increase and Liabilities (cash/currency) will also increase that means "monetary base" also increases.

3. RBI is purchasing extra dollars (from foreign investors coming to India or from exporters) and printing cash/currency (rupee) and paying for it. RBI's assets (dollars) will increase and liabilities (cash/currency) will also increase that means "monetary base" also increases.

Money Supply = Money Multiplier X Monetary Base

Since in the above 3 examples, "Monetary Base" is increasing hence "Money Supply" will (also) increase and "Money Multiplier" may remain constant. Money Multiplier will change only when if there is change in behaviour of people or RBI changing CRR/SLR.

125. (c)
Money with banks, Government and RBI is not part of money supply. Money with public is called money supply.

In the first and second statement, money will reach to government but until and unless government spends that money and it reaches to public, it will not form part of money supply.

In the third statement, money is reaching in the hands of public which will immediately increase money supply.

In the fourth statement, RBI is giving money to banks. So, until banks lend it to public/businesses, it will not increase money supply.

126. (d)
Open Market Operations (OMO) is a monetary policy tool where RBI buys/sells government securities in the secondary (open) market to increase or decrease the money supply.
Due to foreign investments inflow or outflow, money supply in the Indian economy increases/ decreases. To prevent or sterilize the economy from such external shocks, RBI buys or sells government securities to keep the money supply unchanged. This is called sterilization or Market Stabilization Scheme (MSS) and it is not a day-to-day phenomenon, rather less frequently used.

127. (d)

The Liquidity Adjustment Facility (LAF) refers to the Reserve Bank's operations through which it injects/absorbs liquidity into/from the banking system. It consists of overnight as well as term repo/reverse repos (fixed as well as variable rates), SDF and MSF.

Generally, LAF facility is available for all Scheduled Commercial Banks except Regional Rural Banks.

128. (d)
Market Stabilization Scheme is an instrument of sterilisation, which empowered the RBI to **issue** Government Treasury Bills and medium duration Dated Securities for the purpose of liquidity absorption. This instrument of monetary management was introduced in 2004 to absorb surplus liquidity of a more enduring nature arising from large capital inflows. The scheme worked by impounding/taking the proceeds of auctions of Treasury bills and Dated Government securities in a separate identifiable MSS cash account maintained and operated by the RBI. At the same time, interest payments have to be given to the institutions who buy the Market Stabilization Bonds (MSB) (the Treasury bills and Dated securities of govt). Here, for the interest payment, the government allocates money from its budget to the RBI. This expenditure to service interest payment for MSBs is called *carrying cost.* The amounts credited into the MSS cash account by selling MSBs are appropriated only for the purpose of redemption/buying back of the Treasury Bills/dated securities issued under the MSS.

129. (c)

"In terms of Section 42(1) of the RBI Act, 1934 the Reserve Bank, having regard to the needs of securing the monetary stability in the country, prescribes the CRR for Scheduled Commercial Banks (SCBs) without any floor or ceiling rate". The other purpose of CRR is to manage liquidity (RBI can increase CRR to decrease liquidity in the economy) and it also ensures that a part of the bank's deposit is with the Central Bank and is hence, safe.

As a depositor, the CRR and SLR requirements together ensure that some portion of the deposits with Indian banks remain secure, even if banks make poor lending decisions. In absence of the CRR and SLR requirements, to make more profits bank may lend most of the deposits and if there is a sudden rush to withdraw, banks will struggle to meet the repayments to the depositors. The maximum limit for SLR is 40%.

130. (c)

Keeping CRR with RBI provides monetary stability and safety to the public deposits. It also ensures solvency of banks i.e., staying in business and proper functioning of the banks.

Since banks do not earn interest on the CRR, so it is idle money for the banks which increases costs for banks.

131. (a)

The purpose of Statutory Reserve Requirements (CRR & SLR) is to enable the Central Bank to control the amount of advances the banks can create.

The purpose of CRR/SLR is not to prevent banks from making excessive profit but rather monetary stability. Having CRR/SLR makes the people deposits safe and liquid but this is not the intended purpose of maintaining CRR/SLR.

Through CRR or SLR, RBI does not specify any amount of vault cash that the banks need to keep with them. Through SLR, RBI specifies liquid assets in any form like cash, gold or govt. bonds and not any specific amount of vault cash.

132. (d)

The monetary policy framework in India, as it is today, has evolved over the years. A new "**Monetary Policy Framework**" Agreement was signed between the Government of India and RBI in Feb 2015. As per the new monetary policy framework agreement, following are the important points: -

- The objective of the monetary policy is to primarily maintain **price stability**, while keeping in mind the objective of growth
- The monetary policy framework is operated by RBI
- The inflation target is 4% with a band of +/- 2%
- The inflation target is decided by the Government of India in consultation with RBI
- The inflation is the "Consumer Price Index (CPI) – Combined" published by Ministry of Statistics and Programme Implementation (NSO)
- The RBI shall be seen to have failed to meet the Target if inflation is more than 6% or less than 2% for three consecutive quarters
- In case RBI fails to meet the target, it will have to give a written report to Government of India explaining the reasons of failure, remedial actions to be taken and an estimated time period within which the Target would be achieved

133. (a)
The monetary policy framework aims at setting the policy (repo) rate based on an assessment of the current and evolving macroeconomic situation; and modulation of liquidity conditions **to anchor money market rates at or around the repo rate**. Repo rate changes transmit through the money market to the entire the financial system, which, in turn, influences aggregate demand – a key determinant of inflation and growth.

Once the repo rate is announced, the operating framework designed by the Reserve Bank envisages liquidity management on a day-to-day basis through appropriate actions, which aim **at anchoring the operating target – the weighted average call rate (WACR) – around the repo rate**.

Weighted average call rate is also called money market rate.

134. (b)
MPC has the authority to decide only the repo rate and not CRR & SLR or even reverse repo rate. Its decision of repo rate is binding on RBI.

135. (b)
The repo rate is decided by the Monetary Policy Committee (MPC), and MPC keeps the repo rate such that "to primarily maintain price stability, while keeping in mind the objective of growth". MPC does not have any mandate for exchange rate

136. (c)
As per RBI Act 1934, Monetary Policy Committee (MPC) has been constituted consisting of 6 members.

- The Governor of RBI—(Chairperson), Member, ex officio;
- Deputy Governor of RBI, in charge of Monetary Policy—Member, ex officio;
- One officer of RBI to be nominated by the Central Board of RBI—Member, ex officio; and
- Three persons to be appointed by the Central Government—Members.

The decisions are taken with simple majority and in case of tie-up, the Governor gets a casting vote (an extra vote).

The three members appointed by the Central Government shall hold office for a period of four years and shall not be eligible for re-appointment.

The RBI shall organise at least four meetings of the Monetary Policy Committee in a year. As of now, RBI is conducting 6 meetings in a year, once in every two months.

137. (d)
Marginal Standing Facility (MSF): It is a facility under which scheduled commercial banks can borrow additional amount of overnight money from the Reserve Bank by dipping into their Statutory Liquidity Ratio (SLR) portfolio up to a limit (2% of SLR) at a penal rate of interest which is above repo rate (MSF rate = repo rate + 0.25%). This means that if a bank is keeping the minimum SLR requirement of 18% and it wants money/cash from RBI then, the bank can offer 2% of the G-Securities from the SLR reserves (as collateral) to RBI and can get money/cash from RBI. This provides a safety valve against unanticipated liquidity shocks to the banking system.

138. (a)
Whenever banks want, they can deposit money with RBI at SDF and whenever banks want, they can withdraw money from RBI at MSF rate. So, SDF and MSF are available to banks at their discretion.

But Reverse repo (facility) and even repo is available at RBI's discretion. RBI from time-to-time pumps money or sucks out liquidity through repo or reverse repo respectively at its own discretion and not when banks want.

Some feature of Standing Deposit Facility (SDF):

- SDF facility has been introduced by amending the RBI act 1934 (Section 17).
- In SDF, RBI will not provide collateral (of Govt. securities), while in reverse repo rate collateral is provided by RBI. As there is no collateral requirement under SDF, it will strengthen the operating framework of monetary policy
- SDF role is in liquidity management but it also provides financial stability.
- Reverse repo will remain as MPC tool but now it has been made redundant as banks will now deposit money at SDF and not at reverse repo.
- Now the LAF (Policy) corridor will be SDF (repo - .25%) and MSF (repo + .25%)

139. (a)
The Reserve Bank has been conducting Consumer Confidence Survey (CCS) since June 2010. The survey captures qualitative responses on questions pertaining to economic conditions, household circumstances, income, spending, prices and employment prospects. The survey results are based on the views of the respondents and are not necessarily shared by the Reserve Bank of India.

140. (c)
RBI conducts quarterly 'inflation expectation survey' of households wherein RBI gauges the household's expectation regarding inflation for the next one year. These surveys are used for monetary policy purpose.

141. (c)
RBI increases the repo rate when the inflation in the economy increases to reduce the money supply.

When "inflation expectation" of the people is high, i.e., they are expecting that in future inflation will increase, then such a behaviour of the people ultimately leads to higher inflation in the economy. And hence, if the results of 'inflation expectation' survey show that it is high or increasing then RBI increases the repo rate.

142. (a)
When the US Federal Bank increases the interest rate, then the foreign investors sell their investments in India (mostly debt instruments) and move to US. In the process they convert the Rupee into dollars in the forex market and the demand for dollar increases and rupee depreciates.

Money supply in the Indian economy will decrease in this case because foreign investors are selling their investments and taking money out of India.

143. (c)
Rupee-dollar rate is discovered in the forex market. When importers buy dollars in the foreign exchange market, rupee depreciates as the demand of dollars increases in the forex market. But if they directly deal with RBI (and take dollars from RBI) and don't go in the forex market then it may not impact the rupee-dollar rate.

When RBI increases the repo rate, the interest rate in the market increases which may attract foreign investors in debt instruments resulting in rupee appreciation.

When RBI sells dollars in forex market, the supply of dollar increases, and dollar depreciates and rupee appreciates.

144. (c)
Operation Twist is when the central bank uses the proceeds/money from sale of short-term securities to buy long-term government debt papers, leading to easing of long-term interest rates in the economy.

When RBI's objective is to decrease the interest on long term lending, so that the companies are able to borrow at cheaper rate for long term to promote economic growth and investment in infrastructure then RBI purchases debt papers of long-term maturity of government. This results in easy availability of money for long term, hence decrease in long term interest rate.

As the long-term interest rate comes down in the financial market due to Operation Twist, banks cannot keep the lending rate higher for long term due to competition in the market for lending among banks. This will then help in reducing interest rate on long term lending by banks also leading to better monetary transmission.

Monetary Transmission is the pass-through of RBI's policy actions to the economy at large in terms of asset prices and general economic conditions.

Operation Twist is "Open Market Operation" and it is a part of RBIs Monetary Policy.

Before Operation Twist	After Operation Twist
(Banks were having two things) Cash from one year time deposits which banks could have lent only for short term i.e., max one year.	RBI sold Govt. bonds (maturing after one year) to banks and took the cash from banks. *(Banks gave this cash as they have to return money to depositors only after one year)*
Banks have Govt. bonds which are maturing in 2032, which means banks are expecting cash after 10 years.	RBI gave this cash to banks and purchased the bonds from banks which were maturing in 2032. *(Now banks got this cash which they can lend for 10 years as they were expecting cash only after the maturity of bonds in 2032)*

145. (d)
RBI lends to banks @repo rate only up to 0.25% of bank's NDTL for overnight. RBI from time to time, on its own discretion, also lends for long term **at** or **above** the repo rate. In case RBI wants to lend above repo rate then the interest rate is decided by **auction** i.e., if banks want more money, the interest rate will go higher, if few banks are competing for RBIs money, then interest rate will be less, but **it is always above or equal to the repo rate**. RBI, while conducting the auction clearly specifies that bids below the repo rate will be rejected. This is called "**long term repo operation (LTRO)**" which means RBI gives money for a fixed long term. The LTRO is generally at variable rate decided by the auction which is above repo rate but it can be done at repo rate also. (Collateral of government security is required but may not be 100%). Repo is available on a daily basis for banks, but LTRO is for long term and done less frequently only when RBI notifies i.e., on RBI's discretion.

Repo as well as term repo auctions are part of liquidity adjustment facility.

146. (c)
First understand the BASIC CONCEPT regarding MONEY SUPPLY, INFLATION and INTEREST RATE

Generally, when money supply (either in cash or in bank deposits) increases then inflation increases as more money starts chasing the (same) goods/output in the short term. But this will be true only when people are willing to spend money (which is generally true) and purchase goods and services i.e., more money chasing the output.

When inflation increases then generally interest rate in the economy also increases (nominal interest rate = inflation + real interest rate).

So, if a question is there, then you need to understand the concept and context.

NOW, let us understand this question:

The LTRO (long term lending by RBI to banks) will result in increase in money with banks and this increased liquidity/money will result in **decrease in interest rate**. *(When someone says that money has been pumped in the financial system then the first thing which happens is interest rate comes down due to increased supply.)* But, the increased money supply may also result in inflation which then may lead to increase in interest rate.

BUT the impact of LTRO on "**increase in interest rate**" is quite indirect.
And the impact of LTRO on '**money supply**', '**inflation**' and '**decrease in interest rate**' is quite direct.

You should always try to find a DIRECT link while solving Economy questions. And you should also check that which option can be eliminated by seeing the various options.

147. (d)
Liquidity in the banking system refers to readily available cash that banks need to meet short-term business and financial needs. On a given day, if the banking system is a net borrower from the RBI under Liquidity Adjustment Facility (LAF), the system liquidity can be said to be in deficit and if the banking system is a net lender to the RBI, the system liquidity can be said to be in surplus. The LAF refers to the RBI's operations through which it injects (repo) or absorbs (reverse repo) liquidity into or from the banking system.

Explanation of all statements:

1. Bank is giving more loan/credit leads to less cash with the bank
2. Corporates hold money in banks. When they pay advance tax then this money of corporates (which was in bank) moves to Government (with RBI).
3. If credit/loan demand is more than the deposits then definitely it will cause deficit of liquidity in banking system
4. To prevent rupee depreciation, RBI sells dollars in forex market and purchases rupees which results in deficit of (rupee) liquidity in banking system.

148. (b)
As per the RBI Act 1934, RBI follows flexible inflation target of 4% +/- 2%. The Act says "primary objective of the monetary policy is to maintain price stability while keeping in

mind the objective of growth". It means that if inflation is in control, RBI can focus on economic growth of the country and can reduce the repo rate.

The explicit mandate of monetary policy is price stability and not financial stability.

Price stability is not sufficient for financial stability as there may be less inflation but we have huge NPAs and various financial institutions defaulting. *(Like the situation in the last 4/5 years).*

149. (d)
OMO, LTRO, repo and reverse repo are all done at RBI's discretion.

Standing Deposit Facility (SDF) and Marginal Standing Facility (MSF) are at banks discretion.

150. (b)
Monetary policy transmission means when RBI is changing the repo rate (or some other operations like OMO) then how it gets transmitted in deposit and lending rates in financial markets.
When RBI changes repo rate then MSF rate automatically changes by the difference of 0.25%, so that is not called transmission.

151. (d)
Base Rate was introduced in July 2010 replacing the Benchmark Prime Lending Rate (BPLR) system. Base Rate is the minimum rate below which Scheduled Commercial Banks cannot lend. RBI publishes guidelines for calculation of Base Rate and every bank calculates its own base rate.

Base rate calculation methodology was based on various factors like:
- **(Average) Cost of deposits/funds** (interest rate that bank offers to its depositors)
- Cost of maintaining CRR and SLR (if the banks are required to keep higher reserves like CRR and SLR, then they will be able to lend less money & will have to charge higher interest rate)
- Operational Costs of Banks
- Return on Net worth (investment)

From **1st April 2016**, RBI introduced a new methodology for calculation of the Base Rates based on marginal cost of funds rather than average cost of funds. This new methodology is called Marginal Cost of Funds based Lending Rate (MCLR)

MCLR calculation methodology will be based on the following factors: -
- **Marginal cost of deposits/funds**
- Cost of maintaining CRR and SLR
- Operational Costs of Banks
- Tenor Premium (based on the time period for which loan is given)

The basic difference between the previous Base Rate and the new MCLR based rate is the change from average to marginal.

(When RBI reduces the repo rate, generally banks reduce their deposit rate. Earlier the calculation of lending rate was based on ***average cost of deposits*** *to the banks. So, due to reduction in repo rate and further reduction of deposit rates by banks, the average cost of deposits of the banks did not reduce immediately (it may reduce in future when new*

depositors will deposit money at lower deposit rate) because still banks need to pay the higher deposit rate to all its ***previous*** *depositors.*

In the new method banks calculate the lending rate based on marginal cost of deposits i.e., the new deposit rate. So, when RBI reduces the repo rate and banks reduce the deposit rate, the marginal cost of deposit gets reduced and the banks generally reduce the lending rates. This helps in better monetary policy transmission.

The banks shall review and publish their MCLR every month.

152. (b)

153. (c)
Every Bank calculates its own MCLR rate based on marginal cost of deposits, operational costs, reserve requirements and tenor premium. So MCLR (or Base Rate) is an "**internal benchmark**" which varies from bank to bank. Banks link their lending rate with MCLR.

But, the transmission of policy (repo) rate changes to the lending rate of banks under the MCLR framework has not been satisfactory due the various reasons like:

- Banks feared that they will lose the depositors/customers if they will reduce the deposit rate first, and since deposit rate was not reduced, MCLR (or base rate) was also not coming down.
- Government offering higher interest rates on its own small savings schemes like Kisan Vikas Patra, Sukanya Samriddhi Scheme, PPF etc.

Hence, RBI has made it mandatory for banks to link all new floating rate personal or retail **loans** and floating rate **loans** to MSMEs to an **external benchmark** effective October 1, 2019. Banks can choose one of the four external benchmarks – repo rate, three-month treasury bill yield, six-month treasury bill yield or any other benchmark interest rate published by Financial Benchmarks India Pvt. Ltd. Banks are not mandated to link their **deposit rates** with an external benchmark rate.

Now, suppose Axis Bank links its loan rates as per following:

Home Loan	= repo rate + 3%	(3% is called the Spread)
Education Loan	= repo rate + 4%	
Personal Loan	= repo rate + 5%	

Here, the loans are linked to repo rate, which is an **external** benchmark, on which Axis Bank does not have any control. So, the moment RBI changes the repo rate, it will automatically be transmitted to all the lending rates at the same moment for the **new loans** *(Even if the bank links the lending rate with Treasury bill yield; when RBI changes repo rate, the T-bill yield also changes in the market immediately).* The purpose of linking the lending rate with an external benchmark is faster transmission of repo rate into lending rate and this mechanism is more transparent also. Adopting of multiple benchmarks by the same bank is not allowed within a loan category.

Banks are free to decide the components of spread and the amount of spread. But in general, the **spread** consists of **credit risk premium**, **business strategy, operational costs of banks** etc. While the banks will be free to decide on the spread over the external benchmark, credit risk premium can change only when borrower's credit assessment undergoes a substantial change. The other components of the spread like operating cost can be altered once in **three years**.

The interest rate under the external benchmark shall be reset at least once in three months. This means that if a borrower **has already** taken loan on 1st Jan 2022 and RBI changes the repo rate on 1st Feb 2022, then the borrower may not get immediate benefit of the rate cut as the interest rate on his loan will only get revised latest by 1st April 2022 (within three months of the loan taken).
RBI has mandated **banks** to link the lending rate with an **"anchor rate"** like MCLR or repo rate *(while MCLR was internal rate of banks, repo is an external rate)*. But there is **no mandate for NBFCs** to link their lending rates.

154. (d)

155. (d)
When government deviates from the fiscal deficit target and spends more, it results in higher inflation. So even if RBI is trying to bring down the inflation, deviation in the fiscal deficit target will create issues in RBI achieving the inflation target.

To target inflation, RBI changes the repo rate which ultimately increases/decreases the interest rate, resulting in change in money supply. Through change in money supply, RBI tries to achieve its inflation target. So, hindrances in monetary policy transmission may create issues in RBI achieving the inflation target.

In case of supply side challenges like drought, floods or governance issues, just reducing the money supply may not result in bringing down the prices of commodities.

156. (b)
Monetary policy transmission involves two stages:

In the first stage, monetary policy changes are transmitted through the money market to other markets, i.e., the bond market and the bank loan market.
The second stage involves the propagation of monetary policy impulses from the financial market to the real economy - by influencing spending decisions of individuals and firms.

Within the financial system, money market is central to monetary operations conducted by the central bank.

157. (b)
Nominal Interest Rate = Inflation + Real Interest Rate

If inflation is 5% and banks offer deposit rate 5% then nobody will deposit money in banks as whatever banks are offering will be eaten away by inflation. People deposit money in banks to earn something and this is possible only when real interest rate is positive.

So, if inflation is 5% and banks are offering deposit rate 7% then the real interest rate will be 2%. This means the depositors are actually/really getting 2% return.

When real interest rate is positive then it leads to people saving (depositing) money in banks, and somewhat reduction in their consumption.

If banks will not offer some nominal interest rate, then people will never deposit money in banks? People deposit in banks to get some nominal interest rate. Now if the nominal interest rate is positive then real interest rate may be positive or negative depending on inflation.

When the inflation increases a lot and banks do not increase their nominal interest rate then the real interest rate may turn negative.

158. (d)
When inflation in the economy is low, people expenses decreases and they are able to save more.

When per capital income increases it leads to higher savings in the economy.

Growth of financial intermediaries means financial institutions like banks. Increase in banks in the economy leads to increased saving behaviour.

So, all the statements are true.

159. (c)
Inflation premium is the higher return that investors demand in exchange for investing in a long-term security where inflation has a greater potential to reduce the real return.

For example, suppose presently the inflation in the economy is 6% and the bonds are being issued at a coupon/interest rate of 8%. So, basically it will give 2% real interest rate (real return) which is reasonably good and you may be willing to invest in bonds.

But, if most of the people think that going forward in the long run there are chances/risk of inflation going up and hence if they purchase this bond of 8% interest/coupon rate then in future they may lose as because of higher inflation in future their real return will be less than 2%.

So, if people think that there is inflation risk then they will demand some extra interest rate (return) above 8% to compensate for the higher risk of inflation in future. This extra interest/return demanded by the investors is called 'inflation premium'.

160. (c)
If there is inflation in the economy, it leads to loss in the value of currency i.e. currency depreciates.
Nominal interest rate (deposit rate) = Inflation + real interest rate
When inflation increases banks increase the nominal interest rate and generally real interest rate remains same.

161. (d)
Liquidity Trap is a situation where the Central Bank wants to increase the money supply in the economy in case of recession but fails to lower the interest rate as the interest rates (repo rate and bank deposit rates) almost reaches zero. This makes the monetary policy ineffective as further repo rate reduction is not possible.

In such a situation people would like to hold on to their cash (may be in savings deposits in banks that is also called cash and not the fixed deposit) as the interest rate is almost zero. *(Actually, people are not willing to spend and demand in the economy declines, that is why economy enters into liquidity trap).*

When the interest rate has come down to almost zero then the yield will also be close to zero as interest and yield are directly proportional.

162. (b)
- Creditor means the person who has given money to someone
- Debtor means who has taken money from someone

- Depositors means who has deposited money in banks or financial institutions
- Bondholders means person who is holding bonds

When a person holds physical asset, whose price is denoted in Rupees then he benefits from price increase or inflation.

But a person who holds financial assets (like Rs. 100 note) or any financial instrument which guarantees fix return of cash payments in future then he loses from price rise. This is because the purchasing power of the rupee (the fixed money which he is supposed to get) decreases due to inflation.

Hence, in case of inflation, depositors, creditors and bondholders will lose.
So, only **2nd** statement is true

163. (d)
When a country faces inflation, we require more money to purchase a given quantity of goods and services because the purchasing power of rupee decreases. In case of inflation generally wages increase but nothing can be said about the output.

And in case of inflation, the amount of money needed will be more to purchase the same goods and services.
So, **(d)** option is true.

164. (b)
Economy under inflationary pressure means inflation is either increasing or there are chances that it will increase.

Inflation leads to depreciation of currency.

Inflation makes domestic goods costly and exports become less competitive.

Because of inflation in the domestic economy, imports become costlier because of domestic currency depreciation.

When inflation increases then interest rate goes up in the economy and cost of borrowing increases.

165. (c)
If aggregate demand increases by 10 percent and aggregate supply increases by only 8 percent then it leads to an effective increase in demand of 2 percent which results in inflation.
When aggregate/overall output decreases then even if we assume demand as constant then it will lead to an increase in effective demand which results in higher inflation.

Higher employment increases demand in the economy and may result in higher inflation.

166. (b)
Inflation will necessarily occur in case there is effective demand in the economy. If there is increase in aggregate demand, there may not be inflation if the supply also increases.
If output decreases and demand also decreases then it may not result in inflation.
Increased government spending increases aggregate demand rather than effective demand.

167. (b)
Increase in money supply may not necessarily lead to economic growth. But when the supply of money increases, the interest rate comes down (concept of demand and supply).

168. (a)
Deflation is bad for economic growth. Because when prices start declining people postpone their purchase decisions and companies postpone their investment decisions. This leads to decrease in demand in the economy which hurts economic growth.

Low and moderate inflation is good for economic growth as it creates demand in the economy and people are also willing to save money in banks which ultimately increases investment.

Galloping or Hyperinflation eats away the savings of the people as they spend too much money in buying goods and services which ultimately decreases investment.
Banks also do not offer higher interest rate (than inflation) in such cases and people do not keep money in banks as they do not get any real return.

So, only **2nd** statement is true.

169. (d)
In case of low and moderate inflation, people are willing to save money and put in bank deposits because bank offer deposit rates higher than inflation rates. People are willing to sign long term contracts (linked with inflation index) in money terms because they are confident that the relative prices of goods and services they buy and sell will not get too far out of line and it helps in promoting business. As the prices are increasing, people are also willing to consume because if they postpone their consumption, they will have to spend more on consumption at a future date.

170. (d)
When the economy is facing deflation that means prices are decreasing.
In such a situation, whatever I can buy today in Rs. 100, the same Rs. 100 is able to purchase more in the next year. This leads to postponement of purchase decisions by the people and the demand in the economy decreases. When the demand decreases, companies defer their production and investment decisions which lead to increase in unemployment.
So, all the statements are correct.

171. (b)
Stagflation is a rare economic phenomenon that combines two or three negative economic trends that normally do not occur together: high inflation, poor growth and rising unemployment. It has only occurred two or three times in the past 100 years.

"Stagflation" is a combination of two words, "inflation" and "stagnation." An economy in stagflation has high consumer price inflation, low economic growth and, usually, rising unemployment. Stagflation can be caused by:

- A supply side shock like covid-19 lockdown or a sharp rise in the global price of some essential commodity, such as oil. Oil is a good example because higher oil prices increase costs for virtually all businesses.
- Poor economic policies such as too high government spending or too low interest rates. Generally, to bring the economy out of any recession, Government and Central bankers pump too much money in the economy. This results in pulling

economy out of recession but if the supply (of goods and services) could not be increased to match the increased demand (too much money chasing the output) then it may result in higher inflation leading to erosion in purchasing power and stagnation in economy.

Stagflation combines inflation, which lowers the purchasing power of money, with poor productivity, which lowers economic growth. It has been described as causing "misery" because the money people have buys less and less, causing their real cost of living to rise, while the economy's low productivity and high unemployment prevent their wages from rising to compensate. Stagflation erodes people's income and savings while causing businesses to hold down wages and hold back on investments and hiring.

172. (d)
A supply shock is an unexpected event that suddenly changes the supply of a product or commodity, resulting in an unforeseen change in price. Supply shocks can be negative, resulting in a decreased supply, or positive, yielding an increased supply; however, they're often negative.

A supply shock inflation is caused because of the problem (negative supply shock) in supply of goods and services rather than change in demand.

If the exports from India increases that means there is increase in demand by the foreign buyers resulting in demand pull inflation.

Because of increased government expenditure, more money reaches to the public resulting in increased demand and hence demand-pull inflation.

If there is more money/credit creation in the economy then it results in higher demand in the economy resulting in demand pull inflation.

173. (a)
Demand-pull inflation occurs in the economy when the aggregate demand in the economy increases more rapidly as compared to the productive capacity of economy.

Higher govt. spending and lower interest rate both will increase the demand in the economy because of increased money supply.

174. (c)
When the cost of money (interest rate) is cheaper in the economy, it helps in investment. For investment, the main cost is cost of capital i.e., the rate at which capital/money is available.

175. (d)
When the output in the economy is high, that means factories are working at full potential and employing more labour. So, **1st** statement is not true.

When the unemployment in the economy is high, people have less money to purchase goods and services i.e., the demand in the economy decreases which leads to decrease in prices. So, **2nd** statement is also not true.

176. (c)
An overheating economy is an economy that is expanding at an unsustainable rate. The two main signs of an overheating economy are:
(a) rising rates of inflation; and

(b) an unemployment rate that is below the normal rate for an economy (which means there is more demand in the economy)

So, in an overheating economy, inflation is high because of 'demand pull' factors rather than 'cost push' factors.
In case of demand-pull inflation, by raising interest rates, RBI makes it costlier for firms and households to borrow. Demand for investment and consumption goods along with workers comes down, thereby cooling an overheated economy.

But if inflation is because of supply-shock, raising interest rates would risk worsening inflation by impeding supply as interest are cost in themselves.

177. (d)
Reflation is a fiscal or monetary policy designed to expand output, stimulate spending and curb the effects of deflation, which usually occurs after a period of economic uncertainty or recession.

178. (c)
Disinflation is when inflation is decreasing but prices are still increasing. So, in an economy when inflation decreases, the demand of goods and services increases and people spending increases and it supports business activity resulting in decrease in unemployment.
So, all the statements are wrong.

179. (c)
Sovereign Gold Bonds (SGB) are government securities denominated in grams of gold. They are substitutes for holding physical gold. Investors have to pay the issue price in cash and the bonds will be redeemed in cash on maturity. The Bond is issued by RBI on behalf of Government of India.

Suppose somebody is purchasing gold bonds worth Rs. 100 by payment in rupees, then this Rs. 100 bond will also be denominated in grams of gold as per the market price of gold at the time of purchase and the investor will earn a fix interest rate. So, an investor holding gold bonds will get the benefit of price appreciation if the price of physical gold in the market is increasing and interest both but he will lose if the price of gold in the market decreases.

The quantity of gold for which the investor pays is protected, since he receives the ongoing market price at the time of redemption/ premature redemption. The SGB offers a superior alternative to holding gold in physical form. The risks and costs of storage are eliminated. Investors are assured of the market value of gold at the time of maturity and periodical interest (@2.5% per annum paid semi-annually). SGB is free from issues like making charges and purity in the case of gold in jewellery form. It can be purchased from Scheduled Commercial Banks, Post office, BSE and NSE.

180. (d)
- Government will issue SGBs as part of its overall market borrowings for mobilizing resources for green infrastructure.
- The funds raised from SGB (Rs. 16,000 crore) will be part of (included in) the Govt.'s borrowing programme (capital receipts under budget) for 2022-23. These bonds will be debt on Govt. of India
- The proceeds raised from SGB will be deposited to the Consolidated Fund of India (CFI) in line with the regular treasury policy, and then funds from the CFI will be made available for eligible green projects.

- The proceeds will be deployed in public sector projects which help in reducing the carbon intensity of the economy.
- The proceeds from green bonds would be used to fund renewable energy, energy efficiency, clean transportation, water and waste management, pollution prevention and control and green buildings among others.
- Nuclear power generation, landfill projects, alcohol/weapons/tobacco/gaming/palm oil industries and hydropower plants larger than 25 MW have been excluded.
- All eligible 'green expenditures' will include public expenditure by the government in the form of investment, subsidies, grants-in-aid, or tax foregone or select operational expenditures, R&D expenditures in public sector projects that help in reducing the carbon intensity of the economy. Equity is allowed only in the sole case of metro projects under the 'Clean Transportation' category.
- The Ministry of Finance has constituted a Green Finance Working Committee (GFWC) including members from relevant line ministries and chaired by the Chief Economic Advisor. The GFWC will meet at least twice a year to support the Ministry of Finance with selection of projects from those submitted by different departments.
- The Ministry of Finance has constituted a Green Finance Working Committee (GFWC) including members from relevant line ministries and chaired by the Chief Economic Advisor. The GFWC will meet at least twice a year to support the Ministry of Finance with selection of projects from those submitted by different departments.
- SGBs will be eligible for Repurchase Transactions (Repo)
- SGBs will be reckoned as eligible investment for SLR purpose
- SGBs will be eligible for trading in the secondary market
- Non-Residents will also be allowed to invest in SGB
- SGBs will be issued through Uniform Price Auction (at same interest rate)

181. (c)

182. (a)
When FDI/FPI investments (especially FDI) come in the country then it helps in economic growth and export from the country resulting in export earnings under current account. When foreign investors invest in a country then one of the major target is exports from that country.

Foreign investments in Govt. securities will impact capital account.

183. (d)

184. (d)
Integrated Ombudsman Scheme, 2021 integrates the earlier three Ombudsman schemes of RBI namely,

(i) the Banking Ombudsman Scheme, 2006;
(ii) the Ombudsman Scheme for Non-Banking Financial Companies, 2018; and
(iii) the Ombudsman Scheme for Digital Transactions, 2019.

The Integrated Ombudsman Scheme has been framed by the RBI in exercise of the powers conferred on it under the Banking Regulation Act, 1949, Reserve Bank of India Act, 1934 and The Payment and Settlement Systems Act, 2007.

The scheme will provide cost-free redress of customer complaints involving deficiency in services rendered by entities regulated by RBI i.e., banks (commercial as well as urban cooperative) and NBFCs both including digital transactions, if not resolved to the satisfaction of the customers or not replied within a period of 30 days by the regulated entity.

Some of the salient features of the Scheme are:

- It will no longer be necessary for a complainant to identify under which scheme he/she should file complaint with the Ombudsman.
- The Scheme defines 'deficiency in service' as the ground for filing a complaint, with a specified list of exclusions. Therefore, the complaints would no longer be rejected simply on account of "not covered under the grounds listed in the scheme".
- This scheme will be based on 'One Nation-One Ombudsman' with one portal, one email, and one address for the customers to lodge their complaints. Earlier, RBI had three separate ombudsmen — for banks, NBFCs and digital payments. These were operated from 22 RBI ombudsman offices across the country. These will be integrated into one centralised scheme to make the grievance redress mechanism simpler and much more effective. The Scheme has done away with the jurisdiction of each ombudsman office.
- A Centralised Receipt and Processing Centre has been set up at RBI, Chandigarh for receipt and initial processing of physical and email complaints in any language.
- The Executive Director-in charge of Consumer Education and Protection Department of RBI would be the Appellate Authority under the Scheme.
- RBI would appoint the Ombudsman and a Deputy Ombudsman for a period not exceeding three years at a time. Complaints may be made physically or electronically.
- There is no limit on the amount in a dispute that can be brought before the Ombudsman

185. (d)
The Kisan Credit Card (KCC) scheme is an innovative credit delivery mechanism to meet the production credit requirements of the farmers in a timely and hassle-free manner. The scheme is under implementation in the entire country by the vast institutional credit framework involving Commercial Banks, RRBs and Cooperatives and has received wide acceptability amongst bankers and farmers.

Kisan Credit Card Scheme aims at providing adequate and timely credit support from the banking system under a single window to the farmers and fishermen for their following needs:

- To meet the short-term credit requirements for cultivation of crops
- Post-harvest expenses
- Produce Marketing loan
- Consumption requirements of farmer household
- Working capital for maintenance of farm assets and activities allied to agriculture, like dairy animals, inland fishery etc.
- Investment credit requirement for agriculture and allied activities like pump sets, sprayers, dairy animals etc.

The following people are eligible for this scheme

- All Farmers – Individuals / Joint borrowers who are owner cultivators
- Tenant Farmers, Oral Lessees &Share Croppers
- Self Help Groups or Joint Liability Groups of Farmers

186. (d)
The Kisan Credit Card Scheme is being implemented by Commercial Banks, RRBs, Small Finance Banks and Cooperatives.

187. (a)
Share of Commercial banks credit to agriculture sector is around 80%.

188. (c)

189. (d)
Prompt Corrective Action (PCA) is a supervisory framework of RBI where it uses various measures/tools to maintain sound financial health of banks. Based on three parameters (once these parameters cross certain level) RBI puts the bank under PCA. And once RBI puts the bank under PCA, then it can take discretionary actions against the bank.

Earlier three parameters were Capital (Capital Adequacy Ratio), Asset Quality (NPA) and Return on Assets (profit). Now the three parameters are:

- Capital (Capital Adequacy Ratio),
- Asset Quality (NPA), and
- Leverage (equity capital/total assets of bank)

Earlier PCA framework was applicable on all Scheduled Commercial Banks except Regional Rural Banks. Now it is applicable on all Scheduled Commercial Banks except Regional Rural Banks, Payment Banks and Small Finance Banks.

Scheduled Commercial Banks include:

- Public Sector Banks
- Private Sector Banks
- Foreign Banks
- *Regional Rural Banks*
- *Payment Banks*
- *Small Finance Banks*

Once RBI puts a bank under PCA framework then RBI can take the following actions on the bank?

- RBI can put restrictions on Branch expansion, distributing dividends, capping compensation and fees of management and directors.
- In extreme cases, banks may be stopped from lending and there can be a cap on lending to specific sectors/entities.
- May increase the provisioning requirement for banks
- Further, RBI may take steps to bring in new management/Board, appoint consultants for business/ organizational structuring, take steps to change ownership, can also take steps to merge the bank and can supersede the bank board.

The objective of PCA is to facilitate the banks to take corrective measures including those prescribed by the Reserve Bank, in a timely manner, in order to restore their financial health. The framework also provides an opportunity to the Reserve Bank to pay focused attention on such banks by engaging with the management more closely in those areas. The PCA framework is, thus, intended to encourage banks to eschew certain riskier activities and focus on conserving capital so that their balance sheets can become stronger.

RBI has brought in PCA framework for NBFCs also.

190. (c)
Since a lot of urban-cooperative banks (UCBs) were also facing issues, RBI has brought in "Supervisory Action Framework" (SAF) for UCBs in place of PCA for commercial banks. SAF is invoked based on three parameters (NPA level, two consecutive years loss and capital adequacy ratio). SAF in UCB can also be initiated in case of serious governance issues. Once a UCB has been put under SAF, various restrictions on dividend, donation, new loans, capital expenditure etc. can be imposed, which are again similar to PCA restrictions.

191. (d)
Reserve Bank of India invests the reserves in the following types of instruments:

- Deposits with Bank for International Settlements
- Deposits with other central banks
- Deposits with foreign commercial banks
- Debt instruments representing sovereign or sovereign-guaranteed liability
- Other instruments/institutions as approved by the Central Board of RBI

192. (c)
A line of credit is a preset amount of money that a bank has agreed to lend to a company/individual. The company can draw from the line of credit when it needs up to the maximum amount. The company will pay interest only on the amount used.

193. (a)
"Teaser Loans" is the unofficial term used to describe housing loans that carry ultra-low fixed rates in the initial years, but charge market-linked rates thereafter. These products were first launched in 2009-10 by SBI. This scheme was termed a 'teaser loan' scheme by market players because it lured the borrower with low rates in the initial years, only to bump up the rates later.

Home loans in India face very low incidence of default, even amid NPAs. But RBI was worried because in case of a teaser home loan, by offering borrowers ultra-low rates in the first few years, may tempt them to take on a far bigger housing bet than they can afford. In a rising rate cycle, a transition from a fixed to a floating rate can well throw a salary-earner's EMI calculation out of their range.

While such teaser products are not banned by the regulator, the standard asset provisioning requirement is higher for such loans. For normal home loans, the standard **asset provisioning** is 0.4% but for teaser loans it is 2%. RBI, to discourage such products, had increased the provisioning by five times for such loans since these loans are perceived as riskier.

194. (b)
Higher NPAs worsens the financial health of a bank. To tackle the NPA or bad assets problem, RBI has designed several mechanisms. An important among them is the Provisioning norms.

In banking lexicon, provisioning means to set aside (keep separate as reserve) or provide some funds to cover up losses if things go wrong or some of their loans turn into bad assets.

The banks need to provision some funds as a percentage of their loans/advances. For standard asset (which have not turned NPAs), the requirement of provisioning is very less (0.4%) but for NPAs, it may be quite high.

The provisioning coverage ratio is the prescribed percentage of funds to be set aside by the banks for covering the prospective losses due to bad loans –most probably from their profit. For example, if the provisioning coverage ratio is 70% for a particular category of loan, then banks have to set aside funds equivalent to 70% of those loans out of their profits.

195. (a)
RBI has approved 'First Loss Default Guarantee (FLDG)'

FLDG is a contractual arrangement between a Regulated Entity (Commercial Banks, Cooperative Banks, NBFCs) and Lending Service Providers (LSP)/Fintechs or between two Regulated Entities under which the latter (LSP/Fintechs) guarantees to compensate the Regulated Entity, loss due to default up to a certain percentage of the loan portfolio of the Regulated Entity, specified upfront. RBI has approved FLDG cover of maximum up to five percent.

Under FLDG agreements, the fintech originates a loan and promises to compensate the Regulated entity up to a pre-decided percentage in case customers fail to repay. FLDG helps expand the customer base of traditional lenders (Banks/NBFCs) but relies on the fintech's underwriting (risk appraisal) capabilities. The loan is on the books of Banks/NBFCs.

196. (a)
Capital Adequacy Ratio (CAR) is the ratio of a bank's capital to its risk weighted asset ratio. The bank has to maintain this capital so that, if there are defaults then the bank should be able to sustain. RBI mandates how much CAR has to be maintained by banks. As per Basel III norms, banks need to maintain 11.5% CAR.

197. (d)
Additional Tier 1 Bonds (AT-1) bonds have several unusual features, which make them very different from normal bonds.

- One, these bonds are perpetual and carry no maturity date. Instead, they carry call options that allow banks/issuers to redeem them after five or 10 years. But banks are not obliged to use this call (redeem) option and can opt to pay only interest on these bonds for eternity.
- Two, banks issuing AT-1 bonds can skip interest payments for a particular year or even reduce the bonds' face value, provided their capital ratios fall below certain threshold levels. These thresholds are specified in their offer terms.
- Three, if the RBI feels that a bank is tottering on the brink (called point of non-viability) and needs a rescue, it can simply ask the bank to cancel its outstanding AT-1 bonds without consulting its investors.

AT-1 bonds are risky but people invest as it **offers higher interest rate**. In case of Yes Bank crisis, AT-1 bonds worth Rs. 8415 were written down in March 2020. (This means now investors will not get any interest or principal in future on these bonds).

Under Basel III norms, banks need to have 11.5% capital requirement in which 9.5% is Tier 1 capital and 2% is Tier 2 capital. Out of 9.5% Tier 1 capital, Additional Tier 1 capital (AT-1 bonds) can be 1.5%.

In the recent judgement (January 2023), Bombay High Court quashed the 'write-off' of AT1 bonds because these bonds were meant for 'Institutional Investors' and were sold to 'Retail Investors' by the Yes Bank in the guise of 'Super Fixed deposit' or 'as safe as Fixed Deposit' without telling the risks of this bond.

198. (d)

In India, any money you send overseas is subject to controls, as the government is wary of excessive outflows of foreign exchange draining its reserves and destabilising the rupee. But there has been an effort to gradually liberalise these controls.

The window that was opened up in 2004 for **individuals** to remit/send money across the border, **without seeking specific approvals**, was called the **Liberalised Remittance Scheme (LRS)**.

Under LRS, **all resident individuals (in India) can freely remit**/send $250,000 overseas every financial year for a permissible set of current or capital account transactions. Remittances are permitted for overseas education, travel, medical treatment and purchase of shares and property, apart from maintenance of relatives living abroad, gifting and donations. Individuals can also open, maintain and hold foreign currency accounts with overseas banks for carrying out transactions.

However, the rules do not allow trading in "foreign exchange" (for example Dollar and Pound trading).

The LRS represents India's baby steps towards dismantling controls on foreign exchange movements in and out of the country. It has allowed large numbers of Indians to study abroad and diversify their portfolios from purely desi stocks and property.

Ideally speaking, capital controls in any form have no place in a liberalised economy. But for India, which is heavily dependent on imports of critical goods and perpetually spends more foreign exchange than it earns, it is difficult to free up remittances because of the havoc this can wreak on exchange rates.

The LRS gives you the freedom to put your money to work anywhere in the world. Until India is ready to free all capital controls, the LRS remains the most viable way for individuals to legally remit money overseas.

199. (d)

- Foreign Investment means any investment made by a 'person' resident outside India in '**capital instruments**' of an Indian company. Person means foreign individuals, NRIs, companies etc.

- 'Capital Instruments' means **equity shares**, **debentures** (fully, compulsorily and mandatorily convertible debentures), **preference shares** (fully, compulsorily and mandatorily convertible preference shares) and **share warrants** issued by the Indian company.

    - Equity shares: Equity shares represent ownership of the company and voting rights

- Preference shares (fully, compulsorily and mandatorily convertible preference shares): They have preferential rights over dividend and to repayment of the capital in the case of a winding-up of the company. They must be converted into (common) equity shares after some time.

- Debentures (fully, compulsorily and mandatorily convertible debentures): They are like bonds but must be converted into equity shares after some time:

- Share Warrants: Share warrant is a document issued by the company to the investor that gives the warrant holder (investor) a right to subscribe to equity shares of the company at a predetermined price on or after a pre-determined time period. The warrant holder is given a right but not an obligation to subscribe equity shares. If the warrant holder does not exercise his option to subscribe to equity shares, then the initial amount (some percent of the total amount paid by the warrant holder to purchase the warrant) paid stands forfeited.

200. (b)
FDI is into equity shares or bonds/debentures which has a condition for compulsory conversion into equity shares.

Govt. cannot issue equity securities and hence Govt. securities are always of debt in nature. Hence, investment in Govt. securities cannot be classified as FDI

FCCB can be converted into equity hence can be included in FDI.

Global Depository Receipts are shares only, hence included in FDI.

A Financial Lease is an agreement whereby the lessor conveys to the lessee in return for a payment or series of payments the right to use an asset for an agreed period of time. Basically, the lessor takes the asset on behalf of the lessee and gets compensated by the rental payments that are paid by the lessee during the days of the lease. The ownership of the asset is with the lessor, but the lessee gets exclusive right to use the asset in the way desired. For accounting purposes, the lease provides the lessee with economic characters of ownership of the asset. At the end of the lease agreement, the lessee has the option to acquire ownership of the asset.

Financial Lease is a kind of debt instrument and hence not part of FDI.

201. (c)
Foreign Direct Investment (FDI) happens in three ways: -

- A foreign company purchasing shares of Indian company
- A foreign company in collaboration with an Indian company establishing a new company called Joint Venture Company in India
- A foreign company establishing a subsidiary or a child company in India

FDI investors are not allowed to purchase debt securities.

202. (d)

203. (d)

204. (a)

Foreign Direct Investment (FDI)	Foreign Portfolio Investment (FPI)
It happens generally through primary market.	Generally, through secondary market but can happen through primary market as well
Generally new shares are issued and the capital comes to the company through which the company invests in new factory, machines etc.	Generally, only the owners change hands and new capital does not come to the company
The foreign investor appoints Board of Directors and get involved in the decision making (active management) of the company by purchase of large shareholdings	Foreign investors generally do not get involved in the management of the company and purchase minority stakes
Foreign investors try to make the company profitable through their decision making and target the profit of the company	Foreign investors target the share price of the company and derive their gain from change of share prices
It is sector specific. For example, a steel company in US will invest only in a steel company in India and try to make that company profitable through their management and get a share of the profit	It is in general capital market. For example, a foreign investor is not particular about any sector and is willing to invest in any sector/company which gives a chance of share price appreciation
It is a long-term investment as to turn the company profitable, the foreign investor needs to get invested for a long time.	It is generally short-term investment
Generally, there is a lock in period and during this period the foreign investor cannot sell his investment and hence it is quite stable	There is no lock in period and the foreign investor can return any time by selling his investment. It results in exchange rate volatility
It can happen in three ways viz. by purchase of shares, by forming a Joint Venture company or by establishing a subsidiary company	It happens through purchase of shares

205. (c)
Government has accepted the international practice regarding the definitions of FDI and FPI. Where the investor's stake is 10 percent or less in a company it will be treated as FPI and, where an investor has a stake of more than 10 percent, it will be treated as FDI. A single foreign portfolio investor can invest maximum up to 10 percent in an Indian company and all FPIs on aggregate basis can maximum invest up to 24% or the sectoral cap/ statutory ceiling as applicable for that sector under foreign investment. Government now specifies composite cap/ceiling for foreign investors (rather than separate limits for FDI and FPI) in various sectors under which all kinds of foreign investments are allowed.

Foreign Investment in an unlisted company irrespective of threshold limit may be treated as FDI. An investor may be allowed to invest below the 10 percent threshold and this can be treated as FDI subject to the condition that the FDI stake is raised to 10 percent or beyond within one year from the date of the first purchase. The obligation to do so will fall on the company. If the stake is not raised to 10% or above, then the investment shall be treated as portfolio investment. In case an existing FDI falls to a level below 10 percent, it can continue to be treated as FDI, without an obligation to restore it to 10% or more. In a particular company, an investor can hold the investments either under the FPI route or under the FDI route, but not both.

206. (a)
FDI is mostly into equity shares which are classified as non-debt.

Once a foreign investment becomes FDI in India then it will always be treated as FDI even if the investment % falls below 10%. That is why it is said as "Once an FDI always an FDI"

Some students are saying that the above statement should be false because of the following rule:

"*An investor may be allowed to invest below the 10 percent threshold and this can be treated as FDI subject to the condition that the FDI stake is raised to 10 percent or beyond within one year from the date of the first purchase. If the stake is not raised to 10% or above, then the investment shall be treated as portfolio investment*".

But try to understand that in the above case, FDI was conditional that the stakes should be raised to above 10%, it will not become FDI if the stakes are not raised beyond 10%.

But once a foreign investment becomes FDI then it can always remain FDI.

"Once an FDI always an FDI" — This is RBI statement. The rule says that: "*In case an existing FDI falls to a level below 10 percent, it can continue to be treated as FDI, without an obligation to restore it to 10% or more*".

207. (b)
FPI investors require SEBI license/approval for making investments in India. FDI, if happening under 'Govt. approval route' requires approval of specific ministry/department.

Since Both FPI and FDI investment involves foreign currency, so they need to inform about the foreign currency/exchange coming to India to the RBI.

208. (d)
FDI investment happens only in shares but FPI can invest in shares/bonds both.

When an FDI investor comes in India to invest in shares (ownership) then they target the profit of the company.

Now if a country's Nominal Growth in GDP (real growth + inflation) is higher (say 12%) that means all the companies/businesses combined growth in terms of sales/revenue is also 12%. So, if revenue growth is higher say 12% (and costs are also increasing proportionately) then profit will also grow by 12%. And if profit growth is 12% then the FDI investor who has invested in shares (and gets profit every year) will also get good growth of 12% on the amount of money/capital put into shares. But if the FDI investor invests in a country say US and its nominal growth is just 4% then the overall profit of all the companies combined will also grow at just 4% and hence the investor return will also grow at just 4%.

On this logic FDI investors go to those countries where growth is higher (real + inflation). And inflation should be normal say 4% because higher inflation depreciates the currency and when the FDI investor will return then they will lose.

FPI investors invest in shares and bonds both. So, FPI investors invest in shares on the same logic as FDI investors explained above and hence they look for higher growth economies. And when FPI investors invest in bonds then they search for countries where they get higher interest rate. Now, this interest rate is again higher in developing economies (because of relatively higher inflation + real interest rate). Hence, they look for "interest differential between the destination and the home country", which means if interest rate in US is 4% and in India it is 7% then the interest differential is 3% (7% - 4%) which is higher enough to attract FPIs in India.

So, FPIs are attracted both by higher growth and interest differential but FDI investors are mostly attracted by higher growth.

209. (a)
If a foreign investor is coming to India for making investment that means he is going to purchase Land and machinery and other materials in India to set up business/factory.

Now if rupee is depreciating (in nominal terms without increase in inflation) then the foreign investor will get more rupees per dollar and he will be able to purchase more land/machinery/material in the same dollar, so he will get attracted to invest in India. But if rupee depreciates in nominal terms because of higher inflation then the gain from the rupee depreciation (for the investor) will cancel out because of the higher inflation as the price of land/machinery/materials will also increase.

Now if rupee is depreciating in real terms that means our goods (land/machinery/materials) are becoming relatively cheaper so it will attract foreign investors for investment in India.
If rupee is depreciating in real terms that means after taking into account the effect of inflation, rupee is actually depreciating which makes our goods relatively cheaper and attracts investment in India.

If rupee depreciates in nominal terms let us say by 10% and inflation also is higher in India proportionately then both will cancel out and rupee will not depreciate in real terms. But if rupee depreciates in nominal terms by 10% and inflation is higher in India just by 2% then rupee will depreciate in real terms which makes our products competitive i.e. investment in India will be attractive.

210. (d)
All the statements are true.

1. Overseas Direct Investment (ODI) is what Indian residents are investing abroad. This is opposite of FDI. So, this is basically in shares and hence its asset for us but liability on foreign residents.

2. Reserve Assets means the foreign currencies that RBI is holding. Again, this is also an asset for us but liability for other countries

3. Our Portfolio Investments abroad means Indian residents investing in shares and bonds abroad. This is opposite of FPI. If we have purchased bonds and shares of abroad companies then its asset for us.

211. (d)
FPI comes under capital account in Balance of Payment but they bring dollars/foreign currencies and this dollar is used to finance/fund if we have deficit in current account.

When government is listing a PSU on stock exchange for disinvestment, then FPIs can also purchase the PSU's shares in the primary market. So, FPIs help in government's disinvestment plan.

FPI's pay tax on the earnings they derive from gain in shares/bonds prices, called capital gain tax.

212. (d)
Foreign Direct Investment can come through two routes viz. automatic and government approval route. More than 95% of the FDI comes in India through the "Automatic Route" where no government approval is required and are subject to only sectoral laws. Certain sectors that are still under "Government approval route" are scrutinised and cleared by the respective departments and ministries.

In respect of applications in which there is a doubt about the Administrative Ministry/Department concerned, DPIIT shall identify the Administrative Ministry/Department where the application will be processed. In respect of proposals where the respective department/ ministry proposes to reject the proposals or in cases where conditions for approval are stipulated in addition to the conditions laid down in the FDI policy or sectoral laws/regulations, concurrence of DPIIT shall compulsorily be sought by the said Ministry. The Department for Promotion of Industry and Internal Trade (DPIIT), Ministry of Commerce and Industry sets the rules for foreign investment and makes policy pronouncements on FDI through various Press Releases.

Whether FDI is coming under 'Automatic Route' OR 'Government Approval Route', Cabinet Committee on Economic Affairs (CCEA) approval is must if the FDI value is more than Rs. 5000 crores.

213. (c)
External Commercial Borrowings (ECBs) are commercial loans/debt raised by resident entities from recognised non-resident entities. So, it is basically debt denominated in foreign currency or Indian rupee and includes:

1. Bank Loan

2. Trade Credits:
It refers to the credits/loan extended by the overseas supplier, bank, financial institution and other permitted recognised lenders for imports (into India) of capital/non-capital goods permissible under the Foreign Trade Policy of the Government of India. Depending on the source of finance, such Trade Credits are called suppliers' credit and buyers' credit.

3. Bonds, Debentures which should not have condition of fully/compulsorily convertibility.
Bonds/debentures are basically debt but some have option to convert into shares/equity. So, only those debentures/bonds which does not have a condition of fully/compulsorily convertibility are treated as ECB.

4. Preference Shares which should not have condition of fully/compulsorily convertibility:
Preference shares have basically preferential rights over dividend and to repayment of the capital in the case of winding-up of the company. Some preference shares have option of conversion into equity shares after some time. So, in ECB only those preference shares are included which does not have fully/mandatorily convertibility condition. Actually, preference shares features are like bonds for example preferential rights over dividend (a kind of fixed income) and priority over repayment of capital in case of bankruptcy. These characteristics make them a part of ECB but they should not have condition of fully/mandatorily conversion into normal/common equity shares.

5. Foreign Currency Convertible Bonds (FCCB): FCCBs are bonds issued by an Indian company expressed in foreign currency, and the principal and interest in respect of which is payable in foreign currency and subscribed by a non-resident and convertible into ordinary shares of the issuing company.

6. Financial Lease: A Financial Lease is an agreement whereby the lessor conveys to the lessee in return for a payment or series of payments the right to use an asset for an agreed period of time.
   Basically, the lessor takes the asset on behalf of the lessee and gets compensated by the rental payments that are paid by the lessee during the days of the lease. The ownership of the asset is with the lessor, but the lessee gets exclusive right to use the asset in the way desired.

214. (d)
ECB falls under two routes: Automatic Route and Approval Route

Under 'Automatic Route' no approval is required.
RBI has set up an Empowered Committee to consider proposals coming under the 'Approval Route'.

215. (c)
Foreign investment includes 'FDI' and 'FPI' and does not include ECB.

Foreign investments are into 'Capital Instruments' which includes **equity shares**, **debentures** (fully, compulsorily and mandatorily convertible debentures), **preference shares** (fully, compulsorily and mandatorily convertible preference shares) and **share warrants** issued by the Indian company.

FCCB can be part of both ECB as well as 'Foreign Investment'.

216. (d)
Through Masala bonds money is raised from abroad in foreign currency but the bonds are denominated in Rupee.

Masala Bonds are a kind of ECB where the bonds are issued outside India but denominated in Indian Rupees, rather than the local currency. Masala is an Indian word and it means spices. Unlike dollar bonds, where the borrower takes the currency risk, Masala bond makes the investors bear the risk.

<table>
<tr><th>ECB</th><th>MASALA Bonds</th></tr>
<tr><td colspan="2">$1 = Rs. 70 (2019)</td></tr>
<tr><td>$1 Bond was issued to foreign investor and the borrower (Indian company) got $1 for one year. Money is raised in foreign currency and the borrower issued Dollar denominated bond to the foreign investor.</td><td>Rs. 70 Bond was issued to foreign investor and the borrower (Indian company) got $1 (as the rupee dollar rate was $1=Rs.70) for one year. Money is raised in foreign currency but the borrower issued Rupee denominated bond to the foreign investor.</td></tr>
<tr><td colspan="2">$1=Rs. 80 (2020)</td></tr>
<tr><td>In 2020, the borrower needs to return $1 to the foreign investor and for that he will have to spend Rs. 80 to get $1. The conversion/exchange risk is of the borrower (Indian company).</td><td>In 2020, the borrower needs to return dollar equivalent of Rs. 70 (Rs.70/Rs.80* $1 = $0.875) to the foreign investor rather than $1. So, basically the conversion/exchange risk was borne by the foreign investor.</td></tr>
</table>

217. (c)
Through ECB and Masala Bonds, the money is raised in foreign currency which is then sold in the forex market to purchase rupees which leads to rupee appreciation. Restricting FPI investments will reduce the supply of dollar and will have an opposite impact.

When we reduce imports by restricting non-essential items, it leads to reduction in demand of dollars and appreciation of rupee.

218. (d)

- GIFT City has two zones, one is "Domestic" and the other is "SEZ". In domestic zone transactions happen only in Rupee. In 'GIFT-SEZ' all transactions happen only in foreign currency.

- The GIFT SEZ is India's first International Financial Services Centre (IFSC) set up under Special Economic Zones Act, 2005.

- An **IFSC** is a jurisdiction that provides financial services to non-residents and residents, to the extent permissible under the current regulations, in any currency except Indian Rupee.

- Units (entities) related to Banking, Insurance and Capital Markets are considered as IFSC units and hence Banks, Insurers and Capital Market related companies can set up their units in the IFSC (GIFT-SEZ).

- The IFSC in GIFT-City seeks to bring to the Indian shores, those financial services transactions that are currently carried outside India by overseas financial institutions and overseas branches/subsidiaries of Indian financial institutions to a centre which has been designated for all practical purposes as a location having the same eco system as their present offshore location (like London, Singapore etc.), which is physically on Indian soil.

- IFSC (GIFT-SEZ) is the only place in India which allows offshore transactions (i.e., it is treated as outside India transactions)

- IFSC is deemed to be a foreign territory and entities approved as IFSC unit are treated as **non-resident** in India. Therefore, RBI ODI (Overseas Direct Investment, which means investments outside India) Rules are applicable on investments in IFSC. Accordingly, Indian parties are allowed under Automatic route to make investment in IFSC entities and that shall be treated as **ODI**.

- Individual person resident in India is allowed to invest up to USD 2, 50,000 per financial year under Liberalized Remittance Scheme (LRS) outside India or in **IFSC.**

- Bombay Stock Exchange (BSE) has established its subsidiary in IFSC called India International Exchange (India-INX) and National Stock Exchange has established NSE International Exchange (**NSE-IX**) where any **foreign company** or **Indian company** can list its securities (shares/bonds/derivatives). For example, a US based company can list its shares on India INX (various tax incentives are given like no

STT, not LTCG, MAT just 9%) and the securities can be purchased by anyone from outside India or from India through ODI route up to a limit.

219. (d)
In January 2024, Government allowed Indian companies to directly list their **shares** (bonds had already been allowed) on International Exchanges in the GIFT-IFSC and raise foreign capital (in foreign currency). The international exchanges allowed to list securities (equity/shares) of Indian Companies in GIFT-IFSC are:

(i) India International Exchange (BSE)
(ii) NSE International Exchange

Earlier Indian companies had to go to international financial markets like London, Singapore etc. to raise cheaper foreign capital.

So now, Indian companies and foreign companies can list their shares and bonds on the exchanges in GIFT-SEZ and anyone from India or outside can purchase these securities.

220. (d)
When companies (govt. or private) borrow from abroad then it is called External Commercial Borrowing (ECB). ECB can be denominated in 'foreign currency' or it can be denominated in 'rupee' also which are called 'masala bonds'.

Even if masala bonds are denominated in 'Rupee', the money that we get from abroad is in dollars (or foreign currency). "Denominated in rupee" means....the Indian company will issue the bond paper to the foreign investor where it will be written "Rs. 100 bond". But the Indian company will get dollars equivalent of Rs. 100 (say $1.5). This is because Indian currency is not acceptable everywhere so the foreign investors hold dollars and give us dollars. So, at the end of the day, Indian company got dollars and when they bring it to India, it gets converted with RBI (through forex market) and RBI gets the dollars and the Indian company gets the rupee equivalent of dollars. This is a capital account transaction under BoP (as it is a borrowing) and increases our forex reserves, which can be used if India is having deficit in its Current Account. So, basically 'Masala Bonds' help in financing CAD of India. Masala bonds are a kind of ECB and ECB is basically a debt on India (but it is not a debt on Govt. of India).

These Masala Bonds are listed abroad. But now we have "Indian Financial Services Centre" (IFSC) in GIFT CITY SEZ which is a deemed foreign territory and foreign securities can be listed here. So, earlier to list Masala bonds we had to go to say "London Stock Exchange" but now it can be done/listed in GIFT City IFSC and money will be invested by foreign investors.

221. (c)
The term "**Strategic Disinvestment**" means the sale of substantial portion of the Government share-holding of a central public sector enterprise (CPSE) of up to 50%, or such higher percentage (to the strategic partner) along with transfer of management control.
In Strategic Disinvestment, management control must be transferred to the private strategic partner. Strategic disinvestment is a way of privatisation

Other PSUs cannot participate and bid in the strategic disinvestment process of a PSU as it would defeat the very purpose of the disinvestment policy.

222. (c)

223. (d)
All are objectives of Strategic disinvestment policy.

As per the new policy (2019), Department of Investment and Public Asset Management (DIPAM) under the Ministry of Finance has been made the nodal department for the strategic disinvestment. DIPAM and NITI Aayog will now jointly identify PSUs for strategic disinvestment and then it is approved by CCEA.

Government has created an "**Alternative Mechanism**", which is an inter-Ministerial body to fasten the process of strategic disinvestment.

224. (c)
The Balance of Payments (BoP) as a statistical statement that summarises economic transactions between residents of one economy and those of the rest of the world (non-residents) during a specific time period.

The concept of "residence" is central to BoP compilation.

For Households: The residence of an individual is determined by that of the household of which he is a part and not by the place of his work. His status of residence continues till he acquires a centre of predominant economic interest abroad. Normally, the predominant economic interest and, therefore, the status of residence is said to have been acquired by staying or intending to do so for one year or more in a territory.

For Enterprises: As a general principle, an enterprise is resident in an economic territory where the enterprise is engaged in a significant amount of production of goods and/or services.

So, first statement is not true.

Those transactions which happen between Indian residents and Foreigners or non-resident Indians (NRIs) are recorded in India's balance of payment.
In the second statement, an Indian resident is earning income from abroad from a foreign entity and in the third statement also, an Indian family is getting money free from an NRI. So, both will be recorded in India's balance of payments under current account.

225. (d)
Those transactions come under Capital Account (BoP) which creates future obligations/ liabilities or change in assets/liabilities. For example, loans, shares, deposits etc.

Global Depository Receipts (GDRs) are basically shares issued abroad by a domestic company.
NRI deposits create liability on the banks in India.

Securities are basically financial assets, so it will always be included in Capital Account.
So, all are part of Capital Account of BoP

226. (a)
Global Depository Receipts (GDRs) are basically shares issued abroad by a domestic company.

For detailed understanding please refer the Indian Economy book by Vivek Singh.

227. (d)
Masala bonds are issued outside India and money is raised in foreign currency which acts as debt on Indians, so it is part of our capital account. When NRIs are depositing money in Indian banks then it's a transaction between Indian residents (banks) and non-resident Indians and it creates a liability on Indian banks for future, hence it's a capital receipt.
Import of goods or services whether consumption or capital goods are part of current account.

228. (a)
BoP is basically transactions of the residents of the country with the rest of the world. And transfer payments mean anything given for free.

In the **1st** statement, the transaction between Indian resident and Non-Resident Indian (NRI) is for free, without any work done or consideration. So, it is a case of transfer payment and will be recorded in BoP.

In the **2nd** statement, the transaction is between Indian resident (who has gone abroad temporarily) and his family in India. Both are Indian residents, so, this transaction will not be recorded in BoP.

229. (d)
- World Bank publishes 'Migration and Development Brief' twice a year. It provides an update on key developments in the area of migration and remittance flows and related policies over the past six months.
- In 2024, India is received around $129 billion in remittances.
- The United States continued to be the largest source of remittances. The top five remittance recipient countries in 2024 are India ($129 billion), Mexico ($68 billion), China ($48 billion), the Philippines ($40 billion), and Pakistan ($33 billion).

230. (c)
If the Current Account is negative that means we are spending more and earning less (imports are more than exports), then we require foreign exchange to fund the Current Account Deficit.

This foreign exchange can come if we are surplus in Capital Account i.e., there is a net inflow in Capital Account. Or we can also use the foreign exchange reserves of our country.
So, both statements are true.

231. (c)
The currency swap agreement between two countries is entered between the Central Banks of the two countries. One country exchanges its national currency for that of another **or even a third one**. Let us understand this with example.

India and Japan signed currency swap agreement in 2018 worth $ 75 billion. As per the arrangement India can/will get Yen (or even dollars) from Japan worth max $ 75 billion and Japan will get equivalent Indian Rupees as per the market exchange rate at the time of transaction. The exchange will be reversed after an agreed period using the same exchange rate as per in the first transaction.

Whatever amount of Yen/dollars India will take from Japan, India will have to pay interest on that amount and whatever Rupee Japan will take from India, Japan will have to pay interest on that (depending on market interest rate). So, a bilateral currency swap is a kind of **open-ended credit line** from one country to another at a fixed exchange rate. So, under the swap agreement, India got dollars from Japan and Japan may or may not take Rupees from India. As India would be paying interest on the dollars taken from Japan, so it does not matter whether Japan took rupees from India or not. And that is why this currency swap is also called open-ended credit line facility. This currency swap arrangement will allow the Indian central bank to draw **up to** $75 billion worth of yen or dollars as a loan from the Japanese government whenever it needs this money. The RBI can either sell these dollars (or yen) to importers to settle their bills or to borrowers to pay off their foreign loans. The RBI can also just keep these dollars with itself to shore up its own foreign exchange reserves and defend the rupee.

Actually, the rupee was falling against the dollar because of its widening current account deficit. This led to importers upping their demand for dollars far beyond what exporters bring into the country leading to further depreciation of rupee. If RBI would have gone to the market to purchase these dollars (by selling rupees) then it would have further depreciated the rupee. So, RBI approached Japan to get the dollars and hence it is a kind of out of market transaction.

Even if RBI has amassed dollars, having a $75-billion loan-on-demand (as and when needed) from Japan gives the RBI an additional buffer to fall back on, should it need extra dollars. Hence, this currency swap agreement will bring in greater stability to foreign exchange and capital markets in India.

These swap operations carry no exchange rate or other market risks, as transaction terms are set in advance. The absence of an exchange rate risk is the major benefit of such a facility. This facility provides the country, which is getting the dollars, with the flexibility to use these reserves at any time in order to maintain an appropriate level of balance of payments or short-term liquidity.

In July 2020, India and Sri Lanka signed a currency swap agreement worth $ 400 million in which India will give **dollars** to Sri Lanka (as and when needed) and in return India will/can get 'Sri Lankan Rupee' and the facility will be valid till Nov 2022 and then the swap facility will be reversed. The RBI also offers similar swap lines to central banks in the SAARC region within a total corpus of $2 billion. Under the framework for 2019-22, the RBI will continue to offer a swap arrangement within the overall corpus of $2 billion.

232. (c)
As per RBI Act 1934, RBI, in public interest, can supersede the Board of Directors (management) of a non-banking financial company.

(RBI can supersede a bank's board through Banking Regulation Act 1949, but NBFCs are not covered in that Act. ***So, an amendment was done in RBI Act 1934 in July 2019, to allow RBI to supersede the board of NBFCs, in the wake of the crisis faced by various NBFCs like DHFL, IL&FS etc.)***

As per RBI Act 1934 (Section 30), the Central Government can supersede the 'Central Board' of RBI, and thereafter the general superintendence shall be entrusted to such agency as the government may decide and can exercise all the powers exercised by 'Central Board'.

233. (b)
RBI **in general** can issue guidelines for resolution of stressed assets **but it cannot force a banking company to move to IBC 2016 without Govt. of India authorization**. And in case after Govt. approval, RBI is asking a banking company to

move to IBC 2016 for resolution of stressed assets, then it should be in cases of specific defaults.

As per the Supreme Court judgement in 2019:

*"RBI can only direct banking institutions to move under the IBC Code 2016 if there is a central government authorization and it should be in respect of **specific defaults**. Thus, any directions which are in respect of debtors in general, would-be ultra vires Section 35AA of Banking Regulation Act 1949".*

Lenders do not require RBI permission to move to IBC Code 2016.

234. (a)

Committee of Creditors (CoC) consists of only financial creditors (like banks, NBFCs etc.). But the proceeds/money from the resolution process is shared by the financial and operational creditors both. Only CoC will decide how the resolution proceeds will be shared among financial and operational creditors and NCLT will not have any say. NCLT cannot interfere in the merits of the commercial decision taken by the CoC but a "limited judicial review" is possible to see that the CoC had taken into account, inter alia, the fact that the interest of all stakeholders, including operational creditors has been taken care of.

235. (d)

IBC Code 2016 was not applicable for the insolvency of financial service provider like Banks and NBFCs. But since some major NBFCs like DHFL, IL&FS faced crisis, government thought of bringing NBFCs **temporarily** under IBC for resolution. So, GoI, on **15th Nov 2019** notified section 227 under IBC Code which says that the IBC rules shall apply to such financial service providers or categories of financial service providers, as may be notified by the Central Government under section 227, from time to time, for the purpose of their insolvency and liquidation proceedings under these rules.

This is a temporary mechanism because for the resolution of insolvencies of Banks and NBFCs, we have a bill pending, Financial Resolution and Deposit Insurance (FRDI) Bill, which the government is planning to introduce soon.

236. (c)

Section 227 of IBC 2016 says that " *Notwithstanding anything to the contrary examined in this Code or any other law for the time being in force, **the Central Government** may, if it considers necessary, **in consultation with the appropriate financial sector regulators**, notify financial service providers or categories of financial service providers for the purpose of their insolvency and liquidation proceedings, which may be conducted under this Code."*

And the rules also say that to initiate resolution of FSPs under IBC 2016, the appropriate regulator should make an application. This is not applicable in other cases where in case of default, either the creditor or the debtor (company), anyone can move for resolution under IBC 2016.

Since, section 227 got notified, Ministry of Corporate Affairs (GoI) (using the powers under section 227) consulted the regulator (RBI) and said that those **NBFCs** with asset size of more than Rs. 500 crores can be brought under IBC code for resolution. This has been done only for those NBFCs which are regulated by RBI and not for those NBFCs which are regulated by other regulatory bodies like SEBI, IRDAI etc.

237. (a)
As per the amendment done in the Insolvency and Bankruptcy Code (IBC) in November 2017, Wilful Defaulters cannot bid for the companies put up for sale during the resolution process. It also prohibits from bidding any borrower (or promoter) whose account has been identified as an NPA for over a year and has not repaid the dues. But if the borrower/promoter has made payment of all **overdue** amounts with **interest and charges**, then he can bid (submit a resolution plan) for the company.
[Ref: Economic Survey 2017-18 Vol 2 page 52]

238. (c)
Securitisation and Reconstruction of Financial Assets and Enforcement of Security Interest (SARFAESI) Act, 2002 was enacted to regulate securitisation and reconstruction of financial assets and enforcement of security interest. The act allows banks and financial institutions to sell the security in case the debt/ loan is secured and it has become non performing. The provisions have enabled banks and financial institutions to improve recovery by exercising powers to take possession of securities (without moving to court), sell them and reduce nonperforming assets by adopting measures for recovery or reconstruction.

239. (c)
Govt. of India created a 'Bad Bank' named 'National Asset Reconstruction Company Ltd.' (NARCL) in 2021 which is basically an 'Asset Reconstruction Company' (ARC). NARCL will be 51% owned by Public Sector Banks and financial institutions, and the remaining 49% stake will be held by private sector lenders. NARCL is "Government Company", "Public Company" and "Unlisted Company". Another entity, India Debt Resolution Company (IDRCL), has also been set up which is a 'Non-Govt.' Company.

NARCL and IDRCL will together act as bad bank. NARCL will first purchase the bad loans from commercial banks and then IDRCL will try to sell out the bad loans and recover money. A two-entity structure has been created for operational and governance purpose.

Let us understand with an example. Suppose SBI had earlier given loan worth Rs. 1000 crore and it turned into NPA. So, SBI would sell this NPA to the bad bank for recovery and would rather focus on its banking business.

So, Bad bank will purchase this NPA from SBI but not in Rs. 1000 crore. The bad bank will try to estimate how much money it would actually be able to recover from the NPA and accordingly it would quote a price for it. If SBI also agrees then, SBI will sell this NPA/bad loan (paper) to bad bank, let us say in Rs. 300 crore. But the bad bank will not immediately pay in cash Rs. 300 crore to SBI. Rather, the bad bank will pay just 15% of the agreed amount (of the Rs. 300 crore) i.e., Rs. 45 crore in cash and the rest 85% i.e., Rs. 255 crore in securities (a kind of debt paper), which will be paid once the bad bank recovers the money by resolution or liquidation of the bad asset.

But what if the bad bank in future is unable to sell the bad loan or sells the bad loan at a loss (i.e., at less than Rs. 300 crore) and is not able to pay Rs. 255 crore to SBI. So, in that case Govt. of India has agreed to provide "Government Guarantee" on the securities that will be issued by the bad bank.

240. (d)
Pre-Pack Resolution Process (PIRP):
If an MSME has defaulted and the default is of less than Rs. 1 crore then "Pre-Pack" scheme can be used under IBC 2016. Under this scheme the owners of the defaulted

company (MSME) will prepare a resolution plan on their own and initiate the PIRP (with the approval of 2/3 creditors) rather than resolution plan suggested by **outsiders** through open bidding process in which case the company may go to new owners. And during this resolution process, the management of the firm (MSME) will remain with the original promoters. (Under normal IBC proceedings, the management control of the firm passes on to Resolution Professionals). It will adhere to a fix time line of 90 days for submission of resolution plan/mechanism and 30 days for its approval by NCLT, so in total of 120 days.

In case of pre pack resolution process, if the "Operational Creditors" have not been paid their total dues then other "Resolution Applicants" (**outsiders**) will also be allowed to participate in the bid to take over the MSME company (debtor). But the owners of the MSME company will still be asked to match the bid of the other applicants (Swiss Challenge) and if the owners of the MSME match the bid then the company will remain with its (present) owners. And if the MSME owners are not able to match the bid of other applicants then the MSME company will go in the hands of the new owners and the previous owners will lose their MSME company/Investments done in the MSME.

Right now, pre-pack is applicable only for MSMEs and up to a default of Rs. 1 crore but in future other companies may also get included and the default limit can also be increased.

241. (c)
The LCR is calculated by dividing institutions (Banks/NBFCs) high-quality liquid assets (for example cash, govt. securities, securities issued or guaranteed by foreign governments etc.) by its total **net** cash outflow, over a 30-day period.

Suppose a bank's expected cash outflow/spending for the next 30 days is Rs. 150 and cash inflow is expected to be Rs. 50 that means net cash outflow for next 30-day period is Rs. 100. In such a case if bank is holding cash and govt. securities (which are called High Quality Liquid Assets) of Rs. 60, then LCR = (High Quality Liquid Asset)/ (Banks Net cash outflow for 30-day period) = Rs. 60/ Rs. 100 = 60%.

242. (d)
Crypto currencies are just digital assets and are not a currency. Govt. has not made crypto currency legal tender, nor it has legalized the trade in crypto currencies but it is not illegal too to transact in crypto currency. So, govt. is yet to frame any law/rule related to crypto transactions.

But Govt. in the budget 2022-23, has imposed 30% tax on any income from transfer of any virtual digital asset (crypto currencies). And no deduction in respect of any expenditure or allowance shall be allowed while computing such income except cost of acquisition.

But levying of 30% tax on transfer of digital assets does not automatically legalizes crypto currencies. Finance Minister has clarified that imposing tax does not legalize trade in crypto currencies.

As per past court judgements also, *"if the business is illegal, neither the profits earned, nor the losses incurred would be enforceable in law. But that does not take the profits out of the taxing statutes."*

243. (d)
A CBDC is the legal tender issued by a central bank in a digital form. It is the same as a fiat currency and is no different from cash and is exchangeable one-to-one with the fiat currency (bank notes/cash) at par. Only its form is different i.e., digital.

If someone is holding cash and making payment to other person then it does not require any kind of settlement with a third party and the RBI's liability moves from one person to the other person. But when I make payment through cheque/card then it requires inter-bank settlement (through RBI in case of different banks).

CBDCs could bring a lot of benefits like it could make payments faster/instantaneous allowing for immediate settlement and no processing delays

244. (d)
- E-Rupee will be a bearer instrument i.e. whoever is holding the e-Rupee will be assumed to be the owner at any given point of time.
- E-rupee will not earn any interest like cash
- E-rupee would offer features of physical cash like trust, safety and settlement facility
- To introduce 'Central Bank Digital Currency' (CBDC), RBI Act 1934 was amended through Finance Act 2022.

245. (d)
The lending rate in the economy may remain high, in spite of RBI reducing the repo rate because, banks may be offering higher deposit rates to the public, which is basically a cost for banks. So, if the cost is high, banks will keep the interest rate high.

When Government offers higher interest rate on its savings schemes then banks are not willing to reduce their own deposit rate, as they fear that depositors will move towards govt. schemes. When banks don't reduce the deposit rate, they do not reduce lending rate too.

If there is liquidity crunch in the economy i.e., supply is less, so suppliers (banks/FI) will try to charge higher interest rate rather than reducing the lending rates.

246. (c)
For detailed understanding refer the Indian Economy Book by Vivek Singh.

247. (a)
Investments depend essentially on real interest rate. It is the difference in the lending rate and inflation. For businessmen, it is this cost i.e., the real interest rate which matters. If it is high, businessmen will not borrow and invest.
For example, if inflation is 2% and lending rate is 10%, then real interest rate for the businessmen is 8%. For businessmen, it is the real interest rate of 8% that matters. If the real interest is high then it deters investment.

If in the economy, capacity utilization is high that means factories are running at full utilization and then the businessmen plan for increase in capacity so that in future they are able to supply the goods and services in case there is increase in demand. But, if the existing capacity is not fully utilized in the economy, then businessmen defer new investments.

248. (c)
Suppose country A imposed tariff against country B to reduce imports from B. Then it will lead to reduction in demand of currency B for import purpose, which will lead to depreciation of currency B and increasing the competitiveness of products of country B, resulting in negating the effect of tariffs imposed against B.

In a market determined exchange rate, the rate of exchange between two currencies depends only on the demand and supply of the two currencies. But the demand and supply of two currencies may depend on several factors like export and import and foreign people coming in or going out of the country and so on.

249. (a)
If there is inflation in the economy then it means rupee is losing value with respect to goods and services. Now, when rupee has lost value with respect to goods and services in the economy then rupee will lose value with respect to dollars also. This is because now the same rupees will not be able to purchase those goods and services (and the only purpose of rupee is to purchase goods and services in the economy) and hence per dollar the foreigners will demand more rupees leading to depreciation of rupee.

But if rupee is **depreciating**, then it means rupee is losing value with respect to a specific item i.e., dollar. That does not mean that rupee will lose value with respect to all the goods and services in the economy. (*Layman's explanation: If rupee is losing value with respect to onions means onion becoming costlier.......... That does not mean rupee will lose value with respect to all goods and services, and prices of other goods and services will not increase.)*

250. (b)
Advance tax payment means paying a part of the yearly taxes in advance to the government. This reduces liquidity in the economy because the money moves from public to government. *(the logic is money with the government is not part of money supply in the economy)*

In case of GST, the government credits/gives back the taxes paid on inputs, to the suppliers which increase liquidity in the economy.

Front loading of government expenditure means government is spending its yearly targeted expenditure in the starting months rather than in the year end. This increases liquidity in the economy.

Recapitalization of public sector banks means government is putting money in public sector banks which increases the lending capacity of the banks resulting in increase in money supply and liquidity.

251. (c)
In international transactions, generally dollars and some other stable/hard currencies like Euro, Pound, Yen etc. are used/accepted. So, if there is a problem of international liquidity then it means non-availability of these hard currencies.

252. (d)
Whenever something is surplus, its value decreases. So, when there is surplus liquidity (money) in the economy, the value of money decreases, which means money is available at cheaper rate i.e., lesser interest rate.

And since the value of money (Rupee) has decreased, it also means that the same amount of rupee will be able to purchase less dollars i.e., rupee will depreciate. And it also means that purchasing power of rupee will decrease.

[For example, if there are too many flats built in the country then the price of flat will fall and the rentals on flat will also fall].

When the interest rate comes down in the economy then if you will purchase bonds then your return/yield will also be less. This you can also determine as, when the interest rate comes down in the economy, the bond prices go up and return/yield comes down.

253. (c)
Bond yield is dependent on interest rate in the market. When interest rate goes up then (bond price goes down and) bond yield goes up.

But suppose interest rate is not changing in the economy. In this case also, if a lot of bondholders start selling their bonds, then the price of bond will go down and the yield will move up.

254. (b)
If there is a surge in bond yields that means those people holding bonds, their prices are going down, so bondholders will loos.

If the bond yields are increasing (alternatively you can that bonds prices are going down) then definitely it will attract a lot of FPI debt investors to invest in bonds.

When the bond yields move up then investors will shift to debt/bond investments rather than equity investments, so it will hurt government's disinvestment plan.

255. (d)
Typically, yields are higher for longer tenures because one is lending money for longer. If the yields for different tenures of bonds are mapped, it will give an upward-sloping curve ("Normal" in the chart below).

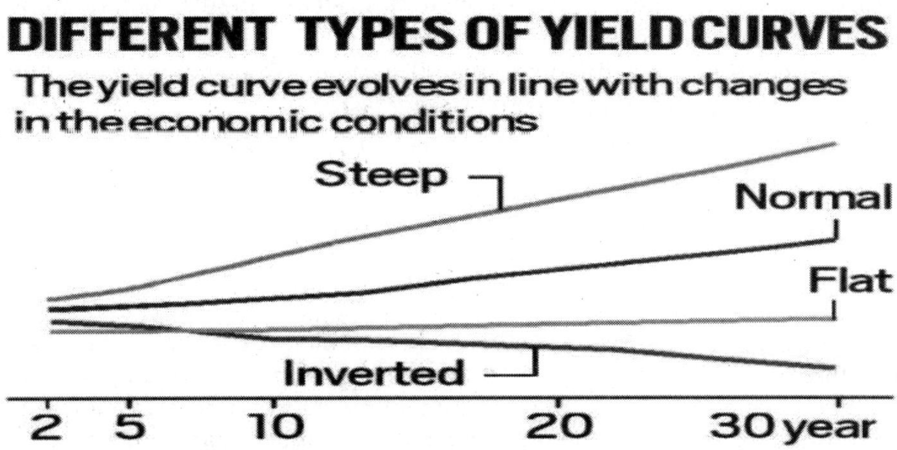

The curves can be flat or steep depending on the money available in the market and the expected overall economic activity. When investors feel buoyant about the economy, they pull money out of long-term bonds and put it into short-term riskier assets such as stock markets. As prices of long-term bonds fall, their yields rise — and the yield curve steepens.

Yield inversion happens when yields for shorter duration bonds are higher than the yields on longer duration bonds. If investors suspect that the economy is heading for trouble, they will pull out money from short-term risky assets (such as stock markets) and put it in long-term bonds. This causes the prices of the long-term bonds to rise and their yields to fall. This process first leads to flattening and eventually the inversion of the yield curve. Yield inversion has long been a reliable predictor of recession in the US

256. (c)

Important features of new guidelines for Micro finance loans published by RBI in March 2022:

- It is applicable to all commercial banks (except payment banks as they do not give loan), cooperative banks and NBFCs

- A microfinance loan is defined as a collateral-free loan given to a household having annual household income up to ₹3,00,000. For this purpose, the household shall mean an individual family unit, i.e., husband, wife and their unmarried children.

- All collateral-free loans, irrespective of end use and mode (either through physical or digital channels), provided to low-income households, i.e., households having annual income up to ₹3,00,000, shall be considered as microfinance loans.

- The Banks/NBFCs should clearly mention a ceiling on the interest rate and all other charges applicable to the microfinance loans. Banks/NBFCs should separate the components of the interest rate such as cost of funds, risk premium and margin, etc. based on objective parameters. Interest rates and other charges/ fees on microfinance loans should not be usurious. These shall be subjected to supervisory scrutiny by the Reserve Bank. *(As such RBI is not fixing/regulating the interest rate on microfinance loan but has given clear guidelines how to do it and put a cap/ceiling).*

257. (a)

- Scheduled commercial banks (SCBs) including small finance banks (SFBs) and regional rural banks (RRBs) (lending both directly as well as through business correspondents (BCs) and self-help groups (SHGs)) and Cooperative Banks [**59.72%**]
- Non-banking financial companies (NBFCs) [**8.71%**]
- Microfinance institutions (MFIs) registered as NBFCs [**30.8%**]
- 'Not for profit' MFIs [**0.78%**]

258. (c)

259. (d)

Financial repression occurs when governments implement policies to channel to themselves funds that in a deregulated market environment would go elsewhere. Policies include directed lending to the government by captive domestic audiences (such as pension funds or domestic banks), explicit or implicit caps on interest rates, regulation of cross-border capital movements, and (generally) a tighter connection between government and banks, either explicitly through public ownership of some of the banks or through heavy "moral suasion" (persuading banks to act in a certain way). Financial repression is also sometimes associated with relatively high reserve requirements (or liquidity requirements), prohibition of gold purchases, or the placement of significant amounts of government debt that is nonmarketable (debt for which there is no secondary market).

260. (b)
Deleverage means reducing the level of debt of a company by selling its assets.

261. (c)
Circuit breakers are pre-defined values in percentage terms, which trigger an automatic check/halt/stop when there is a runaway move in any security or index on either direction (either increase or decrease). The values are calculated from the previous closing level of the security or the index. Usually, circuit breakers are employed for both stocks (share of a particular company) and indices (SENSEX/NIFTY). That means if one company's share fluctuates too much then also circuit breakers can apply or if the overall market i.e., either SENSEX/NIFTY fluctuates then also circuit breakers come into play.

The index-based market-wide circuit breaker system applies at 3 stages of the index movement, either way viz. at 10%, 15% and 20%. These circuit breakers when triggered bring about a coordinated trading halt in all equity and equity derivative markets nationwide. The market-wide circuit breakers are triggered by movement of either the BSE Sensex 30 or the Nifty 50, whichever is breached earlier. This means that if either NIFTY or SENSEX moves beyond 10% then the nationwide markets regulated by SEBI will come to halt. (But in case of a company, only the trading in that company is halted.)

262. (b)

263. (d)
One of the disputed issues in taxation related to MNCs is the area of intra (group) company transactions. The pricing of goods and services between two related companies (companies belonging to the same owner or subsidiaries) is called **transfer pricing**.

Here, a parent company say in Japan may charge a convenient price from its subsidiary in India to minimise its tax payment in India. For example, suppose that Maruti Suzuki India has higher profit and has to pay higher tax to the Government of India. In this case, if Suzuki Japan charges a high price for a component it sold to Maruti, profit of Maruti will come down and the tax payment of the company to GoI will also come down. On the other hand, the revenue of Suzuki Japan will go up. Altogether, the Suzuki Motor Corporation (SMC) group improves its position; but GoI's tax revenue gets affected.

To avoid such a manipulation, tax department of India pre-sets the price charged for different components between Maruti Suzuki India and Suzuki Japan. But this price should follow "**arms-length principle**" i.e., market based. An arm's length transaction refers to a business deal in which buyers and sellers act independently without one party influencing the other. These types of sales assert that both parties act in their own self-interest and are not subject to pressure from the other party; furthermore, it assures others that there is no collusion between the buyer and seller.

At the beginning of the year, the price charged for intra company transactions will be determined in advance and will be kept for the coming five years or so. This price arrangement between Maruti and India's tax department is called **advance pricing agreement**.

An APA is a contract, usually for multiple years, between a taxpayer and at least one tax authority specifying the pricing method that the taxpayer will apply to its **related-**

company transactions. These programmes are designed to help taxpayers voluntarily resolve actual or potential transfer pricing disputes in a proactive, cooperative manner, as an alternative to the traditional examination process. APAs gives certainty to taxpayers, reduces disputes, enhance tax revenues and make the country an attractive destination for foreign investments. These agreements would be binding both on the taxpayer as well as the government. Similarly, they lower complaints and litigation costs.

264. (d)

265. (d)
The National Financial Reporting Authority (NFRA) was constituted on 01st October, 2018 by the Government of India under the Companies Act, 2013. As per the Act, the duties of NFRA are:

- Recommend accounting and auditing policies and standards to be adopted by companies for approval by the Central Government;
- Monitor and enforce compliance with accounting standards and auditing standards;
- Enforce compliance with accounting/auditing standards and undertake investigation of the auditors of listed and unlisted companies
- Protect the public interest and the interests of investors, creditors and others associated with the companies

266. (d)
National Bank for Financing Infrastructure Development (NaBFID) has been established through an act of Parliament as a 'Development Finance Institution' (DFI).

As per the act, *"The financial objective of the Institution shall be to lend or invest, directly or indirectly, and seek to attract investment from private sector investors and institutional investors, in infrastructure projects located in India, or partly in India and partly outside India, with a view to foster sustainable economic development in India."*

Non-recourse debt is made to finance a particular project, with the condition that the project's profits are the only assets out of which the borrower is legally obliged to repay the loan. Unlike non-recourse debt, recourse debt/loans generally require collateral.

267. (d)

268. (c)
Supplementary Demand for Grants: If the amount authorized to be expended for a particular service for the current financial year is found to be insufficient for the purpose of that year or when a **need has arisen** during the current financial year for supplementary or additional expenditure upon some 'new service' not contemplated in the budget for that year then the President causes to be laid before both the Houses of Parliament another statement showing the estimated amount of that expenditure which is called "Supplementary Demand for Grants".

Demand for Excess Grants: If any money **has been spent** on any service during a financial year in excess of the amount granted for the service for that year, the President causes to be presented to Lok Sabha a demand for such excess (which is called "Demand for Excess Grants"). All cases involving such excesses are brought to the notice of Parliament by the CAG through a report on the Appropriation Accounts. The excesses are then examined by the Public Accounts Committee which makes recommendations regarding their regularisation in its report to the House.

*The "**Supplementary Demands for Grants**" are presented to and passed by the House **before** the end of the financial year while the "**Demands for Excess Grants**" are made after the expenditure has actually been incurred and **after** the financial year to which it relates has expired.*

269. (c)
Budget is discussed in two stages - the general discussion followed by detailed discussion.

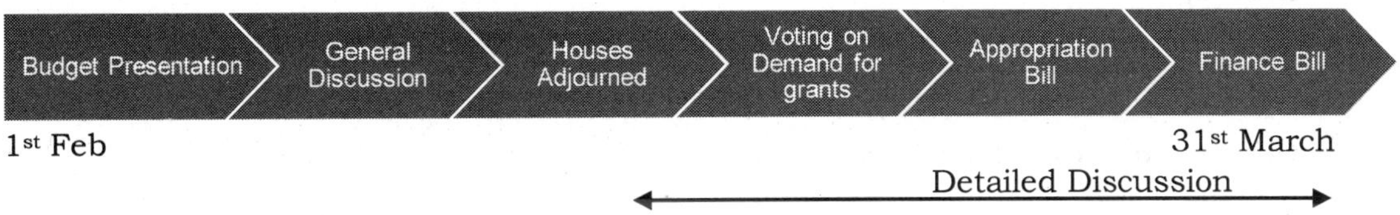

On 1st Feb, Finance bill is also introduced just after budget presentation.

270. (d)
In normal budget, 'Demand for Grants' of every ministry/department is discussed and voted in Lok Sabha (it can be discussed in Rajya Sabha but no voting happens in Rajya Sabha on demand for grants) which basically gives approval of every ministry's expenditure. And then Appropriation Bill is passed to extract that money out of CFI.

But in Vote-on-Account, there is no approval of demand for grants of every ministry/department, but only an approval is taken of the Parliament to extract money out of CFI for expenses purpose of the Govt. for 2/4/6 months.

Taxes from UTs without Assembly get deposited in the Consolidated Fund of India (CFI) and then from CFI amount is spent on various activities of 'UTs without Assembly'. So, just like 'Demand for Grants' of every Union Ministry is passed in the same way a 'Demand for Grants' of every UT without assembly is also passed in the Union Budget and that amount is also included in the Appropriation Bill (to be spent from CFI).

271. (a)
The Public Finance (Central) Division, under Department of Expenditure, Ministry of Finance is responsible for preparation of outcome budgets in consultation with the NITI Aayog. This output-outcome framework (outcome budget) is prepared for all Centrally Sponsored Schemes (CSSs) and Central Sector Schemes (CSs) dealing with identified measurable outcomes in the relevant medium-term framework and physical and financial outputs are targeted on a year to year basis.

For example, suppose if government is budgeting Rs. 30,000 crores for the LPG subsidy for FY 2020-21 then under the outcome budget it may set a target that it is planning to distribute LPG cylinders to 10 crore households.

272. (a)
The "Outcome Budget" reflects the endeavour of the Government to convert "Outlays" into "Outcomes" by planning expenditure, fixing appropriate targets and quantifying deliverables of each scheme. The "Outcome Budget" is an effort of the Government to be transparent and accountable to the people. Outcome budget is presented in the parliament.

273. (b)
The RBI transferred its accumulated surplus reserves (which it was holding since long) to its annual income and then this annual income was transferred to Govt. of India as

dividend. Dividend from PSUs (RBI is a PSU which is 100% owned by Govt. of India) is considered as non-tax revenue receipts.

274. (a)
Grants in aid by the Centre to the States will always be revenue expenditure for the Centre. Whether States spend it on capital expenditure or revenue expenditure, does not matter.

275. (b)
Effective Capital Expenditure = Capital Expenditure by Central Govt. + Grants given to states for creation of capital assets.

Grants given to States (by Govt. of India) is a revenue expenditure for Govt. of India but ultimately it is spent for creation of capital assets by State Governments, so effectively it is capital expenditure for the economy.

This same concept is used to calculate "Effective Revenue Deficit" which is equal to Revenue deficit minus grants given to states for creation of capital assets.

276. (b)
Spectrum auction is a revenue receipt as the spectrum which is asset of Govt. of India is not completely sold out during the auctions rather it is given on lease for 20/30 years of time period.

Revenues of IRCTC are receipts of IRCTC and not of Govt. of India. IRCTC is a PSU and once it gives dividend to Govt. of India then it will be counted in non-tax revenue receipts.

277. (b)
There are certain capital receipts of the Central Government which does not create debt/liability on it. For example, when the government is selling its shares in PSUs it is capital receipts but is not creating debt on Govt. rather it is decreasing its assets.
In the same way recovery of loans is capital receipt but does not create debt.

But, if the Govt. issues securities (treasury bills, dated securities or cash management bills) then it will be debt creating capital receipts. And money received in Public Account is also liability for Govt. of India and are considered as debt creating capital receipts.

278. (c)
Money received in Public Account of India creates liability on Govt. of India and hence it's a part of capital receipt/budget.

India Post Payment Bank is a PSU and funds contributed by Govt. to create a PSU (an asset) will come under capital budget/expenditure of Govt. of India.

A PSU purchasing capital equipment is not part of Govt. of India budget.

279. (d)
Those receipts/expenditures of the government which changes the liability or the assets (physical or financial) of the Govt. comes under capital budget.

Expenditure on acquisition of assets like roads or buildings come under capital expenditure.
Loans received increases the liability and loans given by govt. increases the assets of govt., hence capital budget.

280. (d)
In case of Sovereign Gold Bonds, government issues/creates the gold bond and in return it gets money from the public. This money will come under capital receipt because the gold bond is a kind of liability for the govt. which the govt. must pay in future. Principal payment will come under capital expenditure and interest payment will come under revenue expenditure.

The physical gold which the govt. receives from the pubic in case of gold monetization scheme becomes a liability for the govt. (in return for the physical gold, govt issues a paper which is basically liability for the govt.) which the govt. will have to pay in future either in physical gold form or in cash.

Sovereign Green Bonds are also a kind of borrowing by Govt. of India.

281. (b)
Dividend paid by PSUs is revenue receipts of govt. of India. RBI is also a body corporate and owned by govt. of India and its dividend is also revenue receipts for govt. of India.

PSUs business earnings are not part of govt. of India receipts rather it belongs to the PSU. Sale of govt. land will be capital receipt for govt. because govt's assets get reduced.

282. (a)
The Central Government collects about 60% of the total govt. revenue and has a share of 40% in total Government expenditure.

We can also say that Central Govt. revenue collection is 1.5 times of States and All state government combined expenditure is 1.5 times of Centre. This is possible because Centre transfers funds to States as per Finance Commission Recommendations. So, Central Govt. collects more revenue but States spend more.

283. (d)

284. (a)

$$\text{Tax buoyancy} = \frac{\text{\% Change in Tax Revenue}}{\text{\% Change in Nominal GDP}}$$

If nominal GDP growth is 12% and Tax revenue growth in a particular year is 15% then tax buoyancy will be 15%/12% = 1.25. It tells the growth in tax revenue per percentage change in GDP. If tax buoyancy is greater than one then it is good for economy.

285. (d)
Tax buoyancy = %change in tax revenue/%change in GDP

Since we have progressive tax system, so when GDP increases and people income increases, then their tax increases more as compared to GDP/income. Hence, increase in GDP may lead to increase in tax buoyancy.

All the other factors will increase tax even without an increase in GDP, hence it will also increase tax buoyancy.

286. (c)
The Central Consumer Protection Authority (CCPA) was established in July 2020 under the 'Consumer Protection Act 2019'. CCPA regulates matters relating to violation of rights of consumers, unfair trade practises and false or misleading advertisements which are prejudicial (detrimental) to the interest of public and consumers and to promote and enforce the rights of consumers as a class.

CCPA considers 'service charge' as unfair trade practises and misleading and hence issued guidelines (in July 2022) banning restaurants and hotels across the country from levying service charge.

But the Delhi High Court on July 20 **stayed** the guidelines issued by the CCPA. The court said that the restaurants and hotels have to ensure that the levy of service charge in addition to the food bill and taxes and the obligation of customers to pay it must be displayed prominently on the menu.

The court said hotels and restaurants will undertake not to levy the service charge on takeaway items. The court also said if you don't want to pay, don't enter the restaurant. It is ultimately a question of choice.

287. (d)
Tax Deducted at Source (TDS)
Suppose I work in a company XYZ and it pays me monthly salary of Rs. 1 lakh. So, my total income would be Rs. 12 lakh in a year and I need to pay 'Income Tax' on Rs. 12 lakh. But Govt. asks XYZ that when you are paying salary to Vivek then you deduct some (fix) percent of tax from the monthly salary and pay in Govt.'s account on behalf of Vivek. So, lets say the company XYZ deducts 10% tax (which is called Tax Deducted at Source) and then pays me monthly amount Rs. 90,000. So in one year XYZ deducted Rs. 1,20,000 out of my total salary of Rs. 12 lakh. But if my ' total tax liability' comes out to be around Rs. 3 lakh (as per the income tax slab rates) then I will have to deposit the rest amount (Rs. 3 lakhs - Rs. 1.2 lakhs) of Rs. 1.8 lakh to the Govt. And this amount of Rs. 1.8 lakh needs to be deposited not after the completion of year but during the year (in every quarter), so this Rs. 1.8 lakh is called advance tax.

Tax Collected at Source (TCS)
TCS is the tax that some specified sellers are required to collect from their buyers on exceptional transactions. TCS is collected by the seller as a means to track buyers and minimize tax evasion. Generally, it is not applicable on the common man. It is collected on timber wood, Tendu leaves, Motor vehicles exceeding Rs. 10 lakhs etc.

Example:
Suppose I am purchasing a car whose price is Rs. 15 lakh (it already includes GST) then on this 1% TCS (Rs. 15000) will be charged and the total price of the car would become Rs. 15.15 lakh. So this Rs. 15000 TCS will be deposited by the Seller in Govt. account against the buyers (PAN) i.e. on behalf of buyer.

Now if my total income is Rs. 12 lakh and my total tax liability comes out to be Rs. 3 lakh then I need to pay only Rs. 2.85 lakh as tax because Rs. 15000 has already been deposited by the seller as TCS on my behalf. It may also be possible that the 10% TDS which my employer is deducting is adjusted against TCS i.e. my employer will reduce the TDS amount by the TCS. So, if there are TCS payments made by me then it will reflect in a lower TDS i.e. the paid TCS is adjusted with the total tax liability of the buyer.

TDS and TCS comes under Income Tax Act 1961 and hence are direct taxes.

288. (c)
Receipts under Public Account mainly flow from the sale of Savings Certificates, contributions into General Provident Fund, Public Provident Fund, Security Deposits and Earnest Money Deposits (a kind of security deposits) received by the government. It also includes schemes like Kisan Vikas Patra, Sukanya Samriddhi Scheme etc. In respect of such deposits, the government is acting as a Banker or Trustee and refunds the money after the completion of the contract/ event.

All government borrowings through Treasury bills and Dated securities goes to Consolidated fund of India.

289. (d)
Small Savings Scheme:
The way people deposit money in banks, in the same way there are various schemes through which people can deposit (mostly fixed deposits) money with "Govt. of India" for a fixed tenure and can earn interest and after maturity they get the principal also. But Govt. of India offers these schemes through various Public and Private sector banks and also through Post Offices, and the money goes into "Public Account of India" and is kept separately under "National Small Savings Fund (NSSF)". The rate of interest on these "small savings schemes" has been aligned with G-Security rates of similar maturities. The interest rate is generally a little bit higher than what is offered by banks on fixed deposits and that is why people get attracted but there are certain limits on how much u can keep and no need to go into all these detail.

So, every year Govt. of India receives money in NSSF (under Public Account of India) and it also pays out to those people whose deposits are maturing. The money which Govt. of India receives in NSSF is invested in various Public Agencies like FCI, NHAI etc. and in central and state govt. securities. (Basically, the NSSF fund is used to lend money to Public agencies and Central and State govt.). And whatever interest is received under NSSF (by lending to Public Agencies and central & state govt.), is used to pay interest to the depositors/subscribers of NSSF. The following are the eight small savings scheme run by Govt. of India.

- Post Office Savings Account
- National Savings Recurring Deposit Account
- National Savings Time Deposit Account
- National Savings Monthly Income Account
- Senior Citizens Savings Scheme Account
- Public Provident Fund Account
- National Savings Certificates (VIII Issue) Account
- Kisan Vikas Patra Account
- Sukanya Samriddhi Account

290. (c)

Fiscal Deficit = Total Expenditure - Total Receipts except borrowing
= (Rev Exp. + Cap Exp.) - (Rev Rec. + Cap Rec. except borrowing)
= (Rev Exp. - Rev Rec.) + (Cap Exp. - Cap Rec. except borrowing)
= Revenue Deficit + Cap Exp. - Cap Rec. except borrowing
= Total borrowing
= Domestic market borrowing + borrowing from RBI + Borrowing from abroad

Let us understand with an example.
Suppose, government's total expenditure = 17 lakh crore
and receipts = 13 lakh crore

Then government will have to borrow (17 lakh crore -13 lakh crore) 4 lakh crores to meet its expenditure. And this 4 lakh crore is called the fiscal deficit. That is why fiscal deficit is also equal to the total borrowing i.e., 4 lakh crores.

But this 4 lakh crore which government borrows **becomes part of capital receipt** for the government and it must be included in capital receipts. So, in actual sense government's total receipts will become 17 lakh crores (i.e., 13 lakh crore + 4 lakh crore borrowing).

Hence, in the above example:
Fiscal Deficit = Total expenditure - total receipts **except borrowing**
Otherwise, the difference of total expenditure and total receipts will always be zero.

291. (a)

Fiscal Deficit is equal to total borrowing and the borrowing is part of capital receipts which create debt. So, fiscal deficit is equal to debt creating capital receipts.

292. (a)

Here, budget deficit means fiscal deficit.
Rationalization of subsidies means reducing leakages and wastages in subsidies.

293. (c)

When government incurs fiscal deficit, then it spends more in the economy resulting in increase in total/aggregate demand. But if total supply also increases, then inflation may not increase. So, government's fiscal deficit will necessarily increase aggregate demand but may not increase effective demand.

When the economic capacity is fully (100%) utilized and government spends more then demand increases in the economy, but supply may not immediately increase and the companies will have to set up new capacity which may increase cost, resulting in inflation.

But if the economic capacity is underutilized, because of less demand and then government spends more then the increase in aggregate demand will be met by increased supply, and there may not be inflation.
So, fiscal deficit may or may not cause inflation.

294. (b)

When government postpones its fiscal deficit target or when fiscal deficit increases then interest rate in the economy goes up because government borrows more (demand supply concept). When interest rate in the economy goes up bond yield goes up.

Higher fiscal deficit increases aggregate demand in the economy.

295. (c)
Fiscal Deficit is Govt. of India's borrowing either from domestic sources or from abroad. So, when Govt. of India issues bonds to borrow money, it can be purchased by FPI's and NRIs. But Foreign Direct Investors are not allowed to invest in bonds/debt.

As per FRBM Act 2003, RBI should not fund Govt. of India's fiscal deficit (in primary market) other than in exceptional circumstances. Although RBI can purchase Govt. securities in secondary market.

296. (d)
A 'stimulus' is an attempt by policymakers to kickstart/stimulate a sluggish economy through a package of measures. In case of fiscal stimulus, the Government increases its spending and or slashes tax rates to put more money in the hands of consumers.

A monetary stimulus will see the central bank expanding money supply or reducing the cost of money (interest rates), to spur consumer spending.

297. (c)
Government's fiscal policy can have impact on both current account and capital account under Balance of Payment.

If Government increases spending, then the demand in the economy will increase which may result in increase in imports resulting in current account deficit.
Change in customs duty can also have impact on current account.

Government's change in tax policies may impact FDI/FPI and other investments under capital account.

298. (c)
Government's fiscal policy has big role in stabilizing the economy during business cycles. The two important phases of business cycles are **boom** and **recession**. A recession should not be allowed to grow into a deep recession. Similarly, a boom should not explode bigger. We may say that amplifying the business cycle is dangerous (growing boom and deepening recession). Practically fiscal policy responses using taxation and expenditure can go in two ways in response to the business cycle: Countercyclical and pro-cyclical.

Business Cycle **Fiscal Policy**	**Boom**	**Recession**
Pro-Cyclical	Expenditure increases Tax decreases	Expenditure decreases Tax increases
Counter Cyclical	Expenditure decreases Tax increases	Expenditure increases Tax decreases

299. (b)
Fiscal Consolidation policy is an effort by the Government to bring down fiscal deficit. It is an effort to reduce public debt, raise revenues and bring down wasteful expenses.

300. (d)
Fiscal dominance occurs when central banks use their monetary powers to support the prices of government securities and to keep interest rates at low levels to reduce the costs of servicing sovereign/government debt. Fiscal dominance implies that Fiscal considerations limit the scope for an independent and prudent monetary policy.

This term can be understood in the context of WPI and CPI both are high but still RBI is not willing to increase the repo rate (and reverse repo rate) because it may lead to increase in interest rates and increase in cost of borrowing by the Govt. Recently RBI also scrapped the plan for issuance of Central government securities to raise debt (for govt.) in light of higher interest rate in the market.

301. (d)
As per the FRBM Act 2003, the following three statements should be presented along with the Annual Financial Statement (budget) in both the houses of the parliament:

- Medium Term Fiscal Policy Statement
- Fiscal Policy Strategy Statement
- Macro-economic Framework Statement

But, the 'Medium-term Expenditure Framework Statement' should be laid in the session immediately following the session of the Parliament in which the budget has been presented.

302. (d)
"Monetisation of Deficit" means Govt. borrows from RBI through printing of new currency notes to finance its deficit. So, RBI will print new currency notes and give to Govt. and govt. will give a receipt/proof to RBI that Govt. has taken this much amount of money from RBI. This receipt/proof is called govt. bonds/securities. This is a primary market transaction between the issuer (Govt.) of bonds and investor (RBI).

As the new currency notes given to govt. are liability for RBI, so liability of RBI increases and simultaneously RBI gets the govt's bond which will be asset for RBI. So, RBI's Asset and Liability both will increase by the amount of new printed currency notes.

As ultimately this money will be spent in the economy, it will increase the money supply in the economy resulting in inflation which may result in macroeconomic instability.

This is allowed as per FRBM act 2003 only but only in exceptional circumstances.

303. (d)
Expansionary fiscal policy results in money reaching to the public directly, resulting in inflation which may lead to depreciation of currency.

Expansionary monetary policy may also result in increasing money supply in the economy (and inflation) resulting in depreciation of currency.

Monetisation of Deficit *means government of India will issue bonds to RBI and RBI will print extra cash and give it to government. In RBI's balance sheet, the Govt. bonds will look as assets and the printed currency notes (given to govt.) will become liability for RBI.* This extra cash when govt. spends will go into the economy and may lead to inflation which may lead to depreciation of currency.

Debasement (of currency) refers to lowering of the currency value done by printing more currency notes. Debasement gives more money to the government for spending purpose to meet their financial obligations, but it results in inflation (for the people) in the economy leading to depreciation of currency.

304. (d)
Without any doubt contractionary monetary policy leads to increase in interest rate. This is either by increasing the repo rate which will increase interest rates in market or by reducing the money supply (through OMO etc.) which increases interest rates.

Expansionary Fiscal Policy means Govt. is spending more as compared to its receipts which will result in higher borrowing by Govt. i.e. more demand for funds from the market resulting in higher interest rates.

Now when interest rate increases in domestic economy, it may attract FPI (debt) investors resulting in rupee appreciation.

305. (a)
Before 1997, Government of India used to finance its deficit directly from RBI by issuing ad hoc Treasury Bills to RBI. This is called (direct) monetisation of deficit from RBI.

But this practise was stopped in 1997 by signing a historic agreement between Govt. of India and RBI and a scheme of 'Ways and Means Advance' (WMA) was started wherein govt. can take advances to accommodate temporary mismatches in the government's receipts and payments. So, basically direct monetisation of deficit was stopped.

And it was agreed that henceforth, the RBI would operate **only in the secondary market** through the Open Market Operation (OMO) route. The implied understanding also was that the RBI would use the OMO route not so much to support government borrowing but as a liquidity instrument to manage the balance between the policy objectives of controlling inflation, supporting growth and preserving financial stability.

306. (d)
Tax base is defined as the total value of the financial streams or assets on which tax can be imposed by the government. For example, in case of income tax, the tax base is the minimum amount of annual income that can be taxed by the government (taxable income). If this minimum amount (tax threshold) is lowered, this will automatically increase (widen) the tax base; if it is raised, the tax base will be narrowed. In case of GST, tax base is the value of goods and services on which GST is imposed. In case of property tax, tax base is the value of property on which property tax is imposed. Because the size of the tax base influences the taxable revenues that are available to a government, the size and growth of the tax base is crucial to the planning efforts of any government.

307. (d)
Suppose GST on car of Rs. 5 lacs is Rs. 1 lakh.

Now if I purchase a car then I will pay Rs. 1 lakh tax and if my income is Rs. 10 lacs then tax as a percentage of my income will be:

$$\frac{1 \text{ lakh} \times 100\%}{10 \text{ lakhs}} = 10\%$$

Suppose the same car a rich person purchases whose income is Rs 10 crores then tax as a percentage of his income will be:

$$\frac{1 \text{ lakh} \times 100\%}{10 \text{ crores}} = 0.1\%$$

So, a rich person pays less tax as a percentage of his income, hence GST is regressive. In similar way all indirect taxes are regressive in nature.

Income tax is progressive, as poor people need to pay less tax rate as compared to rich people.

308. (a)
Regressive tax means tax percentage decreases with increase in income.

Inflation is a regressive tax. The logic is same as indirect taxes are regressive in nature. For example, if because of inflation the price of a product increases by Rs. 10 then as a percentage of income, this Rs. 10 will be higher for poor people as compared to rich people.

309. (d)

310. (d)
Consider an example to understand GST in a better way (GST rate 18%):

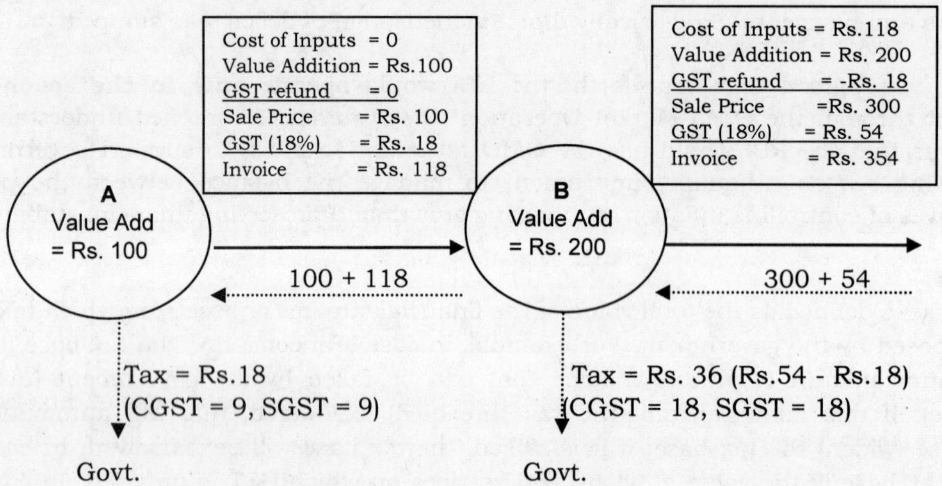

In the above example, A is doing value addition of Rs. 100 and selling the product to B in Rs. 118 and paying Rs. 18 GST to the government. B is doing value addition of Rs. 200 and is paying Rs. 36 GST to the government. *Since GST is a value added tax, so effectively every entity in the value chain shall pay to the government tax only on their value addition.* **Practically** B shows the invoice of Rs. 354 to the government and pays a tax of Rs. 54 to the government but when it produces the tax receipt obtained from A worth Rs. 18 to the government then government credits Rs. 18 to B. This is called **Input Tax Credit Mechanism** as the taxes paid by B on the purchase of inputs from A i.e., Rs. 18 is credited back to B by the government.

Since there is only one tax i.e., GST and credits of input taxes paid at each stage is available in the subsequent stage of value addition **across India** (whereas in case of VAT input credit was available only within the State), hence it will prevent the dreaded cascading effect of taxes. This is the basic feature and advantage of GST.

Important aspects regarding implementation of GST:

- If A belong to one State (say UP) and B and the consumer belong to another State (say Bihar) then all the State GST i.e., Rs. 9 and Rs. 18 (=Rs. 27) will be passed on to the State where the product is being consumed by the consumer i.e., Bihar and the State where A belongs i.e., UP will not get any SGST. This is why GST is also called **consumption based and destination-based tax** as all the SGST is passed on to the consuming State i.e., Bihar.

- If A and B belong to different states then rather than GST, IGST will be levied by the Centre on the transaction between A and B which is again equal to the sum of CGST and SGST and ultimately distributed among the Centre and the consuming State equally. Practically everything remains same, only the tax name changes to Integrated GST (IGST)

- If B, rather than selling the product to the consumer in India, exports the products then IGST will be imposed as IGST is levied on inter-State supplies. The GST paid in the entire value chain and the IGST paid at the end is credited back to the suppliers. So effectively there is no tax on exports and hence we say that exports are "zero rated" supplies. Supplies to SEZs are also zero rated.

- If a trader is importing a product into India then he will have to pay first customs duty and then IGST on the imported product as imports are also considered to be Inter-State supplies.

311. (a)
When Central government was planning to introduce GST, States were worried that after the implementation of GST, tax revenue of States may fall and they will not have the freedom under GST regime to impose extra taxes. So, Government of India calculated the **tax revenue growth** of State's indirect taxes from 2012-13 to 2013-14, 2013-14 to 2014-15 and 2014-15 to 2015-16 i.e. for three years and it found an average annual growth of 14%. So, Govt. of India promised States that if after implementation of GST, the States Indirect Revenue growth is less than 14% annually from 2015-16 (base year) onwards then Govt. of India (through GST council) will impose Cess on luxory and demerit goods and that money it will give to States as compensation for the next five years (1st July 2017 to 30th June 2022). For this purpose, Goods and Services Tax (Compensation to States) Act 2017 was enacted.

Govt of India levies and collects the GST compensation cess in Consolidated Fund of India and then it is transferred under "GST Compensation Fund" in Public Account of India (because it is not Govt. of India's money, and it belongs to States) and then it is transferred to States/UTs.

So, after GST kicked in there was some shortfall and States were compensated. But in Covid, shortfall increased too much and it was not possible to increase the Cess on demerit and luxury goods to compensate the huge shortfall. So, a tussle started in Nov. 2020 regarding how to handle that situation. So, ultimately it was decided that 'Centre' will borrow the (additional) shortfall amount (due to covid) and it will pass (give loan) to States on 'back-to-back' basis. And States will have to pay for the principal and interest amount in future. (When Centre borrows the cost of borrowing is less as compared to States, as Centre can't default and its credit rating is better).

But from where the States will repay this amount (principal and interest) in future. So, it has been decided that for the payment of this 'principal and interest' amount, the cess will be imposed even after 30th June 2022 till 31st March 2026.

States were demanding that in general the cess should be allowed to continue for the next 5 years (starting from 1st July 2022). But Centre said no. The cess will continue only for the repayment of principal and interest which was borrowed by Centre and passed to States on back-to-back basis because of the Covid crisis.

312. (c)
GST has led to reduction in number of taxes and now the same tax rate is applicable across all the country on all goods and services. This is called harmonization of taxes. On exports, Govt credits back the GST paid to suppliers and hence effectively there is no GST on exports in the entire supply chain. This is called exports are 'zero rated'.

313. (c)
Government of India levies 'National Calamity Contingent Duty' (NCCD) on top of Excise and Customs duty, which goes to 'Consolidated Fund of India' and then this amount is appropriated and is transferred to the National Disaster Response Fund (NDRF) established under Public Account of India.

314. (a)
Exports, imports and movement of goods from one state to another state are treated as interstate supply for the purpose of GST. On imports, first customs duty is imposed and then Integrated GST (IGST) is also imposed.

315. (d)
Electronic Way Bill (E-Way Bill) is a document issued by a carrier giving details and instructions relating to the shipment of a consignment of goods like name of consignor, consignee, point of origin of the consignment, its destination, and route. If the value of goods transported is more than worth Rs. 50,000/- then e-way bill should be generated. E-Way Bill is basically a compliance mechanism wherein by way of a digital interface the person causing the movement of goods uploads the relevant information prior to the commencement of movement of goods and generates e-way bill on the GST portal. E-way bill is a mechanism to ensure that goods being transported comply with the GST Law and is an effective tool to track movement of goods and check tax evasion. The E-Way bill under the GST regime replaces the Way bill (which was a physical document) which was required under the VAT regime for the movement of goods.

316. (d)
Composition levy is an alternative method of levy of tax designed for small businesses whose turnover is up to Rs. 1.5 crore (and above 40 lacs). The objective of composition scheme is to bring simplicity and to reduce the compliance cost for the small businesses. It is an **optional** scheme wherein the eligible person can pay tax at 1% flat rate, of his turnover, instead of paying tax at normal GST rate. Similarly, small service providers with turnover of Rs. 50 lakhs can opt for composition scheme and pay GST at 6%. In case of composition scheme, the businesses can't claim input tax credit.

317. (d)
Earlier National Anti-Profiteering Authority (NAA) was dealing with GST related complaints like reduction in GST rates not passed to consumers or input tax credit availed by a registered GST entity not resulting in commensurate reduction in price of product. But now from 1st Dec. 2022, it is being dealt by Competition Commission of India (CCI).

318. (c)

Supreme Court Judgement [May 2022]

- *The recommendations of the GST Council are recommendatory in nature and not binding on the Union and States.*
- *The Parliament and State Legislatures posses' simultaneous power to legislate on GST.*
- *The recommendations of the GST Council are binding on the Government for only secondary/subordinate legislations like changes in tax rates or framing of rules under CGST/SGST/IGST but not for primary legislations. For primary legislations (like amendment in acts.... CGST/SGST), the recommendations have only persuasive value.*

319. (d)

When government borrows more, then there may be a decrease in private investment due to reduction in the amount of savings available to the private sector. This is because if the government decides to borrow from the private citizens by issuing bonds to finance deficits, these bonds (which are risk free) compete with corporate bonds and other financial instruments for the available supply of funds. If people decide to buy government bonds, the funds remaining to be invested in private sector will be less. Thus, some private/corporate borrowers will get "**crowded out**" of the financial markets as the government claims an increasing share of the economy's total savings. This also increases the interest rate for the private sector.

320. (c)

Opposite of crowding out is "**crowding in**" where private investment increases as debt financed government spending increases. If the economy is in slowdown phase or the demand in the economy is less, then an increased government spending boosts the demand for goods which in turn increases the private sector demand for new output sources such as factories, equipment. Thus, the private sector crowds in to satisfy increasing consumer needs.

321. (c)

If the (nominal) growth rate in the economy is higher than the (nominal) interest rate at which government borrows money then the increased (tax) resources through higher growth helps in repayment of debt and leads to lowering of debt. Higher growth also results in increasing the GDP which results in debt sustainability due to lower debt/GDP ratio.

Rollover risk comes into picture when the debt is about to mature and there is no money to repay that debt. In that case the company/Govt. needs to borrow money to repay the debt.
When the maturity profile of the debt is short term then there is a rollover risk.

322. (c)

Inverted Duty Structure: Suppose there is a supply chain, A——>B——>Consumer. Now if the product which A sells to B has more GST rate say 18% and the product which B sells to the consumer has less GST rate say 5%, then we will say that the chain is having "inverted duty structure". Ideally the raw material should have less tax rate and final products should have more tax rate, but if it is not so then it creates an inverted duty structure.

So, suppose B purchased paper as raw material from A on which GST rate is 18% and then converted into book and sold the book to the consumer (on which GST rate is 5%). Now while purchasing the paper B paid more GST but it will collect less GST from the consumer. So, B will claim GST refund which he paid while purchasing the paper (18%)

from A. This is effectively reducing the GST collection of the Govt. on the entire value chain to just 5% while Govt. was expecting to collect 18% GST on paper.

323. (d)
The Aadhaar (Targeted Delivery of Financial and other Subsidies, Benefits and Services) Act 2016 is an Act to provide for, as a good governance, efficient, transparent, and targeted delivery of subsidies, benefits and services, the expenditure for which is incurred from the Consolidated Fund of India or Consolidated Fund of States (States were allowed to transfer benefit through an amendment done 2019), to individuals residing in India (for more than 182 days) through assigning of unique identity numbers.

As per section 7 of Aadhar Act:
"The Central Government or, as the case may be, the State Government may, for the purpose of establishing identity of an individual as a condition for receipt of a subsidy, benefit or service for which the expenditure is incurred from, or the receipt there from forms part of, the Consolidated Fund of India, require that such individual undergo authentication, or furnish proof of possession of Aadhaar number or in the case of an individual to whom no Aadhaar number has been assigned, such individual makes an application for enrolment:
Provided that if an Aadhaar number is not assigned to an individual, the individual shall be offered alternate and viable means of identification for delivery of the subsidy, benefit or service."

Pursuant to the Act, government made Aadhaar Regulations 2016:
"Any Central or State department or an agency which requires an individual to undergo authentication or furnish proof of possession of Aadhar number as a condition of receipt of any subsidy, benefit or service pursuant to Section 7 of the Aadhar Act, shall ensure enrolment of its beneficiaries who are yet to be enrolled, through appropriate measures."

324. (a)
Refinancing means replacing an existing loan with a new loan that pays off the debt of the old loan. So, when a government's debt (public debt) is due, to refinance it, the govt can issue/sell new bonds to raise money.

Alternative definition of refinance: A refinance occurs when an individual or business revises the interest rate, payment schedule, and terms of a previous credit agreement. Debtors will often choose to refinance a loan agreement when the interest rate environment has substantially changed, causing potential savings on debt payments from a new agreement. A refinance involves the re-evaluation of a person or business's credit terms and credit status.

325. (d)
Deficit financing is the budgetary situation where expenditure is higher than the receipts. The expenditure revenue gap is financed by either printing of currency or through borrowing. Nowadays most governments both in the developed and developing world are having deficit budgets and these deficits are often financed through borrowing. Hence the fiscal deficit is the ideal indicator of deficit financing. Deficit financing is very useful in developing countries like India because of revenue scarcity and development expenditure needs.

Since government spends more than receipts, it leads to increase in demand and may result in inflation also.

326. (c) Suppose the price of a product increased from Rs. 30 to Rs. 40 i.e., an increase of Rs. 10. For a poor person earning Rs. 1000, it is 1% tax, but for a rich person earning Rs. 1,00,000, it is just 0.01% tax. So, as a percentage of his income, poor person is paying tax 1% but rich person is paying tax only 0.01%. Hence its regressive (tax % is less for rich people and more for poor people)

327. (d)
Indian Company means a company registered in India under The Company's Act 2013.
A Foreign Company means a company registered outside India.
A Domestic Company means an Indian Company, or it can be a Foreign Company, but it should have made arrangements for the declaration and payment of Dividend in India under Income Tax Act 1961.
The 25.17% tax rate is applicable to **Domestic Companies** only.

Standard Tax Rate = 22%
Surcharge = 10% of 22% = 2.2%
Cess = 4% of (22% + 2.2%) = 0.968%
Effective Tax Rate = 22% + 2.2% + 0.968%= 25.168%= **25.17%**

This rate of 25.17% is applicable to those companies which do not opt for various exemptions provided by the government (and hence there is no MAT). Govt. gives lot of tax exemptions because of which even if the official tax rate was 30% plus cess and surcharge, effectively the tax rate was 25-26% after claiming various exemptions. But it was giving a wrong image to the outside world that India has such a high rate of 30%. So, govt. removed the exemptions and brought the official tax rate down to 25.17%.

328. (b)
Before 2016, only those companies who were registered in India (resident status) used to pay tax in India as per the Income Tax Act 1961. This is because those companies who used to earn from a business activity in India, they had to register their business/office here, then only they could do business in India.

But with the advent of Information Technology, it became possible that "Google" corporation is registered in US and has a resident status in US, but their source of Revenue is from India through digital ads on their websites and others. So, Income Tax Act 1961 was not applicable to the income generated to "Google" (as they did not have any registered office in India and their status was Non-resident in India) through sale of advertisements in India. So, to tax such income generated to such firms, in 2016 India brought "equalization levy" also called "Google tax".

There are various kinds of services under equalisation levy and the clauses under the Income Tax Act 1961 have been made effective with different dates. Three years back, the "sale of digital services (ads)" was notified. And now from 1st April 2020, "equalization levy" is applicable on e-commerce firms also.

So, if an e-commerce firm (say Amazon which is registered in US, and in India its status is non-resident) earns a revenue (profit is different from revenue) of say Rs. 100 from its online platform by sale to Indian people (Indian resident) then out of Rs. 100 they need to give Rs. 2 (2%) to Govt. of India as equalisation levy. On digital ads, the rate is 6% (no need to remember rates).

See, if Amazon would be registered in India, then they would automatically pay "Corporate Income Tax" on their profits as per the Income Tax Act 1961.

"Equalization levy" is a direct tax and is levied on revenue and not "Profit". And this is because for India it will be very difficult to calculate the profit of Amazon as it has lot of operations in US and other countries as well.

329. (d)

Global Minimum Corporate Tax:

- ✓ Big Technology companies shift their profits to such countries where the corporate tax rate is less. The companies do not shift the actual business, but mostly financial transactions are involved. As the competition among the countries is increasing, to attract more business/investment, countries also resort to reduction in corporate taxes. This has led to the loss of tax revenue to the home country government. That is why countries have agreed to implement a Global Minimum Corporate Tax.

- ✓ E.g.: Let us say there is a company XYZ in the US where corporate tax is 20%, and the company shifts its business revenues to another country, say Mauritius where corporate tax is 5%. Now as per GMCT (assuming it to be 15%) US Govt. will have the authority to collect tax from XYZ = 15% - 5%. This means that now if the companies shift their business revenues to tax havens then also they will have to pay a minimum tax.

- ✓ If there is another company which is based in Mauritius, then they can pay 5% tax. GMCT is applicable on companies which have shifted their business to tax havens where tax rate is less.

The Global Minimum Corporate Tax Framework that the countries have agreed has two-pillar package.

- ✓ Pillar 1 will ensure a fairer distribution of profits and taxing rights among countries with respect to the largest Multi-National Enterprises (MNEs), including digital companies. It would re-allocate some taxing rights over MNEs from their home countries to the markets where they have business activities and earn profits, regardless of whether firms have a physical presence there. (So, because of this pillar, Equalization Levy will not be required anymore)

- ✓ Pillar 2 seeks to put a floor on competition over corporate income tax, through the introduction of a global minimum corporate tax rate that countries can use to protect their tax bases. (This is related to GMCT of 15%)

Once the 'Global Minimum (Corporate) Tax' kicks in, India may have to abolish the 'Equalization Levy' which it imposes on multinational technology companies such as Google, Facebook etc.

330. (b)

Public Finance (Central) Division under Department of Expenditure, Ministry of Finance in consultation with the Budget Division, Department of Economic Affairs, Ministry of Finance decides the outlay for Centrally Sponsored Schemes (CSS) and Central Sector Schemes.

331. (d)

- The tax revenues (for ex UTGST) collected from the Union Territories without Legislature goes to the Consolidated Fund of India and is not part of the divisible pool.

- Cost of collection of taxes means the cost incurred by the Central Government in the collection of taxes is also excluded.
- Cess and Surcharge and National Calamity Contingent Duty are also not shared with states.

The following is an image from the XV Finance Commission Report:

2.9 The pool of tax resources of the Union Government to be shared with the States – the divisible pool – excludes the following items from gross tax revenue: cost of collection of taxes, cesses and surcharges including the GST compensation cess, tax revenue of the Union Territories and transfer from the National Calamity Contingency Duty (NCCD) to the National Disaster Response Fund (NDRF). Taking the difference between the projected gross tax revenue and the items to be excluded from the divisible pool, we have estimated that the divisible pool will be around 82.2 per cent of the gross tax revenue in both 2019-20 and 2020-21. The corresponding

332. (d)
For detailed understanding, refer Indian Economy by Vivek Singh

333. (b)
'Income distance' has been computed by taking the distance of each State from the State having highest per capita GSDP. In this case, Goa has the highest per capita GSDP followed by Sikkim. Since they are small and outlier States, the State with the third highest per capita GSDP – Haryana – has been taken as the benchmark to avoid distortions.

This ensures that states with less income get a higher share in order to allow them to provide services comparable to those provided by the richer ones.

334. (d)
As per the FRBM Act 2003, Central Government debt includes the following:

- Total outstanding liabilities of the Central Government on the security of Consolidated Fund of India, including external debt. (This is also called Public Debt)
- The outstanding liabilities in the Public Account of India
- Such financial liabilities of any corporate or other entity owned or controlled by the Central Government, which the government is to repay or service from the Annual Financial Statement. (This is also called off-budget liabilities)

335. (a)
Public Debt of **Govt. of India** includes Central Government's internal and external debt.
Treasury bills and dated securities are Govt. of India's debt because these are bonds issued by GoI.
ECB and FDI relates to companies and PSUs. And NRI deposits are in banks, and it is not a debt of Govt. of India.

So, only **1st** statement is correct.

336. (a)
As commercial banks are required to keep SLR (cash, gold, government securities) of 18%, they keep the maximum percent of government securities. Out of cash, gold and government securities, government securities give the best returns (interest), so they prefer this instrument.
Commercial banks had the highest share (36.6%) of public debt as on Dec 2022, followed by insurance companies and RBI.

337. (d)
India's external debt includes the debt of the Central Government, State Governments, companies (ECB), NRI deposits, debt investments in India like FPIs purchasing bonds etc. So, all the statements are true.

There is difference between "**India**" and "**Govt. of India**".

338. (d)
As on end Sept. 2024, India's external debt stood at $712 billion which was 19.4% of GDP including sovereign debt of 4% of GDP.

Commercial borrowings remained the largest component of external debt.

339. (d)
All are part of India's external debt, and all are denominated in rupees.

Non-Resident External (NRE) Accounts are NRI deposits in India in Rupees.

340. (a)
Currency wise, India's external debt includes:

- US Dollar denominated (53.4%)
- Indian Rupee denominated (31.2%)
- And then some is SDR (5%), Yen (6.6%) and Euro (3.0%).

The Rupee denominated debt is basically FPIs/FIIs purchasing Indian Govt. and companies' bonds in the Indian market and Masala bonds raised by Indian companies in abroad market and some NRI deposits in Indian rupees.

341. (d)
For the first statement which is true please check the trends.

As on 31st March 2025, the total debt of Govt. of India is expected to be around Rs. 181.7 lakh crore and out of this, public debt (internal + external) is Rs. 165.5 lakh crores which is around 91% of the total debt.

All figures in Rs. lakh crore	
Components of Central Govt. Debt	As on 31st March 2025
1) Internal Debt	159.3
2) External Debt	6.2
3) Public A/c Liabilities	16.2
4) Extra Budgetary Resources	Nil
Total	181.7

As per Economic Survey 2022-23, Public debt in India is primarily contracted at fixed interest rates, with floating internal debt constituting only 1.7 per cent of GDP. The debt portfolio is, therefore, insulated from interest rate volatility, which also provides stability to interest payments.

342. (d)
As per Fiscal Responsibility and Budget Management (FRBM) Act 2003, RBI has been prohibited from subscribing Central government securities in the primary market

(except in exceptional circumstances). This has been done so that government should raise money from the market at market interest rate rather than from RBI at cheaper rate.

Central government is not allowed to borrow from RBI to fund its fiscal deficit but if there is a temporary mismatch in government's cash disbursement and cash receipts then, government can take advance (called ways and means advance) from RBI.

Just for Info: FRBM Act 2003 has not been amended in the Budget 2024-25.

343. (a)
States need to take prior approval from Centre for borrowing (from anywhere) only if they have taken debt from Centre and there are pending dues OR there is any outstanding loan on States (from anywhere) with respect to which Central Govt. has given guarantee.

But as almost every state has taken loan from Centre and there are pending dues that is why in the budget document or economic survey it is written that Centre has allowed States to borrow up to this/that limit.

344. (c)
Central Govt. Debt is 59% of GDP as on 31st March 2024.
State Govt. Debt is 28% of GDP
General (Centre + State) Government Debt = 87%

Please refer the trends

345. (a)
Forex reserve includes foreign currency assets, gold, SDR and RTP

Foreign currency assets include US Dollars, Euro, Pound and Yen which are easily accepted worldwide, but mostly it is US dollars.

So, our Forex reserve has several currencies, but it is expressed in terms of US dollars.

So now, suppose we have in our forex reserve, one billion pound also. And the dollar pound rate is: $ 1 = Pound 0.8. So, one billion pound will be $ 1.25 billion in our forex reserve.

Now suppose pound appreciates to $1 = pound 0.75. So, now the same one billion pound will be $ 1.33 billion in our forex. And RBI will say that our forex increased (from $1.25 billion). But if dollar appreciates say, $ 1 = pound 1, then one billion pound will be just $ 1 billion in our forex and RBI will say that our forex reserve decreased (from $ 1.25 billion).

So, if other currencies in our forex appreciate, then our forex reserve increases.
And if other currencies depreciate (or dollar appreciates with respect to other currencies) then our forex reserve decreases.

346. (d)
First, we need to understand few things.
Whatever the Govt. and other entities borrow from abroad acts as a debt/liability for our country.
And if we purchase shares of a company abroad then these **shares are assets for us** (our country) and liability for the other country/company. And hence all the FDI

investments (it happens through shares) happening in India is a liability for the company in India and liability for the country also.

If my company has borrowed from abroad then the debt paper which the foreign bank will be holding, it is an asset for the foreign country/bank and liability for my company/country.

NIIP measures the difference between our nations (includes individual, companies, Govt.) stock of foreign assets and foreigner's stock of our nation's asset.

If the FDI inflow in our country is increasing then it is increasing liability on our company/country or in other way we can say that it is increasing the foreigner's stock of our nation's asset.

If our country has borrowed more from abroad or if FDI investment is more in our country then it is a burden for us and in future we will have to service this by paying interest/principal/dividend.

Forex reserves are the financial assets held by our residents (RBI) which are basically claims on non-residents. So, more foreign currency assets improve our NIIP position.

Our NIIP position as on end June 2024 as a percent of GDP was -11% ($362 billion).

347. (c)
If you have purchased shares/equity of a company then it is the liability of the company towards you.
India's external liabilities include all the investments made in India either in the form of debt or equity. So, it will include everything FDI, FPI (debt and equity both), External Commercial Borrowing, Govt. of India borrowings from abroad, NRI deposits in India.

348. (a)
In view of a higher multiplier effect of capital expenditure and to provide the much-needed resources to the state in the wake of 2nd wave of the COVID-19 pandemic, the scheme 'Special Assistance to States for Capital Expenditure for 2021-22' was launched in April, 2021.

For 2025-26, the allocation is Rs. 1.5 lakh crore to assist the states in catalysing overall investments in the economy. These fifty-year **interest free loans** are over and above the normal borrowings allowed to the states. These loans will form part of capital expenditure of Central Government.

349. (c)
In the budget 2019-20 government had proposed electronic or e-assessment scheme which was notified in September 2019 and to implement this scheme government launched "National e-assessment Centre" (based in Delhi) on 7th October 2019.

There are around 8 crore direct taxpayers. They pay tax and file return (tax document). Taxpayers use various ways to avoid paying taxes and showing their income way below the actual income. So, government has set certain parameters to pick for assessment/review of these cases. For example, those taxpayers whose income is quite high (say 30 lakhs) but tax payment is very less supposing only 2 lakhs or suppose in any particular savings account more than Rs. 10 lakhs got deposited in a financial year etc.

Now suppose there are 5 lakh such cases. Now out of these 5 lakh cases government may pick randomly 50,000 cases for review/assessment (as all cannot be reviewed because of resource constraint). So, government will send notice and you will have to give clarifications. And govt may scrutinise such cases in quite detail and if some wrong doings were found, you may be penalized.

Earlier (before e-assessment scheme was launched), these cases were selected by tax officials and there used to be face to face meetings between tax officials and taxpayers and where taxpayers were used to be harassed. But now all such cases will be randomly picked by computer and no face-to-face grilling would happen but only through electronic mode of communication. So, this will improve transparency and efficiency, and governance and thus improves the quality of assessment and monitoring.

Income Tax Act 1961 was amended to introduce this scheme which implies it is for direct taxes. Recently the Income Tax Act 1961 has been amended to introduce faceless appeal also.

350. (c)
Refer the Trends.
Horticulture production surpassed food grain (rice, wheat, pulses and coarse grains) production since 2012-13. In 2023-24, horticulture production was around 353 MT and food grain production was 332 MT.

351. (a)
Production of foodgrains for 2023-24 is as under:

Rice	138 MT
Wheat	113 MT
Coarse grains	57 MT
Pulses	24 MT
Total	**332 MT**

This has been the trend in previous years too.

352. (a)

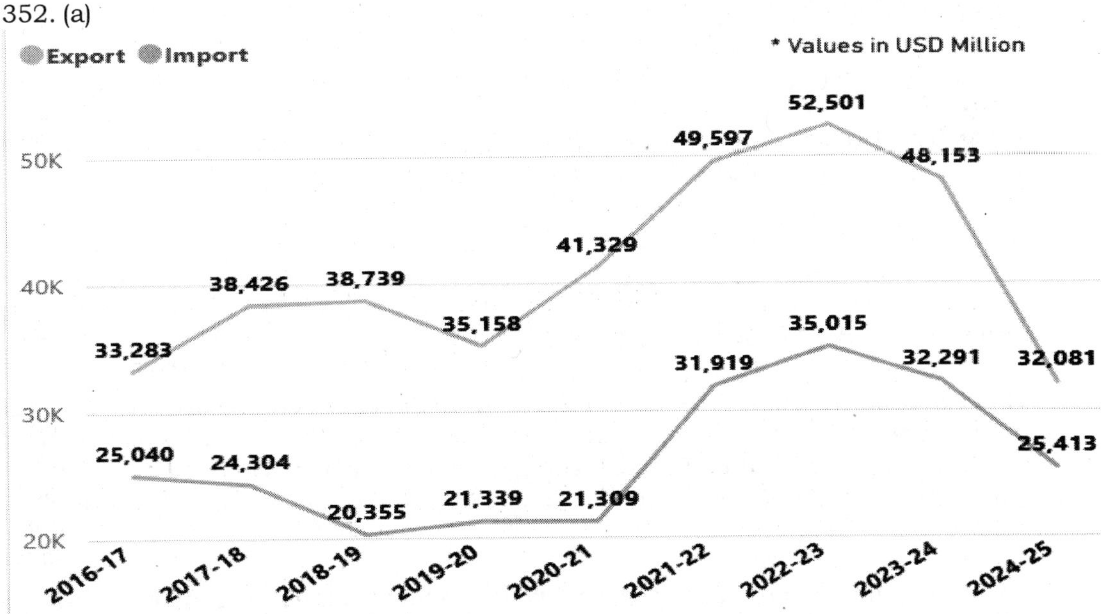

The 2024-25 data is for April to Nov period.

353. (d)

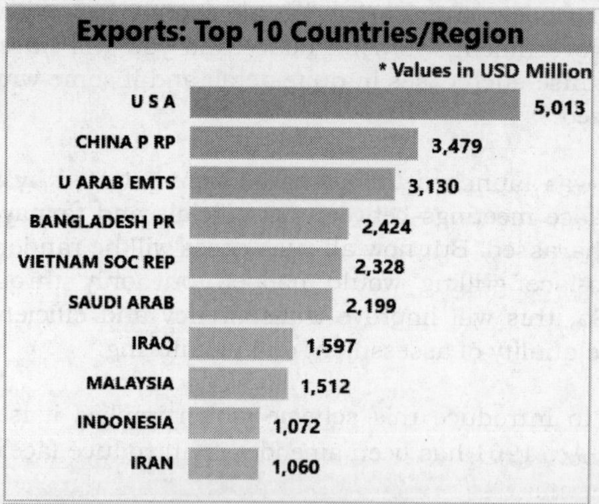

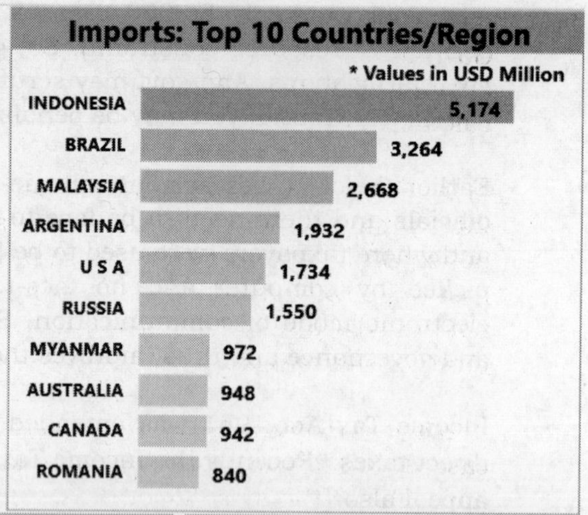

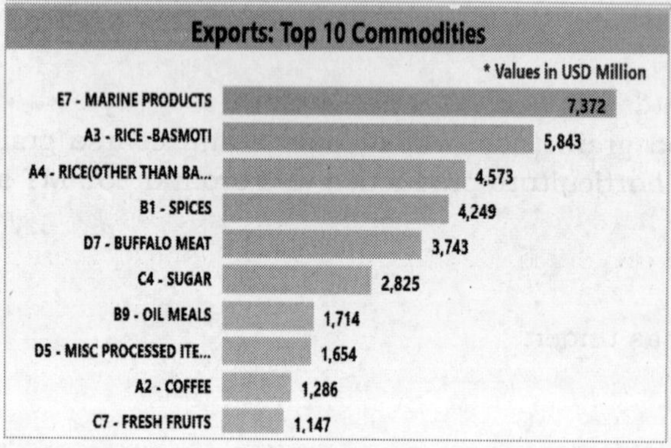

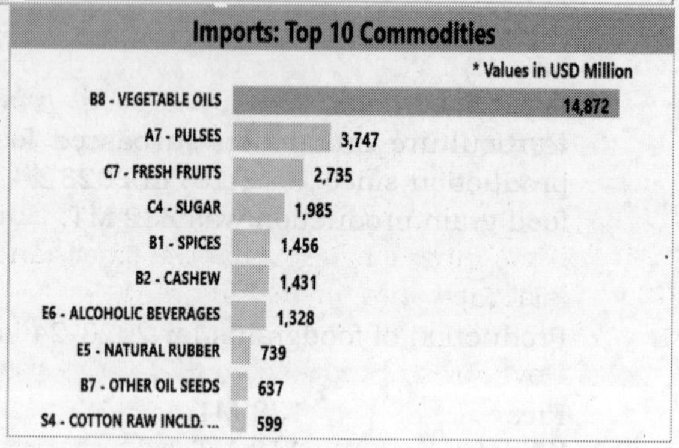

354. (c)
India is the largest producer of millets in the world. India produced 18 MT of Millets last year. Major millets producing states are Rajasthan, Maharashtra, Karnataka, Andhra Pradesh, Madhya Pradesh, etc.

Rajasthan contributes around 28 per cent of the total millet production in India.

India's Pearl Millet production accounts for **40.51** per cent followed by Sorghum 8.09 per cent in the world production of Millets.

355. (c)
National Jute Board as an apex body of the Ministry of Textiles, Govt. of India is responsible for promotion of jute and jute products in India and abroad. It is established under National Jute Board Act 2008.

The Government under the Jute Packaging Materials (Compulsory use in Packing Commodities) Act, 1987 specifies the commodities and the extent to which they are mandatorily packed in Jute Packaging Materials. For the jute year 2021-22, 100% of the foodgrains and 20% of sugar were required to be mandatorily packed in jute bags.

356. (d)
CACP takes into account all the factors while recommending MSP. It may be noted that cost of production is an important factor that goes as an input in determination of MSP, but it is certainly not the only factor that determines MSP.

357. (d)

Govt. announces MSP which is at least 50% over "**All-India weighted average Cost of Production**". (MSP for all over India is same). Now, the cost of production can be calculated in 3 ways.

1) **A2: (Average of actual paid out costs):** It will include expenses on purchase of inputs, electricity, fertilizers, etc. If someone has taken land/equipment on lease and he is paying rent that will also be included. And if a farmer has hired labour then that cost will also be included. But if someone is using family labour then since the farmer is not actually paying from his pocket, so it will not be included in cost. That is why the term says **actual paid out costs**.

2) **A2 + FL (Covers actual paid out cost + imputed value of family labour)**: In this case, if the farmer is using family labour then what we calculate is if the farmer will have to hire the same labour from the market then how much he will have to pay and then it is added in **A2**. This is called imputed value of family labour.

3) **C2 (More comprehensive and includes for the rentals and interest foregone on owned land and fixed capital assets on top of A2 + FL):** This means that if a person has his own land then of course he is not paying rentals and there will be no cost included in either "A2" or "A2+FL". But here in "C2" we will add the cost assuming that if the farmer has to take the same land on rent then what would be the cost, even if he is actually not paying any rent.

Govt. provides MSP of at least 50% above the "**A2 + FL**" cost.

So, from the above we can see that **1st** statement is true and **2nd** statement is not true. Post-harvest activities are not included in the cost hence **4th** statement is not true.

Let us understand the depreciation on agriculture equipment's.

If I am a farmer and producing wheat and I purchased a TRACTOR in year 2020-21, whose price is Rs. 6 lakhs. And suppose I use this tractor for 10 years and after that it is of no use. Now, I should not include the entire Rs. 6 lakhs amount to calculate my cost of production in the year 2020-21. Otherwise, my cost will look too high (this is not good accounting practise). And since I will also be using this equipment for the entire 10-year period, so, ideally I should say that my annual cost of equipment is Rs. 60,000 (6 lakhs/10 years). Basically, average distribution of the equipment cost. This Rs. 60,000 is called depreciation (cost).

Now, the cost of equipment is part of "A2". Because it is the cost incurred (actual paid out) by the farmer. But all the cost is not subtracted in one particular year rather its cost is uniformly distributed over the entire life of the equipment and that cost is called DEPRECIATION (cost).

So, if someone asks that A2 includes the cost on equipment purchase..........then the answer is YES
And if someone asks that A2 includes depreciation of equipment ....then the answer is again YES.

Because practically both means the same thing.

358. (d)
In e-NAM sale, traders from all over India could bid and whoever quotes highest price, the farmer can sell his produce to that trader (it may be across the state). Then farmer will receive the payment in his account and then only the trader can take the physical produce from the mandi. Transportation charge will be on traders account. *(Because of the transportation cost involved, e-NAM would not be able to ensure that the consumers get the agri-commodity at the same price across the country. E-NAM will help that the farmers get the same price across different mandis).*

Even if a farmer wants to sell his produce online through e-NAM, presently, he needs to take the produce in physical APMC mandi and then login to the online portal. Govt is working on the modalities so that the farmers will be able to sell their produce online sitting at their home through their mobile with their physical produce at home, but it may take some time.
But in April 2020, the following new features were enabled in e-NAM through which:

- Farmers stocking their produce in registered warehouses and having Electronic Negotiable Warehouse Receipts (e-NWR), will be able to trade on e-NAM without physically bringing their produce in the APMC mandis
- FPOs can trade their produce on e-NAM, from their collection centre without bringing the produce to APMC mandi.
- E-NAM platform has been made inter-operable with ReMS platform of Govt. of Karnataka
- E-NAM is getting integrated with other platforms to provide transportation and quality services

359. (c)
Food Safety and Standards Authority of India (FSSAI) regulates organic foods in India. FSSAI in Nov 2017, published regulations on organic food which regulates manufacture, sale, distribution and import of organic food in India. As a consequence, any food to be sold as 'organic' in India will have to be certified under **either** of the two prevailing systems. The two systems are National Programme for Organic Production (NPOP) and the Participatory Guarantee System for India (PGS-India).

Prior to application of these regulations, only food products meant for export have to be certified and that too under the NPOP system. The PGS-India system is meant for domestic market only. Drafted with an objective of addressing the problem of fraud and mis-labelling in food claimed as 'organic', *the organic regulations allow import of organic food into India without being re-certified in India if the organic standards of the exporting country have been recognised as equivalent to NPOP.*

Apart from operationalising these regulations, FSSAI has also developed a common logo for organic food from India called '**Jaivik Bharat**' which would integrate the logos of both—the NPOP system and PGS-India.

360. (d)
A Producer Organisation (PO) is a legal entity formed by primary producers, viz. farmers, milk producers, fishermen, weavers, rural artisans, craftsmen. A PO can be a producer company, a cooperative society or any other legal form which provides for sharing of profits/benefits among the members. Ownership control is always with the members/farmers and management is through the representatives of the members. The main aim of PO is to ensure better income for the producers through an organization of their own.

Farmers Producer Organization (FPO) is one type of PO where the members are farmers. Small Farmers' Agribusiness Consortium (SFAC) and NABARD is providing support for promotion of FPOs.

361. (d)

362. (c)
In integrated pest management, Economic Threshold Limit is the insect's population level or extent of crop damage at which the value of the damaged crops exceeds the cost of controlling the pests.
Central Institute of Cotton Research (CICR), Nagpur, in June 2019 said that the Pink Bollworm infestation on cotton crops has crossed the "Economic Threshold limit" in some parts of Maharashtra.

363. (b)
Government has officially deregulated the petroleum products market and the price of petrol/diesel is decided/changed by the market forces on a daily basis based on an average of the previous 15 days' global prices of the crude basket.

Central Govt. imposes Customs Duty on import of crude and Excise Duty on processing of crude and States impose VAT on sales of petrol/diesel. And these fuels are sold by Oil Marketing Companies (OMCs) like IOCL, BPCL, HPCL which are government controlled and few private players also like Reliance/Adani.

Although on paper/officially the prices of petrol/diesel are decontrolled but generally when the crude oil prices go too down then Government increases the Excise/VAT tax (during Covid, crude fell to around $20 per barrel but retail priced did not come down much) and when the crude price goes up then it decreases the tax. So, generally you will not see the impact of crude price change reflecting in retail petrol/diesel prices.

But if Govt. is changing the tax rate, to smoothen the prices then you cannot say that Govt. is controlling the prices, as Govt. has full freedom/right to change the tax. BUT sometimes, when crude prices increase steeply and Govt. is not willing to reduce taxes and it also does not want retail prices to go up (because of elections as as was the case in the last one month) then it indirectly/unofficially forces OMCs like IOCL/BPCL/HPCL (which are controlled by Govt.) to not increase the prices which leads to loss of profit and pricing freedom to the OMCs. And this loss of profit or just loss is called "under recovery" of OMCs. When OMCs do not increase prices then private retailers can also not increase the fuel prices because of competition.

There is 'under-recovery' in case of LPG also when Govt. does not want to increase the subsidy amount while the crude prices move up.

364. (c)
The subsidy amount is transferred into fertilizer's company account upon verification of sale to farmers through Aadhaar. The price of Urea is **regulated** by Central Government and it is Rs. 5.36/kg and the per kg **subsidy** by the government **varies** with the market fluctuations in the price of gas (input).

365. (c)
Nutrient Based Subsidy" is applicable for Phosphatic, Potassic (P&K) and Complex fertilizers only and not for Urea which is a Nitrogenous fertilizer. Govt. fixes the subsidy annually on per kg of nutrient present in the fertilizer. As the **subsidy** given by the Govt. is **fixed**, so the market price of the fertilizers varies with the change in international prices. So, market prices are **not regulated** by the government rather it is decontrolled.

366. (d)

Liquid Nano Urea has been developed and Patented by IFFCO. IFFCO Nano Urea is the only Nano fertilizer approved by the Government of India and included in the Fertilizer Control Order (FCO). To ensure adequate availability of right quality of fertilizers at right time and at right price to farmers, Fertilizer was declared as an Essential Commodity and Fertilizer Control Order (FCO) was promulgated under Section 3 of Essential Commodities Act,1955 to regulate, trade, price, quality and distribution of fertilizers in the country.

- Application of 1 bottle (half litre) of Nano Urea can effectively replace at least 1 bag of Urea (50 kg).
- Presently there is no subsidy on Nano Urea. And the subsidy on normal Urea is around Rs. 15 to Rs. 20 per kg. Presently Govt. regulates the price of normal urea at Rs. 5.36/kg
- When sprayed on leaves, Nano Urea easily enters through stomata and other openings and is assimilated by the plant cells. It is easily distributed through the phloem from source to sink inside the plant as per its need.
- Liquid Nano Urea contains 4% nitrogen by volume and comes in the form of nanoparticle.
- Its efficiency is 85%-90% as compared to 25% for conventional urea
- Unutilized nitrogen is stored in the plant vacuole and is slowly released for proper growth and development of the plant.
- Small size (20-50 nm) of Nano Urea increases its availability to crop by more than 80%.

367. (d)

- Under One Nation One Fertilizer (ONOF) scheme, companies are allowed to display their name, brand, logo and other relevant product information only on one-third space of their bags.
- On the remaining two-thirds space, the “Bharat” brand and Pradhanmantri Bharatiya Jan Urvarak Pariyojana logo will have to be shown.
- The single brand name for UREA, DAP, MOP and Complex Fertilizers (NPK) etc. would be BHARAT UREA, BHARAT DAP, BHARAT MOP and BHARAT NPK etc. respectively for all Fertiliser Companies, State Trading Entities (STEs) and Fertiliser Marketing Entities (FMEs).
- It will bring about uniformity in fertiliser brands across the country.
- The farmer will get rid of all kinds of confusion about the quality of the fertiliser and its availability.

BHARAT Logo:

368. (d)
Government has eliminated the Kerosene subsidy which has traditionally been used to meet the lighting and cooking needs, especially in rural areas. Government has decided to phase out use of kerosene for cooking and lighting in view of the increasing coverage of electricity for lighting needs and LPG as a clean cooking fuel. Post Saubhagya (Pradhan Mantri Sahaj bijli har ghar yojana) and Ujjwala Yojana the use of kerosene is steadily going down.

Out of 37 states/UTs, 11 states/UTs are kerosene free i.e no PDS Kerosene is allocated to these states/ UTs by Ministry of Petroleum and Natural Gas (MOP&NG) [As per Eco Survey 2021-22]. The balance states/UTs are allocated PDS Kerosene by MOP&NG on a quarterly basis. Kerosene is distributed through PDS and is sold at market price with **zero central subsidy**. The allocation varies from State to State depending on factors like LPG penetration, non-lifting of PDS Kerosene, voluntary requests for surrender/reduction. State Government of Tamil Nadu is still subsidizing kerosene through state subsidy.

Effective from 1st March, 2020, the retail selling price of PDS Kerosene is being maintained at NIL under-recovery level on pan India basis and is made available to the states at market prices.

369. (c)
MEP/MIP restrictions are imposed under "The Foreign Trade (Dev. & Reg.) Act 1992" and this Act can also be used to put quantitative restrictions on trade.

370. (c)
To facilitate the procurement of food grains (wheat and paddy), FCI and various state agencies in consultation with the State governments establish a large number of purchase centres at various mandis and key points. The procurement policy is **open ended**. That means, whatever (without any limit) wheat and paddy are offered by farmers, within the stipulated period & conforming to the specifications prescribed by Government of India, are purchased at Minimum Support Price (MSP) by the Government agencies including Food Corporation of India (FCI) for Central Pool.

Central Govt. procures wheat and rice/paddy in two ways:

- One way is "**Centralized Procurement System**" where either FCI procures, or it asks States to procure and hand over the stock to FCI and FCI pays for it. And then FCI stores and distributes under NFSA.
- The second is "**Decentralized Procurement System**" where Centre has asked States to procure, store and distribute under NFSA and other welfare schemes and Centre (FCI) pays to States.

371. (c)
A warehouse receipt is a document which proves ownership of a given commodity that is stored in a recognized location, like a warehouse or a godown. Negotiable warehouse receipts (NWRs) allow transfer of ownership of a commodity stored in a warehouse without having to deliver the physical commodity.

Government of India enacted the Warehousing (Development & Regulation) Act 2007 under which it has constituted the Warehousing Development and Regulatory Authority (WDRA) under Ministry of Consumer Affairs, Food and Public Distribution for the implementation of the provisions of the Act. The main objectives of the Act are to make provisions for the development and regulation of warehouses, negotiability of warehouse receipts and related matters. Any person commencing or carrying on the warehousing business and intending to issue Negotiable Warehouse Receipts (NWRs) has to get the warehouse registered with the Warehousing Development & Regulatory Authority (WDRA). The WDRA checks the warehouse on various parameters and then issues a booklet containing the NWRs. The warehouse then issues these receipts to customers (farmers and people who have stored their produce in the godowns). As these receipts are recognized by the government, banks can easily grant loans against them. The farmer gets an officially recognized receipt against which he can take loan from bank for further farming activities or alternatively sell his produce to a third person by endorsing the receipt, without even taking physical possession.

WDRA has notified 123 agricultural commodities and 26 horticulture commodities for issuing NWRs. In September 2017, Government launched the Electronic Negotiable Warehouse Receipts (e-NWRs). E-NWRs can be traded on e-NAM also.

372. (c)
APEDA was established in 1986 under the Agricultural and Processed Food Products Export Development Authority Act, 1985.

The APEDA under Ministry of Commerce & Industries, Government of India is implementing the National Programme for Organic Production (NPOP) which involves accreditation of Certification Bodies, standards for organic production, promotion of organic farming and marketing etc.

373. (d)
- Govt. is notifying ethanol price (administered price) for blending since 2014 and it is approved by Cabinet Committee on Economic Affairs.
- Since 2018, differential price of ethanol based on different feedstock (ex. C heavy molasses, B heavy molasses, sugarcane juice/sugar/sugar syrup etc.) utilized for ethanol production is being announced by the government.
- Higher ethanol price will help in early payment (of FRP) to cane farmers. Actually, the price of sugar in the market is not that much and hence sugar mills are delaying the payment of Fair and Remunerative Price (FRP) to the farmers. Increasing the

price of by products (ethanol) helps sugar mills to get more revenue and repay the farmers dues.

- The EBP programme will reduce import dependence for energy requirements and give boost to agriculture sector
- Government has advanced the target of 20% ethanol blending in petrol from earlier 2030 to 2025-26 (Ethanol Supply Year)

374. (c)

As per the National Food Security Act 2013, Central Government does procurement (at MSP), transportation from one State to another (from one FCI depot to another FCI depot), and storage and cost is borne by the Central Government through FCI. Then the Central Government (from the Central pool) gives the food grains to States at Rs. 3/kg rice, Rs. 2/kg wheat and Rs. 1/kg coarse grains.

Then the State does intra state movement/transportation of food grains and moves the food grains from FCI depots to Fair Price Shops (including its handling, dealers margin etc.) and the cost for all this is **shared** between the Central Government and the State Government as per the sharing pattern and norms for expenditure on this account as per rules framed under NFSA.

375. (d)

Central Govt. (FCI) procures the food grains at MSP then stores it and then transports it to different States and then gives the foodgrain staock to the States at a price called Central Issue Price (CIP) which is basically Rs. 3/kg for Rice, Rs. 2/kg of wheat and Rs. 1/kg of Coarse grains. So, States pay this price to FCI and get the food grains and then they arrange for within the State transportation and distribution and then this food grains is given to PDS beneficiaries at this same price of Rs. 3/kg rice, Rs. 2/kg of wheat and Rs. 1/kg of Coarse grains. CIP is fixed by Department of Food and Public Distribution, Ministry of Consumer Affairs, Food and Public Distribution.

Let us say MSP of Wheat is Rs. 20/kg and Transportation cost from one State (Punjab) to Assam is Rs. 9/kg and Storage cost is Rs. 10/kg per year then this is called
'Economic Cost' = Rs. 20/kg + Rs. 9/kg + Rs. 10/kg = Rs. 39/kg

And FCI gets Rs. 2/kg of wheat
So, all this burden is borne by the Central Govt. (FCI)

For within the State transportation and distribution, Centre and State share the cost.
So, most of the food subsidy burden is borne by Centre.

Now Pradhan Mantri Garib Kalyan Anna Yojana has been stopped on 31st Dec 2022 and NFSA 2013 is continuing from 1st Jan 2023. From 1st Jan 2023 Central Govt. has started providing foodgrains at zero prices (free of cost) [rather than than at Rs. 3/kg rice, Rs. 2/kg wheat and Rs. 1/kg coarse grains] to the 81 crore beneficiaries.

376. (c)

Under Price Stabilization Fund (PSF) Scheme, Govt. provides budgetary support (interest free loan) for working capital and other incidental expenses for procurement and distribution of agri-horticultural commodities. The intervention is expected to regulate price volatility through procurement by State/UT Government and Central agencies/Central PSUs/Cooperative organisations of selected produce, maintenance of buffer stocks and regulated release into the market.

Govt. has launched 'Bharat Atta' and 'Bharat Rice' 'Bharat Pulses' which is available at all physical and mobile outlets of Kendriya Bhandar, National Agricultural Cooperative Marketing Federation of India (NAFED) and National Cooperative Consumers' Federation of India (NCCF) and will be expanded to other retail outlets and e- commerce platforms.

FCI's Open Market Sale Scheme (OMSS) attempts to sale wheat and rice in the wholesale market, the ultimate aim is ofcourse to bring down the prices in the retail market but OMSS intervention is in wholesale market. But Bharat Brand Atta/Rice/Dal is being sold (intervention) in the retail market under PSF scheme.

377. (d)
National Mission on Agricultural Extension & Technology (NMAET), launched during the 12th plan period, consists of 4 Sub Missions:

1. Sub Mission on Agricultural Extension (SMAE):
2. Sub-Mission on Seed and Planting Material (SMSP):
3. Sub Mission on Agricultural Mechanization (SMAM):
4. Sub Mission on Plant Protection and Plant Quarantine (SMPP):

Sub-Mission on Agricultural Mechanization (SMAM) focuses on farm mechanization. The Sub-Mission is mainly to cater to the needs of the small and marginal farmers and to the regions where availability of farm power is low to offset the adverse economies of scale and high cost of individual ownership through institutional arrangements such as **Custom Hiring Centres**, mechanization of selected villages, subsidy for procurement of machines & equipment, etc.

Custom Hiring Centres (CHCs) are basically a unit comprising a set of costly, advance and bigger farm machinery, implements and equipment (used for tillage, sowing, planting, harvesting, reaping, threshing, plant protection, inter cultivation and residue management) meant for custom hiring by farmers on rental basis who could not afford to purchase the high-end agriculture machineries and equipment. Govt. through SMAM is providing funds/subsidy to Rural level entrepreneurs, SHGs etc. to set up CHCs.

378. (d)
The National Sample Survey (NSS), conducted by National Statistical Office (NSO) is a national socioeconomic survey conducted in **annual rounds** with a cycle of **rotating topics**. For example, the purpose of the 71st round of the National Sample Survey (NSS) conducted in 2014 was to develop indicators on health and education. The purpose of the 68th round (July 2011 - June 2012) of National Sample Survey was household consumption expenditure.

The Household Consumption Expenditure Survey (HCES), generally comes after every five years (quinquennial) during these annual rounds of NSS.

The NSS Household Consumer Expenditure Survey (HCES) generates estimates of household Monthly Per Capita Consumer Expenditure (MPCE) and the distribution of households and persons over the MPCE classes. It is designed to collect information regarding expenditure on consumption of goods and services (food and non-food) consumed by households. The results, after release, are also used for rebasing of the GDP and other macro-economic indicators.

Recently, the 79th Round of NSS started from 1st July 2022 which will be on HCES and will continue till 30th June 2023. This HCES will also collect data on items received free from the Government's welfare programmes.

379. (b)
Economic Census is conducted by NSO, MoSPI and has no fixed periodicity and presently the 7th Economic Census is being conducted (2019). Economic census gives insights on the economic activities being carried out across the country, their geographical distribution, the number and distribution of workers, types of ownership and sources of finance. It covers all structures across the country, whether residential or commercial including informal/unorganized units but excludes certain economic activities such as crop-production, plantation activities, illegal activities, public administration and defence, and activities of extra-territorial organisations.

Periodic Labour Force Survey is conducted by National Statistics Office (NSO) to produce **annual** statistics of employment and unemployment characteristics for both rural and urban areas, along with quarterly estimates for urban areas. Earlier it was conducted after five years.

Household consumption expenditure survey is conducted by National Statistical Office (NSO), after every five years and generates estimates of household Monthly Per Capita Consumer Expenditure.

Census (of the population) is conducted by Registrar General and Census Commissioner under Ministry of Home Affairs after every 10 years. The 2020 census will be digital.
Annual Survey of Industries (ASI) is the most important source of industrial statistics of the registered organized manufacturing sector (Factories registered under Factories Act 1948 i.e. those factories employing ten or more workers using power and those employing twenty or more workers without power) of the economy and extends to the entire country. It is conducted annually by MoSPI.

380. (d)
Employment and Unemployment Surveys (EUS) conducted by NSSO were the primary source of labour market data at National and State level in India. Regular EUS were conducted quinquennially (after every five years) since 1972. Considering the importance of availability of labour force data at more frequent intervals, the Ministry of Statistics and Programme Implementation constituted a committee on Periodic Labour Force Survey (PLFS). Now, National Statistics Office (NSO) is conducting PLFS to produce **annual** statistics of employment and unemployment characteristics for both rural and urban areas, along with quarterly estimates for urban areas. The first annual report based on the data collected in PLFS during July 2017- June 2018 was published in May 2019.

The PLFS is designed with two major objectives for measurement of employment and unemployment.

- The first was to measure the dynamics in labour force participation and employment status in the short time interval of three months for only the urban areas.
- The second was for both rural and urban areas, to measure the labour force estimates on key parameters on an annual basis such as labour force participation rate, worker population ratio etc.

BUT from March 2025 onwards, NSO is planning to release the rural and urban unemployment related data on monthly basis.

381. (b)
AQEES (All-India Quarterly Establishment-based Employment Survey) has been started by **Labour Bureau (Ministry of Labour and Employment)** to provide frequent (quarterly) updates about the employment and related variables of establishments, in **both organized** and **unorganized** segments of **nine** selected sectors. These sectors altogether account for majority of the total employment in the non-farm establishments. These nine selected sectors are Manufacturing, Construction, Trade, Transport, Education, Health, Accommodation and Restaurant, IT/ BPO and Financial Services. There are two components under AQEES:

- **Quarterly Employment Survey (QES):** This is in respect of establishments employing 10 or more workers (mostly constituting the **'organized'** segment)

- **Area Frame Establishment Survey (AFES):** This is to build up a frame in respect of establishments employing 9 or less workers (mostly the **'unorganized'** segment)

AQEES (QES and AFES) will provide employment scenario from demand side at regular intervals which was required for policy planning. **Economic Censuses** are establishment based (demand side) but have been conducted at irregular intervals and do not cover all types of establishments.

382. (c)

383. (b)

384. (b)
Structural unemployment occurs for a number of reasons - workers lacking the requisite job skills, change in government policy or change in technology, or they may live far from regions where jobs are available but are unable to move there or simply unwilling to work because existing wage levels are too low. So, while jobs are available, there is a serious mismatch between what companies need and what workers can offer. Structural unemployment exists when there are jobs available and people willing to do work, but there is not sufficient number of people qualified to fill the vacant jobs.

385. (c)
Frictional unemployment arises due to people moving between jobs, career or location or people entering and exiting the labour force or workers and employers having inconsistence or incomplete information. Actually, people first leave job and then they try to find a new job according to their choice and this process takes some time to apply for new jobs and for employers to make a selection and hence they remain unemployed for this transition period. That is why frictional unemployment is also called as transitional unemployment and it is always present in the economy.

386. (b)
These kind of job losses are because the economy is facing fundamental/structural changes and that is why it is a structural unemployment.

387. (b)
Disguised unemployment arises because more labourers work in the factory/land than are required. And hence productivity i.e., production per unit of labour will be less.
So, **2nd** statement is correct.

In such case if we add more capital then production may increase but if we add more labour then production will not increase.

So, marginal productivity of capital = $\frac{\text{change in production}}{\text{change in capital}}$ = will be positive

but marginal productivity of labour = $\frac{\text{change in production}}{\text{change in labour}}$ = will be zero

388. (d)
When the economy slows down or in recession (due to reduced demand) then production in the economy decreases and employers lay off workers which causes cyclical unemployment.

It is a case of reduced demand, so it generally leads to deflation.
So, **2nd** statement is true.

It can be tackled by increasing the demand in the economy. RBI can increase the demand through expansionary monetary policy i.e., reduction in repo rate. And government can also increase the demand in the economy by expansionary fiscal policy i.e., increase in government expenditure or reduction in taxes. Through both these policies, more money reaches to the people and demand in the economy increases.
So, **3rd** & **4th** statements are also true.

389. (d)
Underemployment is a situation in which a worker is employed, but not in the desired capacity, whether in terms of compensation, skill level, experience, education or their availability. While not technically unemployed, the underemployed are often competing for available jobs. Underemployment is a social problem that affects job growth, poverty level, economic growth and emotional health of underemployed workers.
The major problem that India is presently facing is of underemployment rather than unemployment.

390. (c)
Jobless growth implies that GDP/Output is increasing but job creation is not happening. This means that the same labour is now producing more output. And that implies that Productivity of Labour is increasing (which is defined as Output/Labour)

Employment Elasticity is a measure of the percentage change in employment associated with a 1 percentage point change in economic growth. If employment elasticity is decreasing means with per percentage increase in GDP, employment is not increasing which again implies that more output/GDP is getting produced with the same labour. So, productivity of labour is increasing.

391. (d)
"Demographic Dividend" is the dividend/benefit that a country derives because of the demographic change, and it is measured in terms of **additional Per Capita Income Growth**. *[Ref: Economic Survey 2016-17, Vol I, Page 33]*

392. (c)
Human capital considers education and health as a means to increase labour productivity. Human capital treats human beings as a means to an end; the end being the increase in productivity.

In the human development perspective, human beings are ends in themselves. Human development is based on the idea that education and health are integral to human well-being because only when people have the ability to read and write and the ability to lead a long and healthy life, they will be able to make other choices which they value.

393. (d)

In an endeavour to improve the information flow and bridge the demand-supply gap in the skilled workforce market, the Ministry of Skill Development and Entrepreneurship (MSDE), on 10th July 2020, launched 'Aatamanirbhar Skilled Employee Employer Mapping (ASEEM)' portal (https://smis.nsdcindia.org/) to help skilled people find sustainable livelihood opportunities. ASEEM is an AI-based digital platform to bridge demand-supply gap of skilled workforce across sectors. The portal will map details of workers based on regions and local industry demands.

ASEEM will be used as a match-making engine to map skilled workers with the jobs available. The portal and App will have provision for registration and data upload for workers across job roles, sectors and geographies. The skilled workforce can register their profiles on the app and can search for employment opportunities in their neighbourhood. Through ASEEM, employers, agencies and job aggregators looking for skilled workforce in specific sectors will also have the required details at their fingertips. It will also enable policymakers take more objective view of various sectors.

394. (d)

Important features of e-SHRAM portal

- Ministry of Labour & Employment has developed eSHRAM portal for creating a National Database of Unorganized Workers (NDUW), which will be seeded with Aadhaar.

- These unorganized workers are basically construction workers, migrant workers, street vendors, domestic workers, milkmen, truck drivers, Fishermen, Agriculture workers (nor farmers) and similar other workers.

- The workers will be issued an e-Shram card containing a 12-digit unique number [Universal Account Number (UAN)], which will be valid throughout the country and going ahead, will help in including them in social security schemes

- A worker can register on the portal using his/her Aadhaar card number and bank account details, apart from filling other necessary details like date of birth, home town, mobile number and social category. The registration of workers on the portal will be coordinated by the Labour Ministry, state governments, trade unions and Common Service Centres (CSCs) and it is totally free for workers.

- For the first time in the history of India, a system is being made to register 38 crore **unorganised** workers. It will not only register them but would also be helpful in delivering various social security schemes (being implemented by the Central and state governments) anywhere anytime.

- Central Govt. has sanctioned Rs 2.0 Lakh Accidental Insurance cover on death or permanent disability (and Rs 1.0 lakh on partial disability) to every registered unorganised worker on e-SHRAM Portal.

395. (a)

The Global Gender Gap Index benchmarks the evolution of gender-based gaps among four key dimensions (Economic Participation and Opportunity, Educational Attainment, Health and Survival, and Political Empowerment) and tracks progress towards closing these gaps over time.

The index is released annually by World Economic Forum. As per the 2022 report, India has ranked quite low at 135 out of 146 countries.

396. (c)

397. (a)
Life insurance provides protection against life risk. **General insurance** is a general term used for all the insurance plans that safeguard things **other than life**, such as your valuables against theft, natural disasters, accidents, etc.

In 1956 **Life Insurance sector** was nationalized through the Life Insurance Corporation Act 1956 and Life Insurance Corporation (LIC) came into existence in the same year which absorbed 154 Indian, 16 non-Indian insurers as also 75 provident societies—245 Indian and foreign insurers in all. The LIC had monopoly till the late 90s when the Insurance sector was reopened to the private sector.

398. (c)
General Insurance business was nationalized in 1972 with the passing of the General Insurance Business (Nationalisation) Act 1972 but became effective from 1st January, 1973.

Following the recommendations of the **Malhotra Committee** report, in 1999, the Insurance Regulatory and Development Authority (IRDA) was constituted as an statutory autonomous body to regulate and develop the insurance industry (life and general insurance both) in April 2000.

The key objectives of the IRDA include promotion of competition so as to enhance customer satisfaction through increased consumer choice and lower premiums, while ensuring the financial security of the insurance market. **The IRDA opened up the market in August 2000.**

399. (c)

400. (a)

- The Total Fertility Rate is defined as the total number of children that would be born to each woman if she were to live to the end of her child-bearing years.
- Replacement level fertility is the level of fertility at which a population exactly replaces itself from one generation to the next. Ideally it should be 2.0 but generally it is 2.1 all over the world as we cannot expect all the female children will survive till the child bearing ages.
- As per the latest National Family Health Survey (NFHS), India's TFR has declined to 2.0 which is below the replacement level fertility. But still there will be **positive population growth** in the next two decades due to,

  (a) Population momentum (it occurs because it is not only the number of children per woman that determine population growth, but also the number of women in reproductive age which is more for India.), and
  (b) Continued rise in life expectancy

401. (c)

402. (c)

The global MPI is developed by OPHI with the UN Development Programme (UNDP) for inclusion in UNDP's flagship Human Development Report in 2010. It has been published annually by OPHI and the UNDP.

The Global MPI (2023) report says that there are around 16.4% people in India under multidimensional poverty

As per NITI Aayog Report, which is based on National Family Health Survey (NFHS) 2019-21, the Multidimensional Poverty (MP) has come down.

	2015-16	**2019-21**
Overall MP	24.85%	14.96%
Rural MP	32.59%	19.28%
Urban MP	8.65%	5.27%

India's MPI is not exactly the same as Global MPI. For instance, India's MPI has 12 variables, while the Global MPI has 10. The two additional variables in India's MPI are maternal health and bank account.

403. (d)

Ministry of Rural Development, Govt. of India notifies Mahatma Gandhi NREGA wage rate every financial year for States/UTs in accordance with the provisions of Section 6(1) of the Mahatma Gandhi NREGA. To compensate the Mahatma Gandhi NREGA workers against inflation, the Ministry of Rural Development revises the wage rate every financial year based on change in Consumer Price Index for Agricultural Labour (CPI-AL). The wage rate is made applicable from 1st April of each financial year. However, each State/UT can provide wage over and above the wage rate notified by the Central Government.

Different States can have different MGNREGA wages depending on their minimum wages.

A Committee under the chairpersonship of former Additional Secretary, Ministry of Rural Development was constituted to study among other things the appropriate index for revising MGNREGA wages. The Committee recommended using **Consumer Price Index-Rural** instead of the existing CPI-AL for revising MGNREGA wages every year. The Committee also recommended use of annual average instead of the existing practice of using December month index only. The recommendations of the Committee are under consideration in consultation with the Ministry of Finance

404. (c)

405. (c)

406. (c)

407. (c)

Read the important provisions of the four labour codes from the Indian Economy book.

408. (c)

409. (a)

National Statistical Office (NSO) conducted the first "Time Use Survey" (TUS) in India during January – December 2019.

The primary objective of Time Use Survey (TUS) is to measure participation of men and women in paid and unpaid activities. TUS is an important source of information on the time spent in unpaid caregiving activities, volunteer work, unpaid domestic service producing activities of the household members. It also provides information on time spent on learning, socializing, leisure activities, self-care activities, etc., by the household members. The TUS survey captures how much time is spent by each member (above 6 years) of the household on different activities in twenty-four hours' time slot.

410. (c)
World Bank has introduced the concept of 'Learning Poverty', in coordination with the UNESCO Institute for Statistics. Learning poverty means being unable to read and understand a simple text by age 10.

World Bank believes that all children should be able to read by age 10. Reading is a gateway for learning as the child progresses through school—and conversely, an inability to read slams that gate shut. Beyond this, when children cannot read, it's usually a clear indication that school systems aren't well organized to help children learn in other areas such as math, science, and the humanities. And although it is possible to learn later in life with enough effort, children who don't read by age 10—or at the latest, by the end of primary school—usually fail to master reading later in their schooling career.

There is an urgent need for a society-wide commitment to invest more and better in people. If children cannot read, all education SDGs are at risk. Eliminating learning poverty is as important as eliminating extreme monetary poverty, stunting, or hunger.

411. (a)

412. (b)
Generic Drugs: A generic drug is a medication that has exactly the same active ingredient as the brand name drug and yields the same therapeutic effect. It is the same in dosing, safety, strength, quality, the way it works, the way it is taken, and the way it should be used. Generic drugs do not need to contain the same inactive ingredients as the brand name product, say colour or taste can be different.

However, a generic drug is generally marketed after the brand name drug's patent has expired, which may take up to 20 years. So, during the protection period of 20 years, the patent owner tries to recover its cost which it has spent on research and development and the drug is quite costly during this time as it is produced only by the patent owner under its brand name and others can't manufacture and sell. After the protection period is over, any company can sell the generic versions of the drug and there is fierce competitive which ultimately reduces the price of the drug.

But the (Indian Patent Act 1970) patent laws provide a remedy to the high price issue of branded drugs in the form of licenses to the generic manufacturers even during the protection period of 20 years. This remedy is available in the form of voluntary and compulsory licensing of the drug.

1. Voluntary License: Under this arrangement, a patent holder may give license (on its own) to the third party to manufacture, import and distribute generic versions of the pharmaceutical product and much more. The licensee of the patent will act as an agent of the company. The terms in a voluntary license may set price ranges, royalty from the distribution of the sales etc. [There is no legal provision given under Patent Act 1970 for voluntary license as this license access is done through mutual contractual agreement.]

2. Compulsory License: If the patent owner is exploiting its monopoly position and not manufacturing and supplying the branded drugs in the market or if the drug is not being made available at a reasonably affordable price in the market then government can give compulsory licenses in two ways:

- If a manufacturer himself approaches the government that he can produce the drug (generic versions) at a very cheap price, but only after the negotiation between patent owner and manufacturer has failed for voluntary license. [Section 84 of Patent Act 1970]
- In case of National emergency (pandemic like Covid-19) or extreme urgency, Govt can give notification that it will give compulsory licenses to any manufacturer who wants to manufacture generic versions of the drug with such terms and conditions. [Section 92 of Patent Act 1970]

But in both the cases of compulsory license mentioned above, the manufacturer (the compulsory license holder) will have to pay royalty to the patent owner as decided by the government.

413. (c)

Remission of Duties or Taxes on Exported Products (RoDTEP)

Before GST, any taxes on import (customs duties) of inputs required to manufacture exported products were refunded through Merchandise Export of India Scheme (MEIS) by giving Duty Credit Scrips to exporters. This means if I export goods worth Rs. 100 crores then govt used to give me a paper (Duty Credit Scrip) worth Rs. 2crore (some % of export value) which I could use to pay/adjust my customs duties on import of raw materials. There were certain exemptions on domestic taxes also in case of exports.

But WTO said that the MEIS scheme is not compliant with the WTO trade rules (no need to go into it) and in 2020 it was replaced by **Remission of Duties or Taxes on Exported Products (RoDTEP)**.

Under GST regime, Govt. exempts GST/IGST (taxes paid in case of domestic production and import of raw materials) in case of exports and this is called "exports are zero rated". Because first exporters pay GST/IGST (the standard rate) to the government and then they provide a proof to the government that it is a case of export (sold abroad) and the government reimburses the entire GST hence effectively no tax on exports.

However, certain products are outside GST and the taxes/duties/levies imposed on these products are still not refunded in case of exports even in the present GST regime. These taxes are VAT on fuel used in transportation, Mandi tax, taxes on electricity, petroleum products etc (which becomes embedded in the product price). Under the new RoDTEP scheme, t**hese taxes will be refunded to exporters in their ledger accounts with Customs.** The credits can be used to pay basic customs duty on imported goods/raw materials. The scheme is available for all kinds of exports from 1st Jan 2021.

414. (c)

"Certificate of Origin" (CO) is a document declaring in which country a commodity/ product was manufactured. The CO contains information regarding the product, its destination, and the country of export. It is required by many international treaty/ agreements for cross border trade. CO helps in determining whether certain goods are eligible for free import, or it will be subject to duties.

"**Rules of Origin**" are used in international trade which contains provisions to check the origin of a particular product. For example, if India puts high import duty on goods coming from China but less duty on goods coming from Japan, then it may be possible that a product coming from Japan has most of the value addition/ manufacturing being done in China first and then it moved to Japan where hardly 10% of the value addition was done and then it is being imported in India. This is done to avoid high import duty by China and is possible if India do not have any "Rules of Origin" to check the real source of a product.

So, generally countries specify "Rules of Origin", for example import duty will be applicable as per that country where more than 50% of value addition is done. Then such diversion is not possible. To give effect to the "Rules of Origin", a "Certificate of Origin" is issued.

For exports to countries with which India has Free Trade Agreements (FTA), exporters have to show a certificate that the consignment originated in India. Recently, government launched a common digital platform for the issuance of certificates of origin and now these certificates can be obtained online, and all the issuing authorities will be on the same panel.

415. (a)

416. (a)

417. (d)

418. (b)
BRICS bank has five members but any country which is a member of United Nations is eligible to become a member of BRICS bank.

419. (d)
When a country joins IMF, it is assigned QUOTA which is based on the country's GDP (50%), openness (30%), economic variability (fluctuations in current and capital account) (15%) and international reserves (5%). Quotas are denominated in Special Drawing Rights (SDRs), the IMF's unit of account. India's quota is 2.76% and China is 6.41% while US is 17.46%

A member's quota subscription determines the maximum amount of financial resources the member is obliged to provide to the IMF. A member must pay its subscription in full upon joining IMF: up to 25% must be paid in SDRs or widely accepted currencies (US dollar, Euro, Yen, Pound, Yuan) while the rest 75% is paid in the member's own currency. Quota is supposed to be reviewed after every five years.

The amount of financing a member can obtain from the IMF is also based on its quota. For example, a member can borrow up to 145 percent of its quota annually and 435 percent cumulatively. However, access may be higher in exceptional circumstances. IMF grants loans only to member countries.

Quotas is used to determine the following:

- Subscription (maximum amount of financial resources that a member is obligated to provide to the IMF),
- Voting power/rights in IMF decision making,
- Member country's share of SDR allocations
- Borrowing capacity (financial assistance a member may obtain from the IMF)

In August 2021, IMF did the largest allocation of 456.5 billion SDRs leading to total SDR allocation of around 650 billion. Out of the 456.5 billion SDRs allocated, India was allocated 12.57 billion SDRs (2.75% of allocation).

India's total SDRs holding increased to 13.66 billion SDRs from the previous 1.09 billion SDRs which is a drastic increase.

420. (d)
SDR allocation to a member country is dependent on QUOTA assigned to the member country which depends on the country's GDP and few other parameters.

The IMF allocates each member country SDRs which acts as a debt for the member country.

As the SDR allocation is a debt on Govt. of India given by IMF, so this transaction is recorded in capital account under balance of payment.

In the backdrop of covid-19 to increase global liquidity, in Aug 2021 IMF has created 456 billion more SDRs and allocated to the member countries due to which capital inflows under BoP increased.

SDRs are not present in hard currency and are thus called paper gold or notional currency and can be held only by Govt. entity.

421. (d)
Under WTO agreements, countries cannot normally discriminate between their trading partners. In general MFN means that every time a country lowers a trade barrier (import duties) or opens up a market or gives some country a special favour, it has to do so for the same goods or services from all its trading partners - whether rich or poor, weak or strong. According to the WTO, though the term MFN "suggests special treatment, it actually means non-discrimination." However, exemptions allowed to this rule include free trade pacts and special benefits to poor nations and national security clause.

422. (d)
The Agreement on TRIMs of the WTO is based on the belief that there is strong connection between trade and investment. **Restrictive measures on investment are trade distorting**. Several restrictive measures on investment are prohibiting trade and hence are not allowable like local content requirement, export obligation, domestic employment, technology transfer requirement etc.

423. (d)
Work Programme on e-Commerce under 'Doha Development Agenda':
Members have agreed to maintain the current practice of not imposing customs duties on electronic transmissions until the next Ministerial Conference. Some countries, particularly from the developed world, are demanding a 'permanent moratorium' on imposing duties on electronic transmissions. **India is against such a move** and has put preconditions for extension of such a moratorium. The 'moratorium', which was included in the 1998 'Declaration on Global E-commerce,' at the trade body's second Ministerial Conference, stated that "member countries will continue their current practice of not imposing customs duties on electronic transmission". **This moratorium — which is 'temporary' in nature — gets extended at every biennial MC.**

WTO has agreed to continue the work under the Work Programme on e-Commerce since based on the existing mandate. (India is against any attempt by developed countries to push for negotiations on setting global rules on e-commerce, as domestic rules on e-commerce are in a flux. And at present, India's e-commerce entities lack the strength to compete with giants in China and the developed countries).

424. (a)
Tariff rate quotas (TRQs) allow a pre-determined quantity of a product to be imported at lower import duty rates (in-quota duty) than the duty rate normally applicable to that product.

For example, in the India-UAE FTA, India has given UAE a TRQ of 200 tonnes on gold (imports) from UAE. This means that till 200 tonnes of gold import from UAE, India will impose a concessional tariff and after that, the tariff will be equal to what it is for the rest of the world.

425. (b)
When a government is giving subsidies to its exporters then the importing country can put extra tariff/duty (other than its normal customs/import duty) on those products entering into their market. This extra duty is called "**Countervailing Duty**". It is country specific and is also called **anti-subsidy duty**.

426. (d)
Safeguard Duty are applied when there is a surge in imports of a particular product irrespective of a particular country/ies. Safeguard duty is a WTO compliant temporary measure that is brought in for a certain time frame to avert any damage to a country's domestic industry from cheap imports.

In 2018, India imposed safeguard duty for two years on solar modules to stimulate domestic production.

427. (d)
Trademark is typically a name, word, phrase, logo, symbol, design, image or a combination of these elements. A trademark is a sign that you can use to distinguish your business' goods or services from those of other traders. Through a registered trade mark, you can protect your brand (or "mark") by restricting other people from using its name or logo. Once acquired, a trade mark can last indefinitely. Trademark owner can be an individual, business organization or any legal entity. In India, trademarks are protected through "The Trade Marks Act 1999".

Basically, trademarks are treated as an asset. Therefore, it is transferable from one person to another. An Assignment of a trademark is a permanent process, whereas licensing is treated as a temporary process.

428. (d)
Broadly speaking, any confidential business information which provides an enterprise a competitive edge may be considered a trade secret. The subject matter of trade secrets is usually defined in broad terms and includes sales methods, distribution methods, consumer profiles, advertising strategies, lists of suppliers and clients, and manufacturing processes.
Contrary to patents, trade secrets are protected without registration, that is, trade secrets are protected without any procedural formalities. Consequently, a trade secret can be protected for an unlimited period of time unless it is discovered or legally

acquired by others and disclosed to the public. As per the TRIPS, the following are prerequisites for a trade secret.

- The information must be secret (i.e., it is not generally known among, or readily accessible to, circles that normally deal with the kind of information in question).
- It must have commercial value because it is a secret
- It must have been subject to reasonable steps by the rightful holder of the information to keep it secret (e.g., through confidentiality agreements)

429. (a)
The IMF has taken steps to enhance member country transparency and openness, including setting voluntary standards for dissemination of economic and financial data. The Special Data Dissemination Standard (SDDS) was established in 1996 to guide members that have, or might seek, access to international capital markets in providing their economic and financial data to the public. Data dissemination standards enhance the availability of timely and comprehensive statistics, which contributes to sound macroeconomic policies and the efficient functioning of financial markets. IMF releases "Annual Observance Report (of SDDS)" for each member country annually.

430. (a)
Social mobility is the movement of individuals, families, households, or other categories of people within or between social strata in a society. It is a change in social status relative to one's current social location within a given society. The Social Mobility Index is released by World Economic Forum. India ranked 76th place while Denmark has topped the list of 82 countries in 2020. The five key dimensions used for measuring the countries on this index are:

- Health
- Education (access, quality and equity)
- Technology
- Work (opportunities, wages, conditions)
- Protections and institutions (social protection and inclusive institutions)

431. (b)
As per Ministry of Commerce & Industry (DPIIT), an entity shall be considered as a Startup:

- *Up to a period of ten years from the date of its incorporation*
- *Turnover of the entity since its incorporation has not exceeded Rs. 100 crores in any FY*
- *The entity is working towards innovation, development or improvement of products or process or services, or if it is a scalable business model with a high potential of employment generation and wealth creation*

In August 2020, RBI included 'Startups' under priority sector lending.

432. (c)
Factoring is a transaction where an entity (like MSMEs) sells its receivables (the dues from the corporates/buyer) to a third party (a 'factor' like a bank or NBFC) for immediate funds. So, the bank/NBFCs will provide immediate funds to MSMEs and they purchase the receivables of MSMEs. And then the banks/NBFCs will try to collect/recover the money from the corporates/buyer through these receivables/dues.

Note that credit facilities provided by a bank against the security/collateral of receivables are not considered as factoring business. **In case of 'factoring' the receivables (the dues) are sold rather than kept as collateral to raise finance.**

Factoring is done on an online **TReDS** (Trade Receivables Discounting System) platform initiated by RBI. If the buyer (of goods and services from MSMEs) defaults in payment to the bank/NBFCs then banks/NBFCs do not have any recourse to the MSMEs.

Earlier Factoring could be done by the banks or NBFCs that have a factoring licence (those who do over 50 per cent of business through factoring). Now, as per the "Factoring Regulation (Amendment) Bill, 2021" all NBFCs have been allowed to do factoring business, irrespective of proportion of income from factoring. This, therefore, will bring liquidity into factoring business.

NBFCs' lending to MSMEs is typically against the balance sheet strength of these smaller companies, leading to interest rates which are very high. But in the case of factoring, the NBFC is taking a risk on the customer of the MSME who is generally larger corporate, leading to lower (nearly halving) interest costs.

433. (b)
In Indian Context, the trade is called Merchanting Trade when:

The supplier of goods will be resident in one foreign country
The buyer of goods will be resident in another foreign country
And The merchant or the intermediary will be resident in India

For a trade to be classified as merchanting trade, goods acquired shall not enter the Domestic Tariff Area (India).

434. (a)

Important features of National Monetization Pipeline (NMP)

- NMP estimates aggregate monetization potential of Rs 6.0 lakh crores through **core assets** of the **Central Government and Central Public Sector Enterprises**, over a four-year period, from FY 2021-22 to FY 2024-25.
- Considering that infrastructure creation is inextricably linked to monetization, the period for NMP has been decided so as to be co-terminus (end together) with balance period under National Infrastructure Pipeline (NIP).
- The various sectors under NMP are roads, ports, airports, railways, warehousing, gas & product pipeline, power generation and transmission, mining, telecom, stadium, hospitality, and housing
- The pipeline has been developed by **NITI Aayog**, in consultation with infrastructure line ministries
- The strategic objective of the program is to unlock the value of investments in brownfield public sector assets by tapping institutional and long-term patient capital, which can thereafter be leveraged for further public investments.
- Modality of such unlocking is envisaged to be by way of structured contractual agreements (PPP agreements/concessions) **as against complete privatization** and through Infrastructure Investment Trusts (InvIT). Assets would be handed back to the Govt. at the end of the contract/transaction period.

- NMP consists of brownfield assets, which have been de-risked from execution risks.
- Monetization through disinvestment and monetization of non-core assets have not been included in the NMP
- Asset Monetization needs to be viewed not just as a funding mechanism, but as an overall paradigm shift in infrastructure operations, augmentation and maintenance considering private sector's resource efficiencies and its ability to dynamically adapt to the evolving global and economic reality.
- The end objective of this initiative is to enable 'Infrastructure Creation through Monetization' wherein the public and private sector collaborate, each excelling in their core areas of competence, so as to deliver socio-economic growth and quality of life to the country's citizens.

435. (c)
A private Label/brand is a good that is manufactured for and sold under the name of a specific retailer. A private label product is developed for a specific seller and sold exclusively under that seller's brand. For example, a hotel chain (say Taj), rather than purchasing LOREAL shampoo for its customers, it can ask a third party manufacturer to manufacture shampoo under the brand name of that HOTEL (Taj Shampoo).

Private label (brands) has several advantages like it allows control over marketing, allowing the retailer to tailor a product to local needs and tastes. There's also control over production and image that private branding allows. These brands can create a sense of loyalty as well and are generally more profitable than name-brand goods.

A white label product is developed by a manufacturer and distributed to multiple sellers. Each seller can then apply its name and packaging and resell the product under the seller's brand.

These terms were highlighted during the Corona crisis. When ITC was not able to supply its 'Aashirwad' Atta brand because of Corona crisis then the retailers/sellers asked atta chakkis(flour mills) to supply atta/flour to them which then retailers/sellers packaged under their own brand and sold it to the people (white label).

436. (c)
Let me explain the Production Linked Incentive Scheme (PLIS) with an example.

If a company's sales of goods manufactured in India increases from a particular year (considered as base year) then the Company will get an incentive of 4% to 6% on incremental/additional sales. For example, earlier a company was selling goods worth Rs. 1 lakh in a year and now its sales increased to Rs. 1.2 lakh. Then the company will get incentive of 4% of Rs. 20,000 = Rs. 800. There is also condition of additional investment in plant and machinery under this scheme.

Currently this scheme is available for around 13 sectors, and it is a quite successful scheme.

437. (a)
The scope of the Index of Industrial Production (IIP) as recommended by the United Nations Statistical Office (UNSO) includes mining, manufacturing, construction, electricity, gas and water supply. But due to constraints of data availability, the IIP compiled in India has excluded construction, gas and water supply sectors. *(And Forestry is not part of industrial activity)*

Base Year 2011-12	**Index of Industrial Production (IIP)**		
	Mining	Manufacturing	Electricity
Weights	14.373	77.633	7.994

438. (b)
Industrial Outlook Survey is conducted quarterly by RBI. The survey encapsulates qualitative assessment of the business climate by Indian manufacturing companies and their expectations.

439. (b)
SEBI has introduced the 'Graded Surveillance Measure' to keep a tab on the securities/shares of those companies which witness an abnormal price rise that is not commensurate with the financial health and fundamentals of the company. The underlying principle behind the graded surveillance framework is to alert and protect investors trading in a security, which is seeing abnormal price movements. SEBI may put shares of companies under the measure for suspected price rigging.

The main objective of these measures are to -

- Alert and advise investors to be extra cautious while dealing in these securities and
- Advise market participants to carry out necessary due diligence while dealing in these securities

It became effective from March 2017

440. (c)
The eight core industries comprise 40.27% of the weight of items included in IIP.

In eight core industries, refinery products have the highest weight (28.04%) and fertilizers (2.63%) have the lowest weight.

Core industries index is released by Department for Promotion of Industry and Internal Trade (DPIIT) under ministry of Commerce.

441. (d)

FDI is prohibited in:

a) **Lottery Business including Government/private lottery, online lotteries, etc.**

b) **Gambling and Betting including casinos etc.**

c) **Chit funds**

d) **Nidhi company**

e) **Trading in Transferable Development Rights (TDRs)**

f) **Real Estate Business or Construction of Farm Houses**
'Real estate business' shall not include development of townships, construction of residential /commercial premises, roads or bridges and Real Estate Investment Trusts (REITs) registered and regulated under the SEBI (REITs) Regulations 2014.

g) **Manufacturing of cigars, cheroots, cigarillos and cigarettes, of tobacco or of tobacco substitutes**

h) **Activities/sectors not open to private sector investment e.g.(I) Atomic Energy and (II) Railway operations (other than permitted activities mentioned in para 5.2).**

Foreign technology collaboration in any form including licensing for franchise, trademark, brand name, management contract is also prohibited for Lottery Business, Gambling and Betting activities.

442. (a)
Open access is the non-discriminatory use of transmission and distribution infrastructure of the licensees by consumers for procuring electricity from the source of their choice.

443. (d)
Unified Pension Scheme (UPS) offers assured pension - which is 50 per cent of the average basic pay drawn over the last 12 months prior to superannuation for a minimum qualifying service of 25 years. While in case of NPS, the contribution by employer/govt. (14%) and employee (10%) is invested in market (equity and bonds) and pension is created as per the value of the fund at retirement. In case of UPS, employer/govt. (18.5%) and employee (10%) will have to contribute but they can get an assured pension. In Old Pension Scheme (OPS), there was no contribution from employer/govt. and employee.

Under the OPS, monthly pension is taxable as per the income tax slab rate.

Under the NPS, whatever is the fund value at the time of maturity (60 years or above), you can withdraw 60% one time (lump sum) and for rest 40% you need to purchase annuity. The 60% lump sum amount is exempt from tax.

The 40% fund (is also exempt from tax) but it should be invested in purchase of annuity (annual receipts of payments). This annuity income which you get yearly is taxable as per the income tax slab rate.

444. (b)
The Securities and Exchange Board of India was established on April 12, 1992 in accordance with the provisions of the Securities and Exchange Board of India Act, 1992.

As per the section 4 of IRDAI Act1999, Insurance Regulatory and Development Authority of India (IRDAI) was constituted (in 2000) by an act of parliament, Insurance Regulatory and Development Authority Act 1999.

The Pension Fund Regulatory Development Authority (PFRDA) Act was passed in September, 2013 and the same was notified on 1st February, 2014. PFRDA is regulating National Pension System, subscribed by employees of Govt. of India, State Governments and by employees of private institutions, self-employed professionals and unorganized sectors.

445. (c)
When a company is first time getting listed on the stock exchange then it should release 10% of the shares for trading i.e. Public Shareholding. But within 3 years of listing, the public shareholding should be increased to 25%. Govt. had planned to increase the public shareholding in the listed companies to 35% but was not done. So present rule is Public shareholding should be at least 25% in listed companies.

446. (a)
National Stock Exchange of India received the final approval from the markets regulator Securities and Exchange Board of India (SEBI) to set up a Social Stock Exchange (SSE). The SSE would function as a separate segment within the existing stock exchange and help social enterprises raise funds from the public through its mechanism. It would serve as a medium for enterprises to seek finance for their social initiatives, acquire visibility and provide increased transparency about fund mobilisation and utilisation.

Any non-profit organisation (**NPO**) or for-profit social enterprise (**FPSEs**) that establishes the **social intent** would be recognised as a social enterprise (**SE**) which will make it eligible to be registered or listed on the social stock exchange. Any corporate foundations, political or religious organizations or activities, professional or trade associations, infrastructure and housing companies (except affordable housing) would not be identified as social enterprise.

447. (d)

State-wise Value of Merchandise Exports: Top States in India (FY21 to FY24)				
State	FY 2024	FY 2023	FY 2022	FY 2021
Gujarat	US$134.4 billion	US$146.5 billion	US$124.4 billion	US$60.6 billion
Maharashtra	US$67.2 billion	US$72.5 billion	US$72.9 billion	US$58.4 billion
Tamil Nadu	US$43.6 billion	US$40.76 billion	US$35.0 billion	US$26.2 billion
Karnataka	US$26.6 billion	US$27.9 billion	US$26.1 billion	US$15.1 billion
Uttar Pradesh	US$20.6 billion	US$21.7 billion	US$20.9 billion	US$16.4 billion
Andhra Pradesh	US$19.8 billion	US$19.8 billion	US$19.2 billion	US$16.8 billion
Haryana	US$17.7 billion	US$15.9 billion	US$15.5 billion	US$11.6 billion
Telangana	US$14.0 billion	US$11.4 billion	US$11.0 billion	US$8.7 billion
Odisha	US$11.9 billion	US$11.2 billion	US$16.9 billion	US$10.2 billion
West Bengal	US$11.7 billion	US$12.8 billion	US$13.8 billion	US$9.06 billion

448. (c)

Once a Renewable Power Generator/provider has fed the energy generated into the electricity grid, he receives REC (which can then be sold on the open market as an energy commodity). RECs are a market-based instrument which certifies that the bearer (holder of REC) owns one megawatt-hour (MWh) of electricity generated from a renewable energy resource. RECs are proof that energy has been generated from renewable sources such as solar or wind power etc. When someone purchases RECs, renewable energy is generated on his/her behalf. RECs can go by many names, including Green tag, Tradable Renewable Certificates (TRCs), Renewable Electricity Certificates, or Renewable Energy Credits.

To provide a fillip to the ambitious renewable energy targets of 1,75,000 MW by 2022, obligations have been imposed on entities like power distribution companies, captive power plants (who establish power plants for their own consumption) and other large electricity consumers to purchase energy from renewable sources. These obligations called Renewable Purchase Obligations (RPOs) provide for either purchase of renewable energy certificates (RECs) from Indian Energy Exchange (IEX)/ Power Exchange of India (PXIL) OR purchase of renewable power from the National Load Dispatch Centre (NLDC) by obligated entities . These RPOs are the backbone of India's renewable energy programme. Ministry of Power in consultation with ministry of New and Renewable Energy sets the target of RPOs for States and UTs.

449. (b)

It is a multilateral international initiative to enable instant cross-border retail payments by interlinking domestic Fast Payments Systems (FPSs). India's Unified Payments Interface (UPI) and FPSs of Malaysia, the Philippines, Singapore and Thailand will be interlinked through Nexus. Going ahead, the platform can be extended to more countries.

450. (c)

Dabba trading is an illegal and unregulated form of trading in securities. In dabba trading, traders place deals in securities without the trades actually being executed on any official SEBI recognized stock exchange. These trades are settled internally by the dabba operator and are outside the purview of stock exchanges and regulatory bodies.

Since trades are not executed on official stock exchange platforms, investors can not avail grievances redressal mechanism of stock exchanges.

Dabba trade offers no benefits of safe and guaranteed trades done on Stock Exchanges. Therefore, investor should exercise caution and should not indulge any kind of dabba trading.

TRENDS

1.The following chart represents gross fixed investment (as % of GDP) of India in last ten years.

2015-16	2016-17	2017-18	2018-19	2019-20	2020-21	2021-22	2022-23	2023-24	2024-25
28.70%	28.20%	28.20%	29.50%	28.50%	27.30%	29.60%	30.70%	30.80%	30.10%

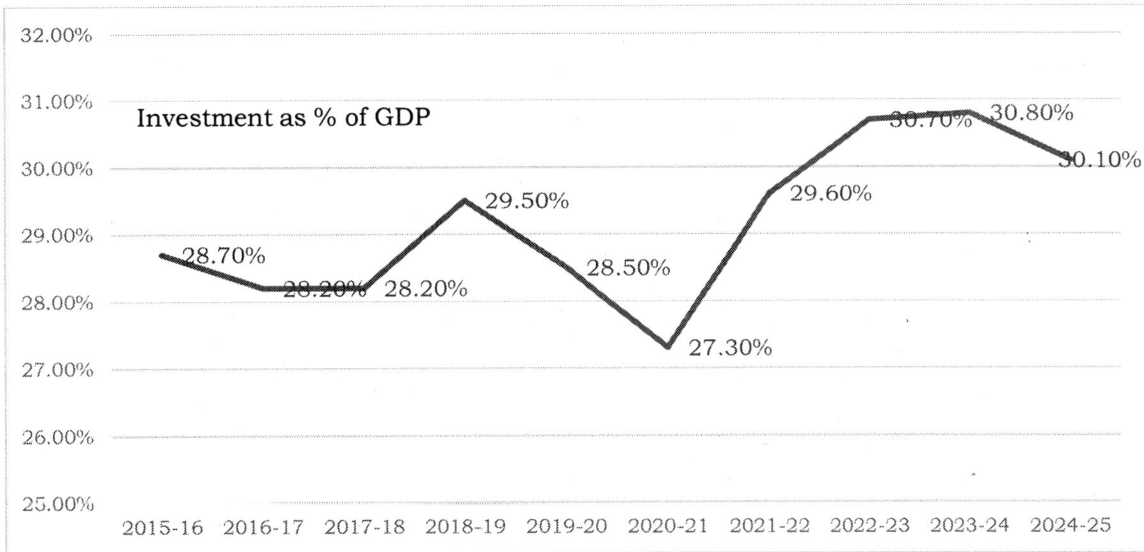

2. The following chart represents Real GDP growth rate of India in the last few years.

2015-16	2016-17	2017-18	2018-19	2019-20	2020-21	2021-22	2022-23	2023-24	2024-25
8.00%	8.30%	6.80%	6.50%	3.90%	-5.80%	9.10%	7.00%	8.20%	6.40%

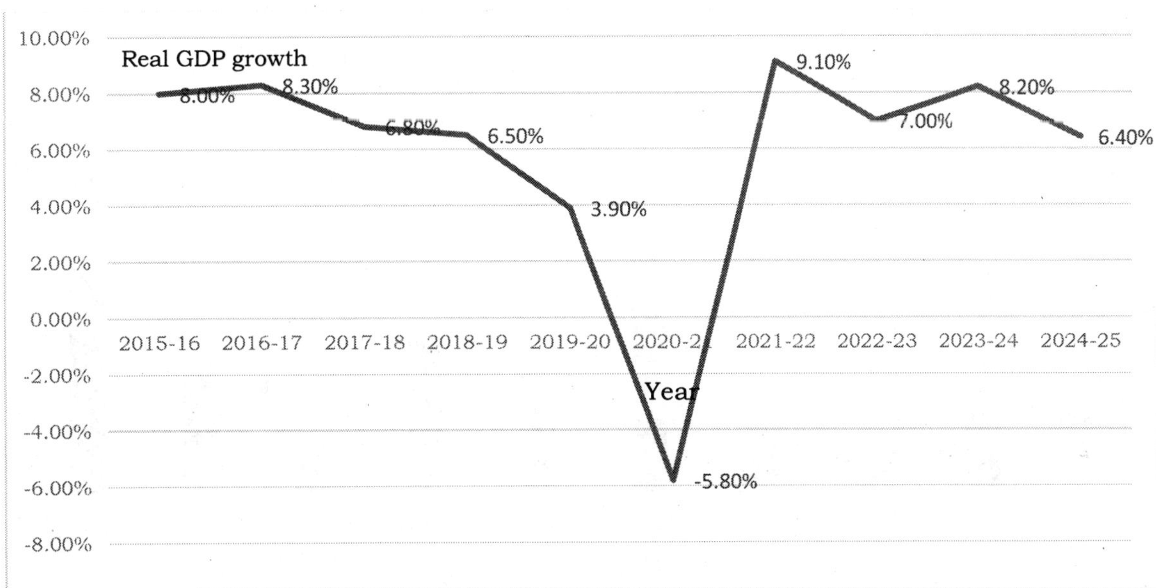

3. Following chart represents agriculture (and allied) sector real GDP growth rate in last few years:

2015-16	2016-17	2017-18	2018-19	2019-20	2020-21	2021-22	2022-23	2023-24	2024-25
0.6%	6.8%	6.6%	2.10%	6.2%	4.10%	3.50%	4.00%	1.40%	3.80%

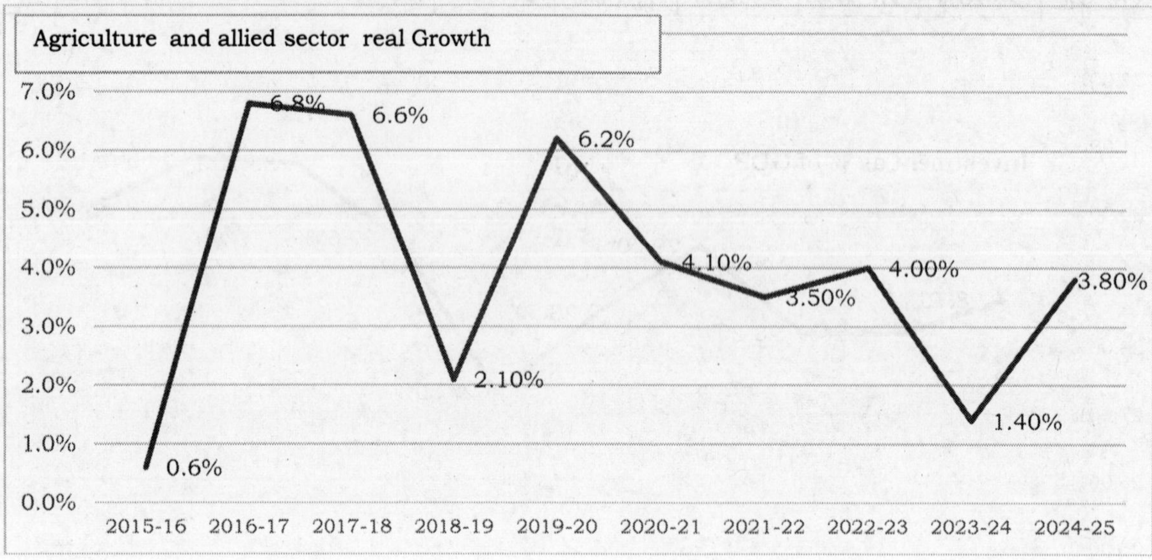

4. The following chart represents RBI's surplus transfer to central government in Rs. Crores.

2015-16	2016-17	2017-18	2018-19	2019-20	2020-21	2021-22	2022-23	2023-24
65876	30659	50000	176000	57000	99000	30307	87416	211000

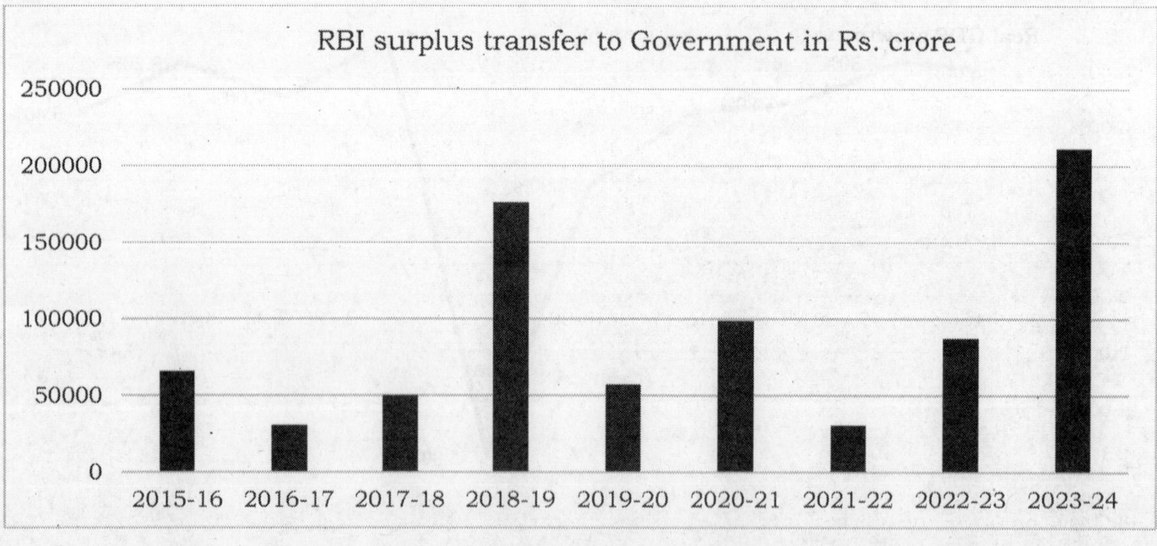

5. The following chart represents Fiscal Deficit (as % of GDP) of Govt. of India in last few years.

2016-17	2017-18	2018-19	2019-20	2020-21	2021-22	2022-23	2023-24	2024-25	2025-26
3.5%	3.5%	3.4%	4.60%	9.20%	6.9%	6.4%	5.6%	4.8%	4.40%

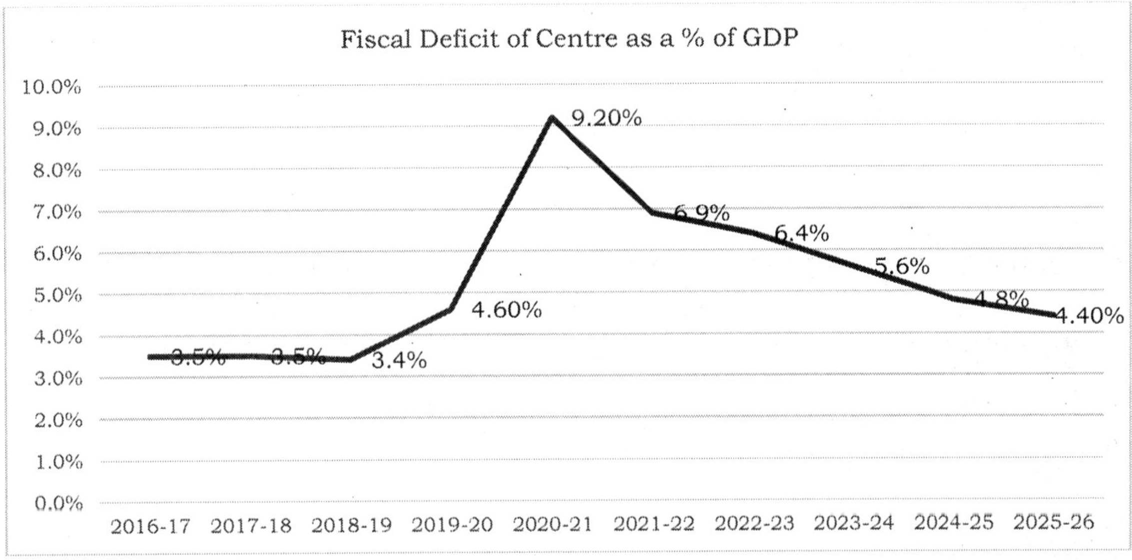

6.Following chart represents Fiscal Deficit (as % of GDP) of State Governments in last few years.

2016-17	2017-18	2018-19	2019-20	2020-21	2021-22	2022-23	2023-24	2024-25
3.50%	2.40%	2.50%	2.60%	4.70%	3.70%	3.40%	3.00%	3.20%

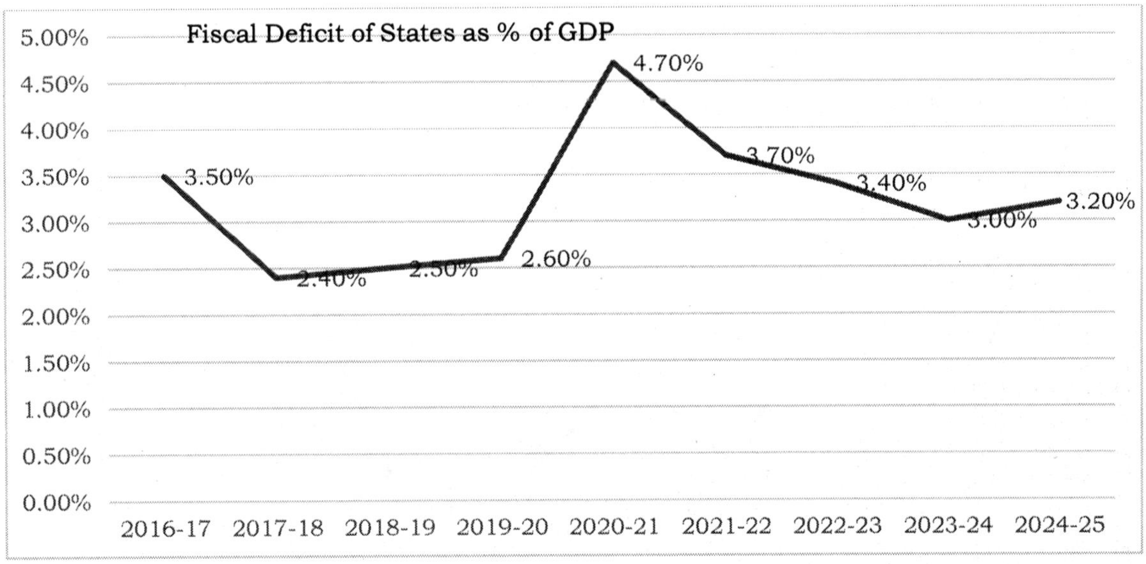

7.The following chart represents Debt to GDP ratio of Centre and states for the last few years:

Debt/ GDP	2016-17	2017-18	2018-19	2019-20	2020-21	2021-22	2022-23	2023-24
Centre	49.6%	46.0%	45.9%	47.80%	59.30%	57.0%	57.10%	59.00%
State	25.1%	25.1%	25.2%	26.30%	31.10%	28.7%	29.5%	28.20%

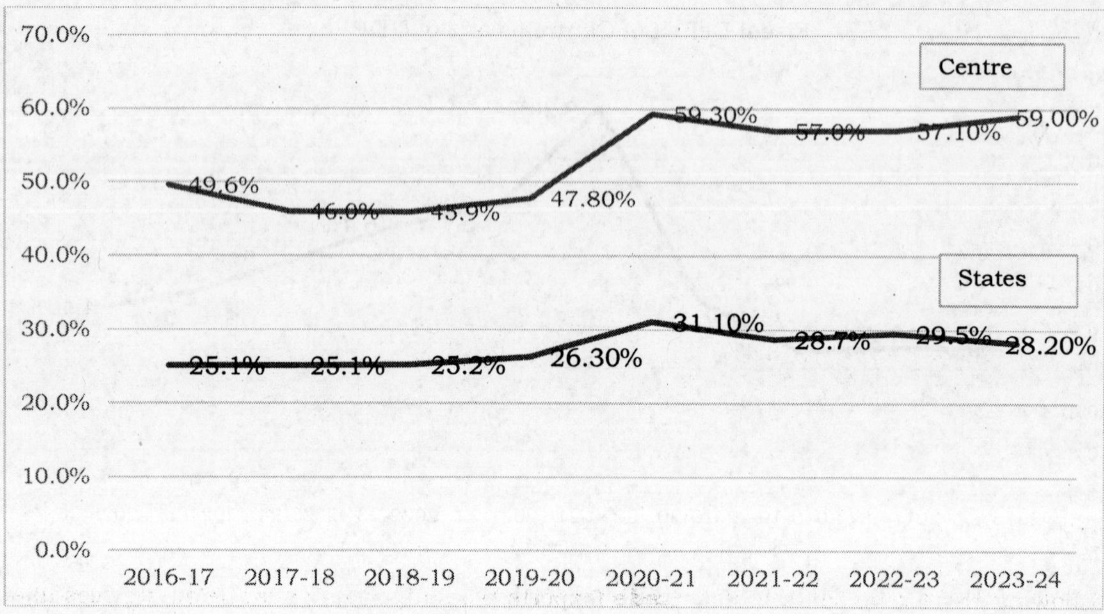

8.Following chart represents India's **exports** of goods and services as per cent of GDP (calendar year, data from World Bank)

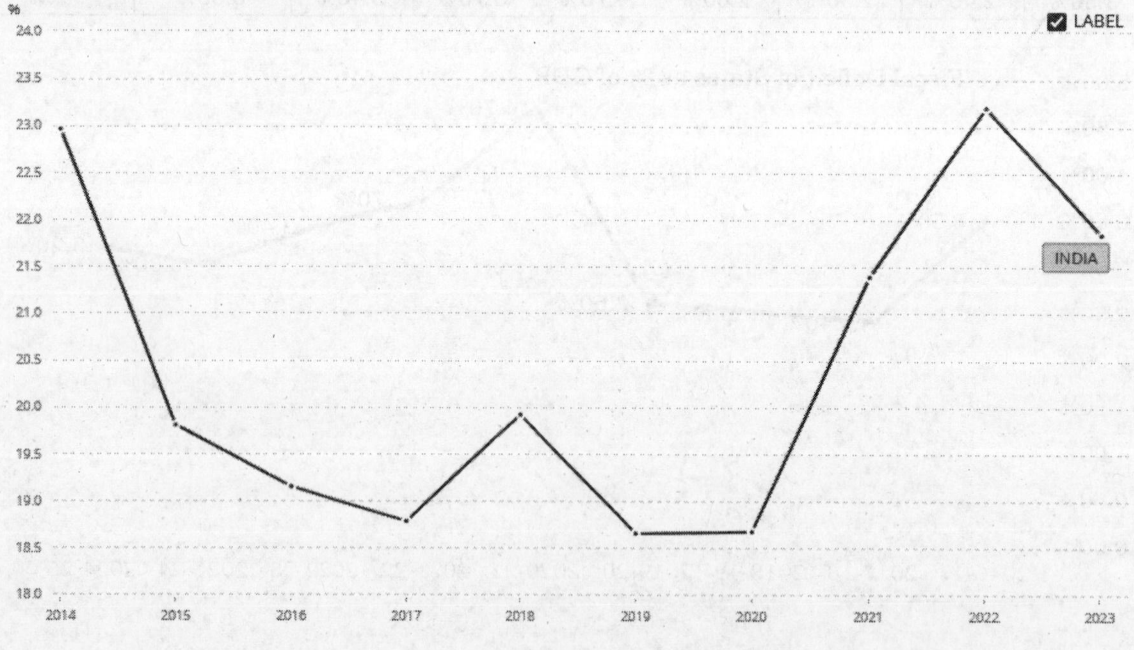

9.Following chart represents India's **imports** of goods and services as per cent of GDP. (Calendar year, data from World Bank)

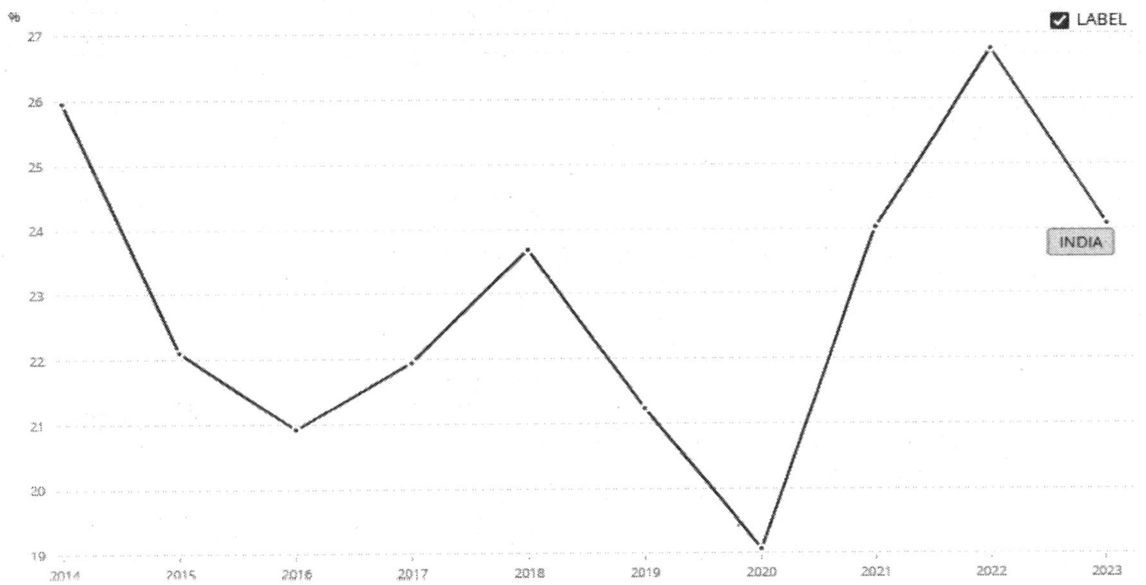

10. Following chart represents India's **trade** (exports plus imports) of goods and services as a per cent of GDP. (calendar year, data from World Bank)

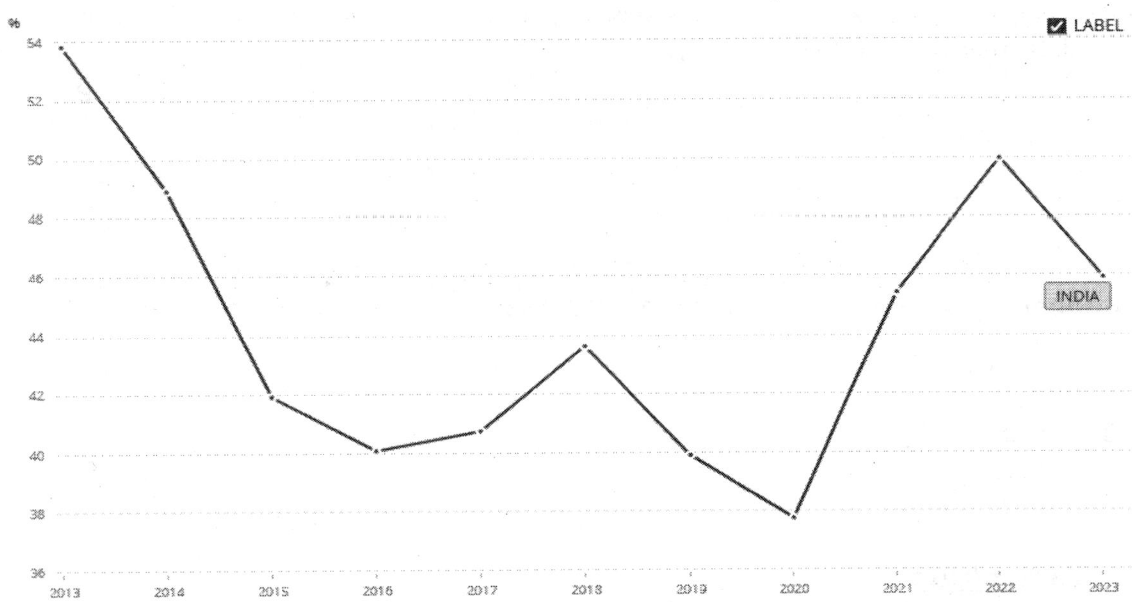

Budget 2025-26 & Economic Survey 2024-25

Central Finances	**2024-25**	**2025-26**
Total Expenditure Budget	Rs. 47.2 lakh cr	Rs. 50.6 lakh cr
• Revenue Expenditure	Rs. 37.0 lakh cr	Rs. 39.4 lakh cr
• Capital Expenditure	Rs. 10.2 lakh cr	Rs. 11.2 lakh cr
Total Receipts	Rs. 47.2 lakh cr	Rs. 50.6 lakh cr
• Revenue Receipts	Rs. 30.9 lakh cr	Rs. 34.2 lakh cr
• Capital Receipts	Rs. 16.3 lakh cr	Rs. 16.4 lakh cr
o Non-Debt Capital Receipts	Rs. 0.6 lakh cr	Rs. 0.7 lakh cr
o Debt Capital Receipts	Rs. 15.7 lakh cr	Rs. 15.7 lakh cr
Fiscal Deficit	4.8% (15.7 lakh cr)	4.4% (15.7 lakh cr)
Revenue Deficit	1.9% (6.1 lakh cr)	1.5% (5.2 lakh cr)
Effective Rev Deficit	1.0%	0.3 %
Primary Deficit	1.3%	0.8%
Nominal GDP	Rs. 324 lakh cr	Rs. 357 lakh cr
Nominal Growth	10.1%	
Gross Tax Revenue (Centre)	Rs. 38.5 lakh crore	Rs. 42.7 lakh crore
Tax to GDP (Centre)	11.9% (Rs.38.5 lcr/Rs.324 lcr)	12.0% (Rs.42.7 lcr/Rs.357 lcr)

Budget Focus on Four Engines of Growth:

- ❑ Agriculture
- ❑ MSMEs
- ❑ Investment
- ❑ Exports

1. Agriculture

- **PM Dhan-Dhaanya Krishi Yojana - Developing Agri Districts Programme**

  Motivated by the success of the Aspirational Districts Programme, Government will undertake a 'Prime Minister Dhan-Dhaanya Krishi Yojana' in partnership with states.

Through the convergence of existing schemes and specialized measures, the programme will cover 100 districts with low productivity, moderate crop intensity and below-average credit parameters. It aims to:

- Enhance agricultural productivity,
- Adopt crop diversification and sustainable agriculture practices,
- Augment post-harvest storage at the panchayat and block level,
- Improve irrigation facilities, and
- Facilitate availability of long-term and short-term credit.

- **Building Rural Prosperity and Resilience**

  A comprehensive multi-sectoral 'Rural Prosperity and Resilience' programme will be launched in partnership with states. This will address under-employment in agriculture through skilling, investment, technology, and invigorating the rural economy. The goal is to generate ample opportunities in rural areas so that migration is an option, but not a necessity. The programme will focus on rural women, young farmers, rural youth, marginal and small farmers, and landless families.

- **Aatmanirbharta in Pulses**

  Government will launch a 6-year "Mission for Aatmanirbharta in Pulses" with a special focus on Tur, Urad and Masoor. Central agencies (NAFED and NCCF) will be ready to procure these 3 pulses, as much as offered during the next 4 years from farmers who register with these agencies and enter into agreements.

- **Comprehensive Programme for Vegetables & Fruits**

  A comprehensive programme to promote production, efficient supplies, processing, and remunerative prices for farmers will be launched in partnership with states. Appropriate institutional mechanisms for implementation and participation of farmer producer organizations (FPOs) and cooperatives will be set up.

- **Makhana Board in Bihar**

  A Makhana Board will be established in the state to improve production, processing, value addition, and marketing of makhana. The people engaged in these activities will be organized into FPOs. The Board will provide handholding and training support to makhana farmers and will also work to ensure they receive the benefits of all relevant Government schemes.

- **National Mission on High Yielding Seeds**

  A National Mission on High Yielding Seeds will be launched, aimed at (1) strengthening the research ecosystem, (2) targeted development and propagation of seeds with high yield, pest resistance and climate resilience, and (3) commercial availability of more than 100 seed varieties released since July 2024.

- **Fisheries**

  India ranks second-largest globally in fish production and aquaculture. Seafood exports are valued at Rs. 60 thousand crores. To unlock the untapped potential of the marine sector, Government will bring in an enabling framework for sustainable harnessing of fisheries from Indian Exclusive Economic Zone and High Seas, with a special focus on the Andaman & Nicobar and Lakshadweep Islands.

- **Mission for Cotton Productivity**

  This 5-year mission will facilitate significant improvements in productivity and sustainability of cotton farming, and promote extra-long staple cotton varieties. The best of science & technology support will be provided to farmers. Aligned with our integrated 5F vision for the textile sector, this will help in increasing incomes of the farmers, and ensure a steady supply of quality cotton for rejuvenating India's traditional textile sector.

- **Enhanced Credit through KCC**

  Kisan Credit Cards (KCC) facilitate short term loans for 7.7 crore farmers, fishermen, and dairy farmers. The loan limit under the Modified Interest Subvention Scheme will be enhanced from Rs. 3 lakhs to Rs. 5 lakhs for loans taken through the KCC.

- **India Post as a Catalyst for the Rural Economy**

  India Post with 1.5 lakh rural post offices, complemented by the India Post Payment Bank and a vast network of 2.4 lakh Dak Sevaks, will be repositioned to act as a catalyst for the rural economy. The expanded range of services will include:

  - rural community hub colocation;
  - institutional account services;
  - DBT, cash out and EMI pick-up;
  - credit services to micro enterprises;
  - insurance; and
  - assisted digital services.

2. MSMEs

- Currently, over 1 crore registered MSMEs, employing 7.5 crore people, and generating 36 per cent of manufacturing, have come together to position India as a global manufacturing hub. With their quality products, these MSMEs are responsible for 45 per cent of our exports. To help them achieve higher efficiencies of scale, technological upgradation and better access to capital, the investment and turnover limits for classification of all MSMEs will be enhanced to 2.5 and 2 times respectively. This will give them the confidence to grow and generate employment for our youth.

₹ in Crore	Investment		Turnover	
	Current	Revised	Current	Revised
Micro Enterprises	1	2.5	5	10
Small Enterprises	10	25	50	100
Medium Enterprises	50	125	250	500

- To improve access to credit, the credit guarantee cover will be enhanced:
  - For Micro and Small Enterprises, from Rs.5 crore to 10 crore, leading to additional credit of Rs.1.5 lakh crore in the next 5 years;
  - For Startups, from Rs.10 crore to 20 crore, with the guarantee fee being moderated to 1 per cent for loans in 27 focus sectors important for Atmanirbhar Bharat; and
  - For well-run exporter MSMEs, for term loans up to Rs.20 crore.

- Credit card for Micro Enterprises
  - Government will introduce customized Credit Cards with a Rs.5 lakh limit for micro enterprises registered on Udyam portal. In the first year, 10 lakh such cards will be issued.

- Measures for Labour Intensive Sectors: To promote employment and entrepreneurship opportunities in labour-intensive sectors, Government will undertake specific policy and facilitation measures:

  - Footwear and Leather: The scheme will support design capacity, component manufacturing, and machinery required for production of non-leather quality footwear, besides the support for leather footwear and products

  - Toy sector
    Make India a global hub for toys: The scheme will focus on development of clusters, skills, and a manufacturing ecosystem that will create high-quality, unique, innovative, and sustainable toys that will represent the 'Made in India' brand.

  - Food Processing
    Govt. will establish National Institute of Food Technology, Entrepreneurship and Management in Bihar. The institute will provide a strong fillip to food processing activities in the entire Eastern region. This will result in enhanced income for the farmers through value addition to their produce and skilling, entrepreneurship and employment opportunities for the youth.

- Manufacturing Mission - Furthering "Make in India"
  - Government will set up a National Manufacturing Mission covering small, medium and large industries for furthering "Make in India" by providing policy support, execution roadmaps, governance and monitoring framework for central ministries and states.

3. Investment

- Expansion of Capacity in IITs
- Day Care Cancer Centres in all District Hospitals
- Bharatiya Bhasha Pustak Scheme: provide digital form Indian language books for school and higher education
- 05 National Centres of Excellence for skilling to be set up with global expertise and partnerships.
- Atal Tinkering Labs: 50 thousand Labs to be set up in government schools in next 5 years.
- Centre of Excellence in Artificial Intelligence for education with a total outlay of ₹500 crore
- Broadband connectivity to be provided to all government secondary schools and primary health centres in rural areas
- Expansion of medical education: 10,000 additional seats with the goal of adding 75,000 seats in the next 5 years.
- PM SVANidhi: To be revamped with enhanced loans from banks, UPI linked credit cards and capacity building support
- Welfare of Online Platform Workers: Registration on the e-Shram portal & healthcare under PM Jan Arogya Yojana.
- Support to States for Infrastructure: With an outlay of ₹ 1.5 lakh crore, 50-year interest free loans to states for capital expenditure and incentives for reforms.
- Power Sector Reforms: Incentivize distribution reforms and augmentation of intra-state transmission. Additional borrowing of 0.5 % of GSDP to states, contingent on these reforms.
- Asset Monetization Plan 2025-30: launched to plough back capital of ₹ 10 lakh crore in new projects.
- Modified UDAN Scheme: Regional connectivity to 120 new destinations and carry 4 crore passengers in the next 10 years.

4. Exports

- Export Promotion Mission: Government will set up an Export Promotion Mission, with sectoral and ministerial targets, driven jointly by the Ministries of Commerce, MSME, and Finance. It will facilitate easy access to export credit, cross-border factoring support, and support to MSMEs to tackle non-tariff measures in overseas markets.

- BharatTradeNet: A digital public infrastructure, 'BharatTradeNet' (BTN) for international trade will be set-up as a unified platform for trade documentation and financing solutions.

- National Framework for GCC: As guidance to states for promoting Global Capability Centres in emerging tier 2 cities.

- Warehousing facility for air cargo: To facilitate upgradation of infrastructure and warehousing for air cargo including high value perishable horticulture produce.

Tax Reforms:

- Direct Taxes

  - Substantial relief is proposed under the **new tax regime** with new slabs and tax rates as under:

Total income	Rate of tax
Upto Rs. 4,00,000	Nil
From Rs. 4,00,001 to Rs. 8,00,000	5 per cent
From Rs. 8,00,001 to Rs. 12,00,000	10 per cent
From Rs. 12,00,001 to Rs. 16,00,000	15 per cent
From Rs. 16,00,001 to Rs. 20,00,000	20 per cent
From Rs. 20,00,001 to Rs. 24,00,000	25 per cent
Above Rs. 24,00,000	30 per cent

  - Those whose income is up to Rs. 12 lakhs, do not need to pay any tax. For salaried employees an additional Standard Deduction is given for Rs. 75,000.

  - New income tax bill will be introduced for reforms in direct taxes regarding making the clauses easier to understand and less ambiguous and reducing compliance burden on tax filing etc.

- Indirect Taxes
  - Rationalisation of Customs Tariff Structure for Industrial Goods

  - Make in India- Exemption to open cell for LED/LCD TV, looms for textiles, capital goods for lithium-ion battery of mobile phones and EVs.

  - Promotion of MRO – exemption for 10 years on goods for ship building and ships for breaking, extension of time limit for export of railway goods imported for repairs.

  - Export promotion – duty free inputs for handicraft and leather sectors

Other Reforms:

- The FDI limit for the insurance sector will be raised from 74 to 100 per cent. This enhanced limit will be available for those companies which invest the entire premium in India. The current guardrails and conditionalities associated with foreign investment will be reviewed and simplified.

- Requirements and procedures for speedy approval of company mergers will be rationalized. The scope for fast-track mergers will also be widened and the process made simpler.
- Jan Vishwas Bill 2.0: to decriminalize more than 100 provisions in various laws.
- A high-level committee will be constituted to propose regulatory reforms
- An Investment Friendliness Index of States will be launched in 2025 to further the spirit of competitive cooperative federalism.

An analysis of budgeted capital expenditure:

- The Capex has been increased from Rs. 10.2 lakh crore (2024-25) to Rs. 11.2 lakh crore (3.1% of GDP) in the budget 2025-26. This capex is only of Central Govt., but Central Govt. gives grants to States for capex under various schemes which increases the effective capital expenditure.
- So, effective capex has been increased from Rs. 13.2 lakh crore in FY25 to Rs. 15.5 lakh crore (4.3% of GDP) in 2025-26
- Capex is also done through CPSEs which is around Rs. 4 lakh crores
- Govt. is planning to bring the National Monetization Pipeline (NMP) for the next five years (2025-26 to 2029-30) which will be double the value of the previous NMP.
- NMP proceeds generally do not go to Consolidated Fund of India (CFI) and is spent outside the budget through PSUs
- Comparison of capital expenditure and revenue expenditure in the last 10 years as a percentage of total central government expenditure:

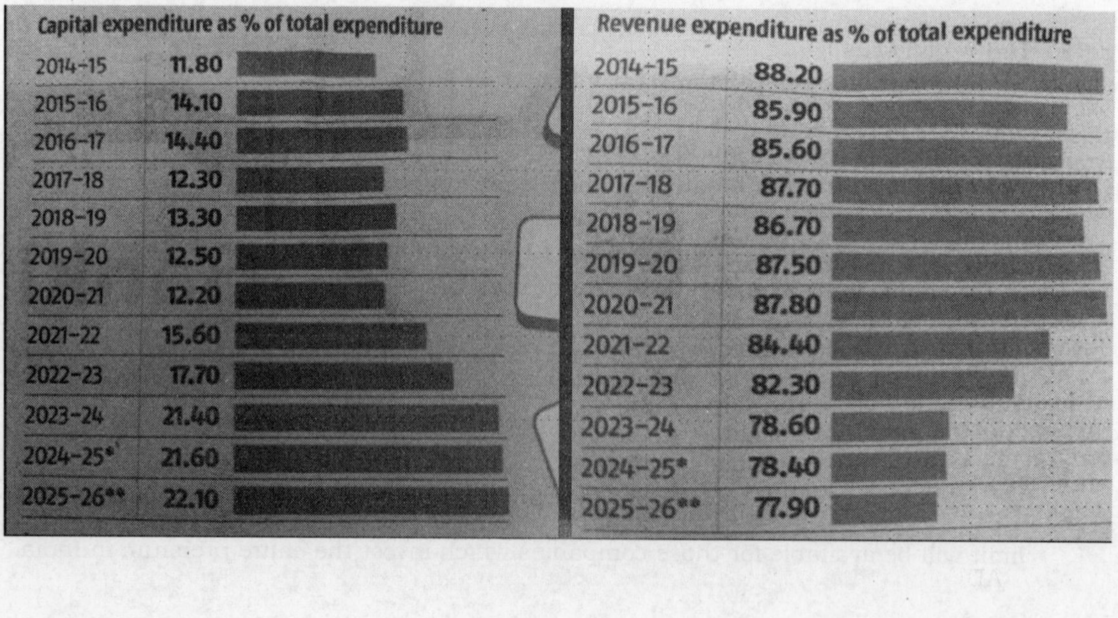

Economic Survey 2024-25:

- Global outlook: The global economy grew by 3.3 per cent in 2023. The International Monetary Fund (IMF) has projected growth of 3.2 per cent and 3.3 per cent for 2024 and 2025, respectively. Growth in the US is expected to remain strong at 2.8 per cent in 2024 and may decline slightly in 2025.

- Indian economy: India displayed steady economic growth. As per the first advance estimates of national accounts, India's real GDP is estimated to grow by 6.4 per cent in FY25. Growth in the first half of FY25 was supported by agriculture and services, with rural demand improving on the back of record Kharif production and favourable agricultural conditions. The manufacturing sector faced pressures due to weak global demand and domestic seasonal conditions. Private consumption remained stable, reflecting steady domestic demand. Fiscal discipline and strong external balance supported by a services trade surplus and healthy remittance growth contributed to macroeconomic stability.

Chart I.20: Despite global uncertainty, India's growth remains close to decadal average (at constant prices)

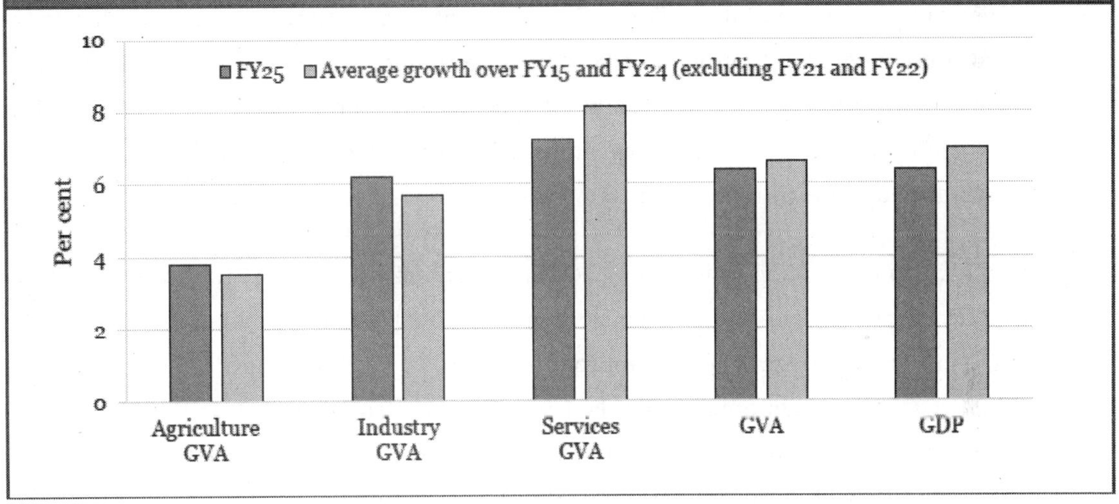

- The merchandise imports outpaced merchandise exports, widening India's merchandise trade deficit. India's services trade surplus has lent balance to the overall trade deficit. India's robust services exports have propelled the country to secure the seventh-largest share in global services exports, underscoring its competitiveness in this critical sector. In addition to the services trade surplus, remittances from abroad led to a healthy net inflow of private transfers. As per the World Bank, India was the top recipient of remittances in the world ($129 billion), driven by an uptick in job creation in OECD economies. These two factors combined to ensure that India's current account deficit (CAD) remains relatively contained at 1.2 per cent of GDP in Q2 FY25.

- The India's monetary and financial sectors have performed well in the first nine months of FY25. Bank credit has grown at a steady rate in the current financial year, with credit growth converging towards deposit growth. There has been a consistent improvement in the profitability of scheduled commercial banks (SCBs) as reflected in a fall in gross non-performing assets (GNPAs) accompanied by a rise in the capital-to-risk weighted asset ratio (CRAR). The government has also achieved significant progress in financial inclusion, with the Financial Inclusion Index of the Reserve Bank of India (RBI) increasing from 53.9 in March 2021 to 64.2 at the end of March 2024.

- India's external sector continued to display resilience amidst global headwinds of economic and trade policy uncertainties. Total exports (merchandise and services) have registered a steady growth in the first nine months of FY25, reaching USD 602.6 billion (6 per cent growth). Growth in services and goods exports, excluding petroleum and gems and jewellery, was 10.4 per cent. Total imports during the same period reached USD 682.2 billion, registering a growth of 6.9 per cent on the back of steady domestic demand.

- On the capital front, foreign portfolio investments (FPIs) have shown a mixed trend in FY25 so far. Uncertainty in the global markets and profit taking by foreign portfolio investors led to capital outflows. However, strong macroeconomic fundamentals, a favourable business environment, and high economic growth have kept FPI flows positive overall. Gross foreign direct investment (FDI) inflows have shown signs of revival in the first eight months of FY25, though net FDI inflows declined relative to April-November 2023 due to a rise in repatriation.

- India's Global Capability Centres (GCCs) are emerging as strategic hubs reshaping the Indian corporate landscape while influencing global business dynamics. The number of GCCs in India has grown from approximately 1430 in FY19 to over 1700 in FY24. As of FY24, GCCs in India employ nearly 1.9 million professionals. Over the past five years, India has remained at the forefront of the global GCC expansion strategy, with more than 400 new GCCs and around 1100 new units established.

- GCCs are fundamentally altering the technology landscape. Leading organisations are centralising their tech ecosystems in India. This is particularly evident in sectors like aerospace, defence, and semiconductors, where companies are advancing their engineering efforts to focus on next-generation platforms, products, and technologies. Over the last five years, the setup rate of engineering research & development GCCs has grown 1.3 times faster than the overall GCC setup, highlighting a continued shift towards high-value-added work.

- India has established itself as a prominent player in leveraging its vast talent pool, which accounts for 28 per cent of the global (science, technology, engineering, mathematics) STEM workforce and 23 per cent of the global software engineering talent. Over the past decade, the GCC ecosystem in India has matured significantly, advancing into high-end engineering roles such as product managers and architects, with 35 per cent of transformation hubs exhibiting a strong presence of architects. Furthermore, global roles within GCCs are expanding rapidly, expected to grow from currently 6,500 to over 30,000 by 2030, supported by robust training programs to develop leadership. The adoption of Artificial Intelligence (AI) and Machine Learning (ML) and the establishment of AI centres of excellence further enhance the GCC landscape by tapping into India's strong middle-management talent.